Cyber Security in Parallel and Distributed Computing

Scrivener Publishing
100 Cummings Center, Suite 541J
Beverly, MA 01915-6106

Publishers at Scrivener
Martin Scrivener (martin@scrivenerpublishing.com)
Phillip Carmical (pcarmical@scrivenerpublishing.com)

Cyber Security in Parallel and Distributed Computing

Concepts, Techniques, Applications and Case Studies

Edited by

DacNhuong Le
Haiphong University, Haiphong, Vietnam

Raghvendra Kumar
LNCT College, India

Brojo Kishore Mishra
C. V. Raman College of Engineering, Bhubaneswar, India

Manju Khari
Ambedkar Institute of Advance Communication Technologies & Research, India

Jyotir Moy Chatterjee
Asia Pacific University of Technology & Innovation, Kathmandu, Nepal

Scrivener
Publishing

WILEY

Wiley Global Headquarters
111 River Street, Hoboken, NJ 07030, USA

For details of our global editorial offices, customer services, and more information about Wiley products visit us at www.wiley.com.

Limit of Liability/Disclaimer of Warranty
While the publisher and authors have used their best efforts in preparing this work, they make no representations or warranties with respect to the accuracy or completeness of the contents of this work and specifically disclaim all warranties, including without limitation any implied warranties of merchantability or fitness for a particular purpose. No warranty may be created or extended by sales representatives, written sales materials, or promotional statements for this work. The fact that an organization, website, or product is referred to in this work as a citation and/or potential source of further information does not mean that the publisher and authors endorse the information or services the organization, website, or product may provide or recommendations it may make. This work is sold with the understanding that the publisher is not engaged in rendering professional services. The advice and strategies contained herein may not be suitable for your situation. You should consult with a specialist where appropriate. Neither the publisher nor authors shall be liable for any loss of profit or any other commercial damages, including but not limited to special, incidental, consequential, or other damages. Further, readers should be aware that websites listed in this work may have changed or disappeared between when this work was written and when it is read.

Library of Congress Cataloging-in-Publication Data
ISBN 978-1-119-48805-7

Cover images: Pixabay.Com
Cover design by: Russell Richardson

Set in size of 11pt and Minion Pro by Exeter Premedia Services Private Ltd., Chennai, India

10   9 8 7 6 5 4 3 2 1

To our parents

Contents

List of Figures   xv

List of Tables   xvii

Foreword   xix

Preface   xxi

Acknowledgments   xxv

Acronyms   xxvii

Part 1   Cybersecurity Concept

1   Introduction on Cybersecurity   3
Ishaani Priyadarshini

1.1   Introduction to Cybersecurity   5
1.2   Cybersecurity Objectives   6
1.3   Cybersecurity Infrastructure and Internet Architecture (NIST)   8
1.4   Cybersecurity Roles   10
1.5   Cybercrimes   17
     1.5.1   Overview   17
     1.5.2   Traditional Computer Crime and Contemporary Computer Crime   18
     1.5.3   Combating Crimes   21
1.6   Security Models   23
1.7   Computer Forensics   25
1.8   Cyber Insurance   27
     1.8.1   Digital Citizenship   29
     1.8.2   Information Warfare and Its Countermeasures   31
     1.8.3   Network Neutrality   33
     1.8.4   Good Practices and Policies   34
     1.8.5   Cybersecurity and Human Rights   35
1.9   Future of Cybersecurity   36
1.10   Conclusion   36
    References   37

2   Steganography and Steganalysis   **39**
Ho Thi Huong Thom, Nguyen Kim Anh
2.1   Introduction   40
2.2   Steganography   41
    2.2.1   Method for Evaluating Hidden Information
        Schema Security   41
    2.2.2   Peak Signal-to-Noise Ratio   42
2.3   Steganalysis   42
    2.3.1   Blind Detection Based on LSB   43
    2.3.2   Constraint Steganalysis   45
2.4   Conclusion   46
References   46

3   Security Threats and Vulnerabilities in E-business   **51**
Satya Narayan Tripathy, Sisira Kumar Kapat, Susanta Kumar Das
3.1   Introduction to e-Business   52
    3.1.1   Benefits of e-Business   52
    3.1.2   Business Revolution   53
3.2   Security Issues in e-Business   54
    3.2.1   Vulnerabilities   54
    3.2.2   Security Attacks   55
    3.2.3   Malware as a Threat   55
3.3   Common Vulnerabilities in e-Business   55
    3.3.1   Phishing   55
    3.3.2   Cross-Site Scripting (XSS)   56
3.4   Threats in e-Business   56
    3.4.1   Ransomware   56
    3.4.2   Spyware   56
    3.4.3   Worms   57
    3.4.4   Trojan Horse   57
3.5   Prevention Mechanism   57
3.6   Conclusion   58
References   58

4   e-Commerce Security: Threats, Issues, and Methods   **61**
Prerna Sharma, Deepak Gupta, Ashish Khanna
4.1   Introduction   62
4.2   Literature Review   63
4.3   e-Commerce   63
    4.3.1   Characteristics of e-Commerce Technology   63
    4.3.2   Architectural Framework of e-Commerce   64
    4.3.3   Advantages and Disadvantages of e-Commerce   66
4.4   Security Overview in e-Commerce   67
    4.4.1   Purpose of Security in e-Commerce   67
    4.4.2   Security Element at Different Levels of e-Commerce System   67

4.5 Security Issues in e-Commerce 68
  4.5.1 Client Level 68
  4.5.2 Front-End Servers and Software Application Level 68
  4.5.3 Network and Server Level 68
4.6 Security Threats in e-Commerce 69
4.7 Security Approaches in e-Commerce 72
4.8 Comparative Analysis of Various Security Threats in e-Commerce 73
4.9 e-Commerce Security Life-Cycle Model 73
4.10 Conclusion 75
References 76

5 Cyberwar is Coming 79
T. Manikandan, B. Balamurugan, C. Senthilkumar,
R. Rajesh Alias Harinarayan, R. Raja Subramanian
5.1 Introduction 80
5.2 Ransomware Attacks 82
  5.2.1 Petya 83
  5.2.2 WannaCry 83
  5.2.3 Locky 84
5.3 Are Nations Ready? 85
5.4 Conclusion 88
References 88

Part 2 Cybersecurity in Parallel and Distributed Computing Techniques

6 Introduction to Blockchain Technology 93
Ishaani Priyadarshini
6.1 Introduction 94
6.2 Need for Blockchain Security 95
6.3 Characteristics of Blockchain Technology 96
6.4 Types of Blockchains 97
6.5 The Architecture of Blockchain Technology 97
6.6 How Blockchain Technology Works 100
6.7 Some Other Case Studies for Blockchain Technology 102
6.8 Challenges Faced by Blockchain Technology 103
6.9 The Future of Blockchain Technology 105
6.10 Conclusion 106
References 106

7 Cyber-Security Techniques in Distributed Systems, SLAs and other Cyber Regulations 109
Soumitra Ghosh, Anjana Mishra, Brojo Kishore Mishra
7.1 Introduction 110
  7.1.1 Primary Characteristics of a Distributed System 110
  7.1.2 Major Challenges for Distributed Systems 111

7.2	Identifying Cyber Requirements	112
7.3	Popular security mechanisms in Distributed Systems	113
	7.3.1 Secure Communication	113
	7.3.2 Message Integrity and Confidentiality	115
	7.3.3 Access Controls	116
7.4	Service Level Agreements	118
	7.4.1 Types of SLAs	118
	7.4.2 Critical Areas for SLAs	119
7.5	The Cuckoo's Egg in the Context of IT Security	122
7.6	Searching and Seizing ComputerRelated Evidence	124
	7.6.1 Computerized Search Warrants	124
	7.6.2 Searching and Seizing	125
7.7	Conclusion	126
	References	126

8   Distributed Computing Security: Issues and Challenges   **129**
Munmun Saha, Sanjaya Kumar Panda and Suvasini Panigrahi

8.1	Introduction	130
8.2	Security Issues and Challenges	131
	8.2.1 Confidentiality, Integrity and Availability	131
	8.2.2 Authentication and Access Control Issue	132
	8.2.3 Broken Authentication, Session and Access	132
8.3	Security Issues and Challenges in Advanced Areas	133
8.4	Conclusion	136
	References	136

9   Organization Assignment in Federated Cloud Environments based on Multi-Target Optimization of Security   **139**
Abhishek Kumar, Palvadi Srinivas Kumar, T.V.M. Sairam

9.1	Introduction	140
9.2	Background Work Related to Domain	141
	9.2.1 Basics on Cloud computing	141
	9.2.2 Clouds Which are Federated	141
	9.2.3 Cloud Resource Management	141
9.3	Architectural-Based Cloud Security Implementation	142
9.4	Expected Results of the Process	144
9.5	Conclusion	146
	References	146

10   An On-Demand and User-friendly Framework for Cloud Data Centre Networks with Performance Guarantee   **149**
P. Srinivas Kumar, Abhishek Kumar, Pramod Singh Rathore, Jyotir Moy Chatterjee

10.1	Introduction	150
	10.1.1 Key Research Problems in This Area	150
	10.1.2 Problems with Interoperability	151

10.2	Difficulties from a Cloud Adoption Perspective		151
10.3	Security and Privacy		151
	10.3.1	Resource Provisioning	152
	10.3.2	How Do We Define Cloud?	153
	10.3.3	Public vs Private Cloud-Based Services	153
	10.3.4	Traffic-Aware VM Migration to Load Balance Cloud Servers	154
10.4	Conclusion and Future Work	157
References		157

Part 3   Cybersecurity Applications and Case Studies

11   Cybersecurity at Organizations: A Delphi Pilot Study of Expert Opinions About Policy and Protection   163
Holly Reitmeier, Jolanda Tromp, John Bottoms

11.1	Introduction	164
	11.1.1	What is Cybercrime?	164
	11.1.2	What is Cybersecurity?	165
	11.1.3	Purpose of This Cybersecurity Pilot Study	165
	11.1.4	Methods of Cybersecurity Professionals	165
11.2	Shocking Statistics of Cybercrime	166
	11.2.1	Role of the Internet Crime Complaint Center	166
	11.2.2	2016 Global Economic Crime Survey Report	168
	11.2.3	Inadequate Preparation at Organizations	168
	11.2.4	Organizations: Be Aware, Be Secure	168
11.3	Cybersecurity Policies for Organizations	169
	11.3.1	Classification of Cybersecurity at an Organization	171
	11.3.2	Pyramid of Cybersecurity	171
11.4	Blockchain Technology	172
11.5	Research Methodology	173
	11.5.1	Quantitative and Qualitative Data Collection	173
	11.5.2	Design of the Study	174
	11.5.3	Selection of the Delphi Method	174
	11.5.4	Procedure of Utilization of the Delphi Method	175
	11.5.5	Delphi Activities (Iteration Rounds) of This Pilot Study	175
11.6	Results of the Cybersecurity Delphi Study	176
	11.6.1	Results from Round One	176
	11.6.2	Results of Round Two	178
	11.6.3	Discussion and Limitations Based on the Results	181
11.7	Conclusion	183
	11.7.1	The Literature in the Field	183
	11.7.2	Next Steps for Future Research	184
References		184

**12   Smartphone Triggered Security Challenges - Issues, Case Studies
and Prevention   187**
*Saurabh Ranjan Srivastava, Sachin Dube, Gulshan Shrivastava,
Kavita Sharma*

12.1   Introduction   188
12.2   Classification of Mobile Security Threats   188
    12.2.1   Physical Threats   189
    12.2.2   Web-Based Threats   189
    12.2.3   Application-Based Threats   189
    12.2.4   Network-Based Threats   190
    12.2.5   Data Transfer-Based Threats   191
    12.2.6   Improper Session Management-Based Threats   191
    12.2.7   Bluetooth-Based Threats   191
    12.2.8   Application Platform-Based Threats   192
12.3   Smartphones as a Tool of Crime   192
12.4   Types of Mobile Phone-Related Crimes   193
12.5   Types of Mobile Fraud   196
12.6   Case Studies   198
    12.6.1   Mobile Identity Theft   198
    12.6.2   Data Theft by Applications   200
    12.6.3   SIM Card Fraud   200
12.7   Preventive Measures and Precautions   201
    12.7.1   Against Physical Loss and Theft of the Mobile Device   201
    12.7.2   Against SMiShing Attacks   202
    12.7.3   Against App-Based Attacks   203
    12.7.4   Against Identity Theft and SIM Card Fraud   203
12.8   Conclusion   204
References   205

**13   Cybersecurity: A Practical Strategy Against Cyber Threats,
Risks with Real World Usages   207**
Anjana Mishra, Soumitra Ghosh, Brojo Kishore Mishra

13.1   Introduction   208
13.2   Cyberwar   209
13.3   Arms Control in Cyberwar   210
13.4   Internet Security Alliance   211
13.5   Cybersecurity Information Sharing Act   212
13.6   Market for Malware   214
13.7   Mobile Cybersecurity   215
13.8   Healthcare   216
13.9   Human Rights   217
13.10 Cybersecurity Application in Our Life   218
13.11 Conclusion   219
References   219

14 Security in Distributed Operating System: A Comprehensive Study **221**
Sushree Bibhuprada B. Priyadarshini, Amiya Bhusan Bagjadab,
Brojo Kishore Mishra
14.1 Introduction to Security and Distributed Systems 222
14.2 Relevant Terminology 225
14.3 Types of External Attacks 225
14.4 Globus Security Architecture 228
14.5 Distribution of Security Mechanism 229
14.6 Conclusions 230
References 230

15 Security in Healthcare Applications based on Fog and
Cloud Computing **231**
Rojalina Priyadarshini, Mohit Ranjan Panda,
Brojo Kishore Mishra
15.1 Introduction 232
15.2 Security Needs of Healthcare Sector 233
15.2.1 Data Integrity 233
15.2.2 Data Confidentiality 233
15.2.3 Authentication and Authorization 233
15.2.4 Availability 234
15.2.5 Access Control 234
15.2.6 Dependability 234
15.2.7 Flexibility 234
15.3 Solutions to Probable Attacks in e-Healthcare 234
15.3.1 Jamming Attack 235
15.3.2 Data Collision Attack 235
15.3.3 Desynchronization Attack 235
15.3.4 Spoofing Attack 236
15.3.5 Man-in-the-Middle Attack 236
15.3.6 Denial-of-Service (DoS) Attack 237
15.3.7 Insider Attack 238
15.3.8 Masquerade Attack 238
15.3.9 Attacks on Virtual Machine and Hypervisor 239
15.4 Emerging Threats in Cloud- and Fog-Based Healthcare System 240
15.4.1 Software Supply Chain Attacks 240
15.4.2 Ransomware Attacks 240
15.4.3 Crypto-Mining and Crypto-Jacking Malware 240
15.5 Conclusion 241
References 241

16   Mapping of e-Wallets with Features   **245**
Alisha Sikri, Surjeet Dalal, N.P Singh, Dac-Nhuong Le
    16.1   Introduction   246
            16.1.1   e-Wallet   246
            16.1.2   Objectives   247
    16.2   Review of Literature   250
    16.3   Market Share of e-Wallet   251
            16.3.1   Technical Features   252
            16.3.2   Legal Features   252
            16.3.3   Operational Features   253
            16.3.4   Security Features   253
    16.4   Research Methodology   253
    16.5   Result Analysis   255
    16.6   Conclusions and future work   256
    References   256

List of Figures

2.1	Classification of Steganography	40
3.1	Product flow structure in traditional business	53
3.2	Communication cycle in e-business, from manufacturer to customer	54
4.1	Two-tier e-commerce architecture	65
4.2	Three-tier e-commerce architecture	65
4.3	DDOS attack	69
4.4	SQL injection attack	70
4.5	Price manipulation	71
4.6	Session hijacking attack	71
4.7	Cross-site scripting attack	72
4.8	Security engineering life cycle	75
5.1	Virus alert!	80
5.2	Petya ransomware	83
5.3	WannaCry ransomware	84
5.4	Motives of the attackers over the years	85
6.1	Blockchain architecture diagram	98
6.2	Network architecture of blockchain	99
6.3	How transactions get converted to blocks	99
6.4	Cryptocurrency transaction using blockchain technology	101
6.5	How double spending may occur	102
6.6	Blockchain generation from unordered transactions	102
7.1	Challenges of a distributed system	111
7.2	Shared secret key-based authentication	113
7.3	Role of KDC in authentication	114
7.4	Public key encryption based on mutual authentication	115
7.5	Digital signature	116
7.6	Schematic of a sandbox and a playground	117
9.1	Overview of MQMCE	142
9.2	MQMCE scheduler process	143
9.3	Obtained non-dominated solutions for the parallel workflow	144
9.4	Obtained non-dominated solutions for the hybrid workflow	145
9.5	Obtained non-dominated solutions for the synthetic workflow	145
11.1	Internet Crime Complaint Center(IC3) public value of overall statistics 2016	167
11.2	Pyramid of cybersecurity 2017	171
11.3	Expert-level-awareness of cybersecurity	177
11.4	Effective incident response plans	177

11.5   Federal government cybersecurity initiatives   177
11.6   Blockchain secure Internet transactions   178
12.1   Classification of mobile security threats   188
12.2   Various mobile phone-related crimes   193
12.3   The schematic sequence of a SMiShing attack   195
12.4   Types of mobile frauds   197
13.1   Issues of cybersecurity [4]   208
13.2   Cybersecurity attacks occurring in different years [8]   208
13.3   Malware attacks on smartphone OSes   215
14.1   Logical organization of distributed systems into various layers   222
14.2   Basic elements of information system security   222
14.3   Schematic showing the exchange of information
       in distributed systems   223
14.4   Types of external attacks   225
14.5   Types of DoS attacks   227
14.6   Globus security policy architecture   229
15.1   General architecture of healthcare monitoring systems   232
15.2   Categorization of attacks in healthcare system   235
15.3   Schematic diagram of a captured communication by
       an eavesdropper in fog environment   237
15.4   Schematic diagram of a distributed denial of service attack   238
15.5   Masquerade attack   239
16.1   Ecosystem for setting up of an Open, closed and semi-closed
       e-wallet respectively [2]   247
16.2   Research Model for the mapping of features of E-wallets with
       the types of e-wallets   255

List of Tables

2.1	Relationship between PSNR and MOS values	42
4.1	Advantages of e-commerce	66
4.2	Disadvantages of e-commerce	66
4.3	Comparative analysis of various security threats in e-commerce	73
9.1	Reasons for the federation of cloud	142
10.1	Graph theory in computer networks	155
10.2	Grap theory in cloud	156
11.1	The major findings from Round 1 and the 4 key insights presented to the respondents	178
11.2	Cybersecurity policy within an organization	179
11.3	Effective cyber incident response plan mandates	179
11.4	Federal government cybersecurity initiatives	180
11.5	Blockchain technology for secure Internet transactions	180
13.1	A contrast of the smartphone oses market share over the era of 2011-2017	215
15.1	Security attacks and their existing solutions	240
16.1	Examples of types of e-wallets	247
16.2	Electronic cash payment systems	249
16.3	Technological features of e-wallets in India	252
16.4	Legal features of e-wallets in India	252
16.5	Operational features of e-wallets in India	253
16.6	Security features of e-wallets in India	253
16.7	Mapping framework of e-wallet features	254

Foreword

With the widespread applicability of cyberspace in today's world, malefic activities like hacking, cracking or other malicious use of cyberspace have become more sophisticated and so critical that, absent a proper and organized plan to protect against such activities, overcoming them is impossible.

Today cybersecurity is one of the prime concerns for any organization, whether governmental or private sector; and for the sake of security and safety, it may be considered of national importance for a country. Many components of cyberspace are disreputable and therefore vulnerable to an expanding range of attacks by a spectrum of hackers, criminals, terrorists, and state actors. For example, both government agencies as well as private sector companies, irrespective of their size and nature, may suffer from cyber thefts, cyber vandalism and attacks like denial-of-service or other service-related attacks, since they incorporate sensitive information. Many of a nation's critical infrastructures, like the electric power grid, air traffic control system, financial systems, and communication networks, depend extensively on information technology for their operation. Nowadays, threats posed by the vulnerabilities of information technology and its malicious use have increased along with technological advancements. Following the infamous September 11, 2001 attacks against the United States, the importance of maintaining a properly fashioned security environment has been realized in light of increased cyber espionage directed at private companies and government agencies. National policy makers have become increasingly concerned that adversaries backed by considerable resources will attempt to exploit cyber vulnerabilities in the critical infrastructure, thereby inflicting substantial harm on a nation.

Numerous policy proposals have been suggested in the past and a number of bills have been introduced to tackle the challenges of cybersecurity. Although the larger public discourse sometimes treats the topic of cybersecurity as a new one, the Computer Science and Telecommunications Board (CSTB) of the National Research Council has extensively recognized cybersecurity as being a major challenge for public policy. Therefore, for over more than two decades the CSTB has offered a wealth of information on practical measures, technical and nontechnical challenges, as well as potential policy concerning cybersecurity. Drawing on past insights developed in the body of work of the CSTB, a committee has produced a report entitled *Cybersecurity Primer: Leveraging Two Decades of National Academies Work*, which acts as a concise primer on the fundamentals of cybersecurity and the nexus between cybersecurity and public policy.

Full Professor Valentina E. Balas
Department of Automatics and Applied Software
Aurel Vlaicu University of Arad, Romania

Preface

The main objective of this book is to explore the concept of cybersecurity in parallel and distributed computing along with recent research developments in the field. Also included are various real-time/offline applications and case studies in the fields of engineering and computer science and the modern tools and technologies used. Information concerning various topics relating to cybersecurity technologies is organized within the sixteen chapters of this book.

Chapter 1 discusses the difference between traditional and contemporary computer crimes observed over the last few years. The general evolution of cybercrimes has led to internet-based risks affecting businesses, organizations, etc., exposing them to potential liability. The recent concept of cyber insurance, which promises coverage when organizations suffer as a result of internet-based risk, is discussed in this chapter. Later on in the chapter, readers will become familiarized with security policies and various security models, such as the Bell-LaPadula and Biba models, that enforce them. Furthermore, readers will also become acquainted with the concepts of network neutrality and human rights, as they go hand in hand. With the risks and aftereffects of cybercrimes in mind, we also explore the legal aspect of cybercrimes by analyzing the concept of computer forensics. Some best practices pertaining to countermeasures to information warfare are also discussed.

Chapter 2 presents an overview of the research and solutions relating to the problem of hidden image detection.

Chapter 3 focuses on the security aspects of data mining and possible techniques to prevent it. Moreover, some privacy issues due to data mining, such as intrusion detection, are also highlighted.

Chapter 4 addresses different types of specific security threats, security challenges, and vulnerabilities at various levels of the system. Furthermore, it throws light on how to deal with these various security threats and issues, and presents a comparative analysis of various methods used in e-commerce security, including how to perform secure payment transactions in an efficient manner.

Chapter 5 notes that although the likelihood of conventional warfare has been reduced due to diplomatic efforts, the fear of reduced resources and monetary greed are still very much in evidence. With resources becoming increasingly digitalized due to the development of technologies like 5G, the internet of things, smartphones, smarter cities, etc., cyberattacks from ransomware such as WannaCry, NotPetya, Bad Rabbit, etc., are also on the rise. With everything connected to the internet, it has become a battlefield on which the civilians of all nations are connected, unwittingly placing them on the battlefield. This connectivity is a bigger threat, as it can cause massive devastation in rising digital economies, affecting everyone and everything, even our brains, which, along with the internet's ever-encroaching war on human emotions, is evidence that a war is coming – a cyberwar.

Chapter 6 introduces the concept of blockchain technology and how it is crucial to the security industry. We delve into the details concerning the characteristics of blockchain technology, its structure, types, architecture and workings. Since Bitcoin is one of the most widespread applications of blockchain technology, this chapter also highlights its workings. The chapter concludes with a few of the challenges facing this technology and its future scope.

Chapter 7 focuses on the need for service level agreements (SLAs) to prevail between a service provider and a client in relation to certain aspects of the service such as quality, availability and responsibilities. The Cuckoo's Egg lessons on cybersecurity by Clifford Stoll, as well as various amendments to curb fraud, data breaches, dishonesty, deceit and other such cybercrimes, are also thoroughly discussed.

Chapter 8 examines various security issues and challenges in distributed computing security, along with security issues in advanced areas like heterogeneous computing, cloud computing, fog computing, etc. Moreover, we present the methods/schemes/protocols used to address various security issues and possible methods of implementation.

Chapter 9 demonstrates the administration task issue in unified cloud situations as a multi-target enhancement issue in light of security. The model enables shoppers to consider an exchange between three security factors—cost, execution, and hazard—when appointing their administrations to CSPs. The cost and execution of the conveyed security administrations are assessed utilizing an arrangement of quantitative measurements which we propose. We then address utilization of the preemptive streamlining technique to assess clients' needs. Reproductions have demonstrated that this model aides in decreasing the infringement rate of security and execution.

Chapter 10 investigates chart hypothesis applications in PC systems with a particular spotlight on diagram hypothesis applications in distributed computing. Included in this chapter are the fundamental asset provisioning issues that emerge in distributed computing situations along with some applied hypothetical diagram recommendations to address these issues.

Chapter 11 explores the concepts of cybercrime and cybersecurity, and presents the statistical impact they have on organizations, demonstrating the importance of an effective cybersecurity policy manual. It also describes the methodology used for this research, analyzes the data provided by expert testimonials, and introduces the development of a new innovative technological method (blockchain) to minimize the risks of the cyber world. The analyses cover the extent to which Blockchain applications could help strengthen cybersecurity and protect organizations against cyberattacks, and what kind of research directions are essential for the future.

Chapter 12 classifies and details the various types of smartphone device security threats. Further case studies about the exploitation of smartphones by terrorists, user data theft and smartphone-based fraud are presented. The chapter concludes with measures to improve the security of mobile devices and prevent user data from being exploited by attacks.

Chapter 13 highlights some strategies for maintaining the privacy, integrity, confidentiality and availability of cyber information and its real-world impacts such as mobile security software for secure email and online banking, cyber health check programs for business, cyber incident response management, cybersecurity risk management and cyber security schemes and services.

Chapter 14 discusses security policies and mechanisms, various categories of attacks (e.g., denial-of-service) and Globus security architecture, along with distribution of security mechanisms. Furthermore, the various attack strategies that frequently occur in any information system under consideration are also investigated.

Chapter 15 lists some of the security issues which have arisen in the healthcare sector and also discusses existing solutions and emerging threats.

Chapter 16 presents and analyzes various types of models operating in the e-commerce/ebusiness domains in India. This chapter tries to give a brief insight into the various technological, operational, legal and security features available in different types of e-Wallets. It can be concluded from the information presented that all three wallets have the same security features, which include Anti-fraud, 3D SET or SSL, P2P, data encryption and OTP.

Among those who have influenced this project are our family and friends, who have sacrificed a lot of their time and attention to ensure that we remained motivated throughout the time devoted to the completion of this crucial book.

Dac-Nhuong Le
Raghvendra Kumar
Brojo Kishore Mishra
Manju Khari
Jyotir Moy Chatterjee

Acknowledgments

We would like to acknowledge the most important people in our lives, our grandfathers and grandmothers, and thank our wives. This book has been our long-cherished dream which would not have been turned into reality without the support and love of these amazing people. They have encouraged us despite our failing to give them the proper time and attention. We are also grateful to our best friends, who have encouraged and blessed this work with their unconditional love and patient.

Dr. Dac-Nhuong Le
Deputy Head, Faculty of Information Technology
Haiphong University, Haiphong, Vietnam

Acronyms

APIs	Application Programming Interfaces
AR	Post-Traumatic Stress Disorder
AES	Advance Encryption Algorithm
ACL	Access Control Lists
APT	Advanced Persistent Threats
ATM	Automated Teller Machine
AS	Autonomous System
ACE	Access Control Entries
B2B	Business-to-Business
B2C	Business-to-Consumer
BAN	Body Area Networks
CA	Certifying Authority
C2B	Consumer-to-Business
C2C	Consumer-to-Consumer
C2G	Consumer-to-Government
CSPs	Cloud Service Providers
CV	Consumer Version
CPPS	Cyber-Physical Production System
COMSEC	Communications Security
CDI	Constrained Data Item
COI	Conflict of Interest
CDMA	Code-Division Multiple Access
CDC	Cloud Data Center
CISA	Cybersecurity Information Sharing Act
C3I	Command, Control, Communications and Intelligence
CFOs	Chief Financial Officers
CPU	Central Processing Unit
CoF	Cloud based Card-on File
CRC	Cyclic Redundancy Checksum
DAC	Discretionary Access Control
DAO	Decentralized Autonomous Organizations
DMZ	Demilitarized Zone
DFD	Degree of Security Deficiency
DDoS	Distributed Denial of Service
DoS	Denial of Service
DSC	Digital Signature Certificate
DHS	Department of Homeland Security

ETG	Enterprise Topology Graphs
ECMA	European Computer Manufacturers Association
ECDA	Elliptic Curve Diffie-Hellman
ECC	Elliptic Curve Cryptography
ESN	Electronic Serial Number
EPROM	Erasable Programmable Read-Only Memory
EWF	Energy Web Foundation
FBI	Federal Bureau of Investigation
FIPB	Foreign Investment Promotion Board
FC	Fog Computing
FI	Financial Institution
FEMA	Foreign Exchange Management Act
GUI	Graphical User Interface
GPS	Global Positioning System
HTML	Hypertext Markup Language
HMI	Human-Machine Interface
HAIL	High-Availability and Integrity Layer
HTTPS	Hypertext Transfer Protocol Secure
IoT	Internet of Things
ICCPR	International Covenant on Civil and Political Rights
ICMP	Internet Control Message Protocol
IPS	Intrusion Prevention Systems
IDS	Intrusion Detection System
IMPS	Immediate Payment Service
IP	Internet Protocol
ISP	Internet Service Provider
IT	Information Technology
IC3	Internet Crime Complaint Center
ISA	Instruction Set Architecture
IaaS	Infrastructure as a Service
ICERT	Indian Computer Emergency Response Team
IE	Internet Explorer
IEEE	Institute of Electrical and Electronics Engineers
KDC	Key Distribution Center
KYC	Know Your Customer
LAN	Local-Area Network
LSB	Least Significant Bit
MAC	Mandatory Access Control
MBR	Master Boot Record
MTBF	Mean Time Between Failures
MTTR	Mean Time to Recovery, Response, or Resolution
MIN	Mobile Identification Number
MiM	Man-in-the-middle Attack
NCSA	National Cyber Security Alliance
NCP	Network Control Protocol
NFC	Near Field Communication
NBFC	Non-Banking Financial Companie

NIST	National Institute of Standards and Technology
OS	Operating System
OTP	One-Time Password
PLC	Programmable Logic Controller
PIN	Personal Identification Number
PGP	Pretty Good Privacy
PwC	PricewaterhouseCoopers
PC	Personal Computer
POS	Point-on Scale
PKI	Public Key Infrastructure
P2P	Peer-to-Peer
PPI	Prepaid Payment Instruments
PaaS	Platform as a Service
PDA	Personal Digital Assistant
QoS	Quality of Service
RFID	Radio-Frequency Identification
RBAC	Role-Based Access Control
RBI	Reserve Bank of India
RSA	Rivest-Shamir-Adleman
SCADA	Supervisory Control and Data Acquisition
SET	Secure Electronic Transaction
SLA	Service Level Agreement
SMB	Server Message Block
SYN	Synchronization
SSID	Service Set Identifier
SQL	Structured Query Language
SSL	Secure Sockets Layer
SMS	Short Message Service
SIM	Subscriber Identity Module
SPV	Simple Payment Verification
TCPAC	Trusted Computing Platform Alliance
TCB	Trusted Computing Base
UDI	Unconstrained Data Item
UDP	User Datagram Protocol
UDHR	Universal Declaration of Human Rights
VM	Virtual Machine
VPN	Virtual Private Network
XSS	Cross-Site Scripting
XML	eXtensible Markup Language
XACML	eXtensible Access Control Markup Language

PART I

Cybersecurity Concept

Introduction on Cybersecurity

ISHAANI PRIYADARSHINI

University of Delaware, Newark, Delaware, USA
Email: IshaaniPriyadarshini@udel.edu

Abstract

In a world ruled by speed and perfection, technology relies primarily on computer science. Be it a simple act of sending an email or a critical act of conveying billions of dollars, almost everything is merely a click away. The world of computer science keeps people engaged in activities like gaming, website surfing, social media, banking, digital citizenship, etc., with a grip spanning many domains such as hardware, software, network, data, etc. Because so many activities rely on computers, they attract criminals, which ultimately leads to cybercrime, which could be as elementary as basic hacking or as elaborate as ransomware attacks or financial cybercrimes. The consequences may vary from loss of personal or sensitive information to loss of massive amounts of money. Thus, the need to ensure cybersecurity is paramount. In this chapter, we will take a look at the concept of cybersecurity, its causes, consequences and principles. The idea of cybersecurity is not only limited to small firms and educational institutions, but also spreads across various industries and governments, making it one of the most significant areas of study. In the past, certain objectives have been proposed to safeguard such critical cyber infrastructures. Certain standards, guidelines and practices have found their place in cybersecurity frameworks to ensure that the cyber infrastructure and architecture is secure. Since the operations are multiple as well as insightful, they must be carried out by accountable personnel, such as the security administrator or incident response team, who are usually given roles in the cyber infrastructure depending on the nature of their work. Some of the anticipated roles

Dac-Nhuong Le et al. (eds.), Cyber Security in Parallel and Distributed Computing, (3–262)
© 2019 Scrivener Publishing LLC

of accountable personnel are defined in this chapter. The nature of cybercrimes over the last few years has changed drastically owing to the change in motives behind the crimes, tools and techniques involved and the overall consequences. We have observed the contrast between traditional and contemporary computer crimes over the last few years. The general evolution of cybercrimes has led to internet-based risks affecting businesses, organizations, etc,. which are potential liabilities that are harmful to property. The concept of cyber insurance is recent and promises coverage when organizations suffer internet based risks, which we have essayed in this chapter. In the later part of the chapter we will familiarize ourselves with the concept of security policies and various security models that enforce them. Few security models like the Bell La Padula and the Biba model will be discussed in this section. Further, we will acquaint ourselves with the concept of network neutrality and human rights as they go hand in hand. Keeping in mind the risks and after effects of cybercrimes, we will also explore the the legal aspect of cybercrimes by analyzing the concept of computer forensics. Some best practices pertaining to countermeasures for information warfare have also been discussed.

In a world ruled by speed and perfection, technology relies primarily on computer science. Be it a simple act of sending an email or a critical act of conveying billions of dollars, almost everything is merely a click away. The world of computer science keeps people engaged in activities like gaming, website surfing, social media, banking, digital citizenship, etc., with a grip spanning many domains such as hardware, software, network, data, etc. Because so many activities rely on computers, they attract criminals, which ultimately leads to cybercrime, which could be as elementary as basic hacking or as elaborate as ransomware attacks or financial cybercrimes. The consequences may vary from loss of personal or sensitive information to loss of massive amounts of money. Thus, the need to ensure cybersecurity is paramount. In this chapter, we will take a look at the concept of cybersecurity, its causes, consequences and principles. The idea of cybersecurity is not only limited to small firms and educational institutions, but also spreads across various industries and governments, making it one of the most significant areas of study. In the past, certain objectives have been proposed to safeguard such critical cyber infrastructures. Certain standards, guidelines and practices have found their place in cybersecurity frameworks to ensure that the cyber infrastructure and architecture is secure. Since the operations are multiple as well as insightful, they must be carried out by accountable personnel who are usually given roles in the cyber infrastructure depending on their nature of their work such as the security administrator or the incident response team. We will look forward to some of the roles in this chapter. The nature of cybercrimes over the last few years has changed drastically owing to the change in motive behind the crimes, tools and techniques involved and the overall consequences. We observe the contrast between traditional computer crimes and contemporary computer crimes over the last few years. General evolution of cybercrimes has led to internet based risks affecting businesses, organizations etc. which have the potential to harm liability and properties. Therefore, cyber insurance is discussed in this chapter, which is a recent concept that promises coverage when organizations suffer internet-based risks. Later on in the chapter, security policies and various security models that enforce them are explained. A few security models, such as the Bell-LaPadula and Biba models, will be discussed in this section. Furthermore, the reader will become acquainted with the concepts of network neutrality and human rights, as they go hand in hand. Keeping in mind the risks and aftereffects of cybercrimes, we also explore the legal aspects of cybercrimes by analyzing the concept of computer forensics. Some best practices pertaining to countermeasures for information warfare are also discussed.

Keywords: Cyber infrastructure, cybercrimes, cyber insurance, computer forensics, security models

1.1 Introduction to Cybersecurity

Cybersecurity may be defined as the ability to defend against and recover from cyberattacks. According to the National Institute of Standards and Technology (NIST), cybersecurity is the ability to protect or defend the use of cyberspace from cyberattacks [1]. The entire cyberspace consists of several interdependent networks of the information systems infrastructure which could be the internet, telecommunications network, computer systems, embedded systems or controllers. Thus, cybersecurity is concerned with critical infrastructure, network security, cloud security, application security, the internet of things and several other domains where the need to ensure security is paramount.

1. **Critical infrastructure**: Security in critical infrastructure deals with cyber physical systems and real-world deployments. Industries like automation, aviation, healthcare, traffic lights, electricity grids etc are prone to cyberattacks like eavesdropping, compromised key attacks, man-in-the-middle attacks and denial-of-service attacks [2].

2. **Network security**: Network security deals with measures and concerns to protect information systems. It guards against unauthorized intrusions and protects the usability and integrity of network and data. cyberattacks on networks could be passive like port scanning, wiretapping and encryption, and active, like phishing, cross-site scripting and denial of service attacks.

3. **Cloud security**: Cloud security takes into account several control-based technologies and policies to protect information, data applications and infrastructure within the cloud. Since cloud is a shared resource, cyberattacks on clouds may lead to data breaches, system vulnerabilities, malicious insiders, data loss and shared technology vulnerabilities. Some attacks on the cloud computing environment are account hijacking, phishing, denial-of-service attacks and compromised credentials.

4. **Application security**: Security of an application is ensured by mitigating security vulnerabilities. Since an application development has several stages, like design, development, deployment, upgrade and maintenance, each stage being susceptible to cyberattacks. Common attacks pertaining to web application security are cross-site scripting, SQL injection, buffer overflows and distributed denial-of-service attacks. In mobile applications, attacks like spyware, botnets, ad hoc and click fraud and malware infections take place.

5. **Internet of Things security**: The internet of things (IoT) consists of computing, mechanical and digital devices with unique identifiers capable of transferring data over the network without human interference. IoT security safeguards these connected devices and networks in IoT. The attacks include spyware and botnets.

The CIA (*Confidentiality, Integrity, Availability*) triad is the unifying attribute for cybersecurity which is used to evaluate security of an organization using the three key areas related to security namely confidentiality,integrity and availability. These three attributes have specific requirements and operations.

1. **Confidentiality**: Fairly similar to privacy, confidentiality ensures that information is accessed by authorized personnel. The idea is to prevent sensitive information from being accessed by unauthorized people. Attacks on confidentiality could be credit card fraud, identity theft, wiretapping, phishing, and social engineering. User IDs, passwords, encrypted data, access control lists (ACL) and policy-based security measures evade attacks against confidentiality.

2. **Integrity**: Integrity ensures consistency, trustworthiness and accuracy of data. The idea is to prevent modification of data by those who are unauthorized to do so. It also ensures data authenticity and nonrepudiation. Some attacks on integrity are man-in-the-middle attacks, session hijacking attacks and salami attacks. Establishing user access controls, checksums, data encryption and hashing are some means to ensure data integrity.

3. **Availability**: Availability refers to timely and reliable access to resources. The information concerned should be readily accessible to authorized personnel. Some attacks against availability are denial-of-service attacks, SYN attacks and ICMP (*Internet Control Message Protocol*) flood attacks.

Cybersecurity revolves around the human and operational side of technology. It takes into account 3Ps, namely people, plan and practice.

1. **People**: The main idea about people being involved in cybersecurity is to prepare human resources against cyber threats and for data protection. It is not uncommon for organizations to be victims of phishing. Educating masses and awareness efforts in the form of classroom training, emails, tips and tricks can lead to constituting such a compelling environment.

2. **Plan**: In order to respond to a cyber incident, there should be a plan that answers significant questions like *"Is there a technical way to deal with some issue."* Using a plan could assist in recovering data and restoring operations. It can guide, establish protocols and organize the approach to certain responses.

3. **Practice**: Testing of plans requires exercises. Practicing refers to preparing the team with exercises in order to identify weaknesses in the plan. Exercises may incorporate hypothetical situations, series of clues, implementations, decision making and response processes.

1.2 Cybersecurity Objectives

The concept of cybersecurity strives to maintain a secure cyberspace so as to safeguard the critical infrastructure. To recover from cyber incidents and attacks, there should be appropriate response, resolution and recovery. A legal framework ensures secure cyberspace. Following are a few objectives that lead to prevention from cyber threats and protection against cyberattacks.

1. **Prevent threats**: In order to prevent threats, it is important to analyze the attacks and ensure designing, deployment and operation of required network control protocols (NCP). Threat indicators must be identified and certain incident reporting guidelines must be established. Adopting best practices and identifying malicious technology combined with research may be used to avert certain threats.

2. **Identification and system hardening**: One of the primary objectives of cybersecurity is to identify threats in order to harden the system. The process ensures risk assessment and adoption of security measures. The purpose of system hardening is to mitigate certain risks associated with security. Sometimes an advanced system hardening approach is used, which incorporates reformatting of hard disks and installing only specific programs into the system.

3. **Conduct operational, architectural and technical innovations**: Introducing dynamic approaches towards cyber risk management protects cyber infrastructure from specific cyberattacks.

4. **Prepare for contingencies**: The idea of contingency planning is basically preparedness for cyberattacks. It may contain policies, best practices, procedures and recovery plans.

5. **Allocation of information**: The information that is supposed to be circulated in the entire system must be effective. Cyber threats, vulnerabilities and incidents could be reported by issuing alerts. The information may be successfully distributed among several platforms.

6. **Specialized security training**: The workforce must be equipped with specialized security training. The information and services must be provided to the joint federal partners so that the workforce is strong enough during cyber incidents.

7. **Strengthen system fault tolerance**: Fault tolerance of a system may be computed by performing vulnerability assessment. High-assurance systems may possibly withstand cyberattacks.

8. **Reduce vulnerabilities**: Several security practices assist in reducing vulnerabilities. Patching, use of firewalls and using strong passwords can prevent malicious access to the systems.

9. **Improve usability**: The term usability is defined as the degree to which something is easy to use. Usability requirements may be incorporated into the systems along with trusted technology.

10. **Authentication in cyberspace**: Verification of the identity of a user or process is an important process in cybersecurity. Depending on the device, one factor or multifactor authentication may be deployed. Authentication supports what we have, what we are and what we know.

11. **Automate security procedure**: Automation leads to efficiency, better prediction of behavior and faster execution. Appropriate implementation of automation leads to prevention of cyberattacks. Automation can correlate data, promote prevention quicker than the spreading of attacks and identify network infections.

12. **Guarantee interoperability among devices**: Interoperability is the ability of systems to coordinate in order to work together or across organizations. Ensuring interoperability leads to information being distributed effectively in the organization.

13. **Highlight unfavorable events in cyberspace**: It is important to highlight unfavorable events in cyberspace so as to find solutions in order to prevent the systems from being

vandalized. Information regarding the cause, extent and impact of unfavorable events may be listed for future use.

14. **Introduce security measures**: By introducing security measures, one can detect cyberattacks, prevent them and correct them. Some security measures are network segmentation and use of firewalls, secure remote access, access controls, password protection, ensuring training programs and defining policies [3].

1.3   Cybersecurity Infrastructure and Internet Architecture (NIST)

Since cyberattacks are becoming more and more sophisticated, there is a need to introduce standardized practices to ensure security.The National Institute of Standards and Technology (NIST) incorporates certain policies, standards, guidelines and best practices to address cybersecurity issues [4]. This framework is divided into framework core, implementation tiers and profiles.

1. **Framework core**: The framework core comprises of certain schemes leading to specific outcomes. It may be in the form of functions, categories, subcategories and informative references.

    - *Functions*: In order to secure systems and respond to attacks, the five basic functions are to identify, protect, detect, respond and recover, which we will be discussing later in this section.

    - *Categories*: Different functions have corresponding categories for identifying different operations and activities. For example, in order to protect, one can make use of access control, software updates and anti-malware programs.

    - *Subcategories*: Categories with specific goals are termed as subcategories. For example, the process of software updating could have specific operations like proper configuration or manual updating of machines.

    - *Informative references*: Informative references include policies, standards and guidelines. For example, certain steps that require manually updating Windows system.

2. **Implementation tiers**: Following are the four tiers of information:

    - Tier 1 or Partial Implementation handles organizational risks inconsistently due to ad hoc cybersecurity infrastructure.

    - Tier 2 implementation deals with risks, plans and resources to protect cyber infrastructure at a deeper level than partial implementation.

    - Tier 3 or Repeatable Implementation can repeatedly tend to cyber crises. Policies may be implemented at the same level and cybersecurity awareness can minimize cyber-related risks.

    - Tier 4 or Adaptive Implementation is responsible for detecting threats and predicting issues with respect to the security infrastructure.

3. **Profiles**: A cybersecurity framework has some specific goals. Profiles summarize the status of an organization's cybersecurity. Multiple profiles in a cybersecurity framework ensure identification of several weak spots that are a part of the cybersecurity

implementation. They can also support the connection among functions, categories and subcategories to resources and risk tolerance of organizations.

As discussed before, we will now take a look at the functions of the framework core. They are as follows:

1. **Identify**: Identification refers to development of understanding in order to manage cybersecurity risks to systems, assets, data and capabilities. The identify function has the following categories:

   - *Asset management*: Identification of data, devices and systems that assist an organization for business purposes.
   - *Business environment* It prioritizes the objectives, mission and activities of an organization. The information plays a key role in decision making for cybersecurity roles, responsibilities and risk management.
   - *Governance*: These are the mandatory guidelines essential for managing an organization's environment and identifying the cybersecurity risks.
   - *Risk assessment*: The organization must be able to infer the risks related to its operations and infrastructure.
   - *Risk management strategy*: Several constraints, tolerances and assumptions affect security risk decisions.

2. **Protect**: Organizations must be equipped with several defense mechanisms during a cybersecurity event. Ensuring controlled access, awareness, training, proper network configuration, deploying protective tools and technology, etc., can ensure protection of cybersecurity infrastructure and systems. Following are a few of the categories for protection:

   - *Access control*: Authorized users may access devices, processes, activities and transactions.
   - *Awareness and training*: Awareness and training of the employees of the organization along with policies and guidelines can ensure protection from cyber issues.
   - *Data security*: Confidentiality, integrity and availability of data should be maintained throughout its lifetime.
   - *Information protection*: Policies, procedures, guidelines and processes can protect information.
   - *Maintenance*: Maintenance of the system could be performed using certain policies and procedures.
   - *Protective technology*: Policies, procedures and agreements, along with technical solutions, lead to system security.

3. **Detect**: To identify cybersecurity events, proper measures must be adopted by organizations. Monitoring and threat identification are a few ways to detect security issues in systems. The following categories pertain to detection:

   - *Events and anomalies*: Analyzing the events in a timely manner can ensure detection of anomalous activities.
   - *Monitoring*: Monitoring the system at different intervals can assist in identifying issues and also verify the effectiveness of solutions proposed.

- *Other detection techniques*: Several processes and procedures may be tested to detect malicious behavior in a system.

4. **Respond**: In the case of cyber incidents occurring, organizations must be able to contain the impact. Chalking out response plans, establishing communication lines, and collecting and analyzing information are several response strategies. We look at a few categories.

   - *Response planning*: Execution of processes and procedures to detect cybersecurity events.
   - *Communication*: Information and response activities across the organization can be coordinated if communicated properly.
   - *Analysis*: Analyzing data ensures proper response and recovery.
   - *Mitigation*: Several events which have the potential to cause security issues in the system must be mitigated. The cyber incidents and their aftereffects must be mitigated.
   - *Improvement*: Analyzing the current and previous detection-response activities can greatly enhance future response activities.

5. **Recover**: Cybersecurity events have the potential to affect services and capabilities of systems. Therefore, organizations must introduce effective strategies or recovery plans to restore the system. Following are some categories that do the same:

   - *Recovery planning*: Execution of recovery processes and procedures and maintenance leads to timely restoration of systems affected by malicious events.
   - *Improvements*: Upgradation of current processes and procedures leads to improvement in future systems for recovery.
   - *Communications*: Communication within an organization ensures coordination of restoration activities.

1.4   Cybersecurity Roles

As discussed in the previous sections, we know that cybersecurity spans a vast domain. In order to secure an organizational infrastructure, checkpoints are introduced at every step, thereby making security a significant element throughout the organization. Since security in an organization is introduced from top to bottom, there are several roles and responsibilities that are undertaken by cybersecurity professionals. In this section we will take a look at all the roles that are a part of cybersecurity. For that we must categorize the specific operations that take place in a cyber infrastructure. We will further specify the important fields that are a part of the operations involved. Based on the fields we will highlight the corresponding roles [5]. The cybersecurity operations that take place in a cyber infracture are presented below.

Secure provisioning:: Involved in the process of secure provisioning are secure configuration, deployment and management of the incorporated resources. Following are some specialty areas for secure provisioning in cybersecurity:

1. **Risk management**: The risk management process is used to identify threats and vulnerabilities, so that specific solutions may be adopted to secure a system. The roles pertaining to this specialization are:

- *Authorizing official*: These officials are responsible for functioning of the overall system with tolerable risk to organization and individuals.

- *Security control assessor*: These officials assess operations, technicality and management of the system controls deployed in the organization.

2. **Software Development**: Developing software from a cybersecurity perspective results in secure software design. The idea is to identify weakness in the software development life cycle so that it does not affect the software. Following are the security roles pertaining to software development:

   - *Software developer*: Responsible for creating, coding and maintaining software.

   - *Secure software assessor*: Sees to it that existing computer applications are secured.

3. **Systems architecture**: System architecture specifies security design to highlight the risks involved in a system. It analyzes whether the system requires security controls. Some security roles that are involved in system architecture are as follows:

   - *Enterprise architecture*: Involved in designing systems and processing information that is required by the system.

   - *Security architecture*: A security architecture designs systems and ensures system security while the software is developed.

4. **Research and development**: Due to increasing sophisticated cyber threats, it is important to research security in cyberspace and continuously develop strategies to overcome security issues. The role that falls into this category is as follows:

   - *Research and development specialist*: Conducts research to find vulnerabilities in existing systems and also develops techniques to ensure cybersecurity in certain infrastructures.

5. **Systems planning and development**: The process of system planning and development is initiated by gathering the requirements for the system design and based on the functionalities required, developing a system. The following roles are a part of this specialization:

   - *Requirements planner*: Takes into account the functional requirements for the system and processes the requirements into technical solutions.

   - *Systems developer*: Is assigned the task of designing, developing, testing and evaluating the system throughout the life-cycle of system development.

   - *Information systems security developer*: Is assigned the task of designing, developing, testing and evaluating the system security throughout the development of the system life cycle.

6. **Systems testing and evaluation**: This can help to understand how vulnerable a system is. It is carried out using certain tests, analysis, findings, examinations and developing combating strategies. Those taking on this role are as follows:

   - *Testing and evaluation specialist*: The responsibility of a testing and evaluation specialist is to plan, prepare and test a system in order to evaluate results. The test results are analyzed based on specifications in order to ensure security of a system.

Operate and maintain: The process of operation and maintenance ensures support, administration and maintenance for efficient system performance and security. The specialization areas in this domain are as follows:

1. **Database administration**: This takes into account storage, query, protection and utilization of data. Hence, sensitive data must be secured. Following are the roles that ensure security in database administration

    - *Database administrator*: Administers databases and is concerned with data management systems.

    - *Database analyst*: Develops and implements algorithms along with processing of data sets for data mining and research.

2. **Knowledge management**: Refers to the analysis and technical support of cybersecurity practices. The practices include identifying, creating, depicting and conducting good practices to promote a secure environment. One of the knowledge management roles is as follows:

    - *Knowledge manager*: Manages and administers processes and tools in order to identify, access and present information.

3. **Customer service and support**: The aim of customer service and support is to address technical problems related to cybersecurity for a system or an organization. One of the roles is as follows:

    - *Technical support specialist*: May assist in installing, configuring, troubleshooting and maintaining a system in order to offer technical assistance.

4. **Network services**: The work of network services is to protect the information technology infrastructure from various threats and vulnerabilities. Network services are used to manage the network, including hardware and software. Those that perform these kinds of tasks are known by the following title:

    - *Network security specialist*: Concerned with planning, implementing and operating network services to ensure security.

5. **Systems administration**: This field is responsible for providing advice to organizations regarding their infrastructure and security loopholes. It usually provides information about the weaknesses in a system. Those that take on this role are known by the following title:

    - *System administrator*: A system administrator is responsible for administering system accounts and is capable of installing, troubleshooting and maintaining a system.

6. **Systems analysis**: This is the study of existing systems, procedures and design to come up with solutions to ensure efficiency, security and effectiveness. Those that perform this role are known by the following title:

    - *Systems security analyst*: These officials develop and analyze integration, testing, operations and maintenance of systems in order to promote security.

Oversee and govern: The process of overseeing and governing assists in providing leadership, development, management and advocacy (*law and order*) for proper working of an organization. Some of the specialized fields and their corresponding roles are described as follows:

1. **Cyber law and advocacy**: This deals with all the legal procedures in order to provide consultancy on specific information technology-based issues and acts. The laws and policies have a direct impact on human rights and may also address cybercrimes. The roles that are specific to cyber law and advocacy are as follows:

   - *Cyber legal advisor*: Is responsible for providing legal advice and solutions to issues that pertain to cyber law.

   - *Privacy compliance manager*: Develops privacy compliance programs which highlight privacy issues.

2. **Training and education**: With cyberattacks growing rampantly, securing data and infrastructure requires highly trained professionals who must be academically and technically sound. The roles that form a part of this field are as follows:

   - *Cybersecurity curriculum developer*: Chalks out and evaluates cybersecurity training and education courses and techniques.

   - *Cybersecurity instructor*: Conducts classroom training and education of people who require cybersecurity knowledge and skills.

3. **Cybersecurity management**: This refers to procedures, operations and functions undertaken by an organization to ensure security in its infrastructure. It is used for thwarting issues like cyberattacks, intrusions, data breaches and malware. The roles belonging to this field are as follows:

   - *Information systems security manager*: Ensures security of a program or organization.

   - *COMSEC manager*: Communications security (COMSEC) resources of an organization is taken care of by COMSEC manager.

4. **Policy making**: The process of policy making ensures that a system is properly placed such that it can guard against critical attacks. This is done by implementing procedures and guidelines in order to protect a system as well as identify threats. The responsibilities of those taking on this role are as follows:

   - *Cyber workforce developer and manager:* Develops plans and strategies to support the education and training required for staff and professionals. Those in this role can also perform changes to existing policies.

   - *Cyber policy planner:* Develops and plans cybersecurity policies that align with the needs of security infrastructure.

5. **Cyber leadership**: The aim of cybersecurity project management is to direct to cybersecurity activities [6]. The following role belongs to this field:

   - *Executive cyber leadership:* These officials are responsible for conducting decision-making and directing the operations for an organization's security.

6. **Project management**: The aim of cybersecurity project management is to direct security projects with respect to an organization's needs and goals. The role taken up for this field are as follows:

   - *Program manager:* Plays a lead role in coordinating, communicating and integrating the program and is accountable for it.
   - *Project manager:* Manages the product throughout its life cycle.
   - *Product support manager:* Ensures that the functionalities are embedded into the system and that the system is operationally capable.
   - *Investment manager:* Manages a portfolio that highlights the details of the system capabilities and ensures that the needs are met.
   - *Program auditor:* Takes care of evaluations of the system and its individual components to ensure that the system is updated.

Protect and Defend: The protection and defense approach in cybersecurity is concerned with identifying and analyzing a system for threats and vulnerabilities in order to mitigate them. Following are a few areas and roles concerned with this specialization:

1. **Defense analysis**: The idea of defense analysis is based on the use of defensive tools and techniques in order to identify, analyze and report issues in a system that might potentially serve to corrupt information or system. The responsibility for this role is taken on by the following specialist:

   - *Defense analyst:* Collects data using defense tools like firewalls, intrusion detection systems, alerts, etc., to analyze events that may promote cyber issues in the system.

2. **Defense infrastructure:** The defense infrastructure takes into account testing, implementation, maintenance and administration of infrastructure hardware and software. The professionals efficient in this ability assume the following role:

   - *Defense infrastructure specialist*: Tests, implements, deploys and maintains infrastructure hardware and software.

3. **Incident response:** The incident response is a strategic method of addressing and managing the aftereffects of a security breach. The system must be handled in a way that has minimum damage and recovery time. The professionals pertaining to this field take on the following role:

   - *Defense incident responder:* Is concerned with investigating, analyzing and responding to cyber issues in a system.

4. **Vulnerability assessment and management:** The process of defining, identifying and classifying vulnerabilities in a system or infrastructure is referred to as vulnerability assessment. It is important to manage such systems as the weakest links may prove to be troublesome. The following role specializes in such operations:

   - *Vulnerability analyst:* Assesses systems and identifies those systems which deviate from appropriate configurations.

Analyze: Analyzing a system and its infrastructure involves studies that provide, procedures, designs and solutions to impart security, efficiency and effectiveness to the system.

The various ways through which a system is analyzed, along with the corresponding roles, are as follows:

1. **Threat Analysis**: Threats lead to interruption, interference and damage to a system and its resources. Hence, analyzing threats is very important. Threat analysis is performed to identify elements of risks that could prove to be destructive for the system. The title of those that perform this role is as follows:

   - *Warnings Analyst:* Generates indicators of compromise to identify the threats in a system. Collects, identifies and analyzes data that could potentially be regarded as threats.

2. **Exploitation Analysis**: In exploitation analysis, information is collected and analyzed to identify vulnerabilities that could lead to probable exploitation. The title assigned to this role is as follows:

   - *Exploitation Analyst:* Identifies access and collection gaps. Relies on reverse engineering and penetration testing techniques to find out if a system is being exploited.

3. **Source Analysis:** In source analysis, threat information which is a part of multiple sources is scrutinized. A description of those that perform this role is as follows:

   - *Source Analyst:* Prepares the environment based on analysis of data from multiple sources. Handles information requests and submits requirements needed for planning and operations.

4. **Target Analysis**: Target analysis refers to identification of probable cyber targets. A description of those that perform this role is as follows:

   - *Target Analyst*: Collects and analyzes open source data to study targets and their activities. Target analysts obtain information on the movement, communications and operations of targets.

5. **Language Analysis:** The idea of language analysis is to apply language and technical expertise for the process of collection of information, analysis and other cybersecurity activities. A description of those that perform this role is as follows:

   - *Language Analyst:* Analyzes information deduced from a language, voice or graphical representation. Language analysts have language-specific databases and they deliver subject matter expertise in specific languages.

Operate and Collect: The operate and collect process issues specialized contradictory and deceitful operations along with cybersecurity data, which may assist in developing intelligence. It includes those areas aimed at protection of unclassified information which may prove to be unfavorable in the future. Given below are some areas of interest with roles along the same lines.

1. **Collection Operations**: The collection operations process is based on conducting strategy-based collections that take into account the priorities involved. It is usually performed through a collection management process. The roles of those that ensure collection operations are as follows:

- *All-source Collection Manager:* Is responsible for identifying collection authorities and including significant information in the collection management process. All-source collection managers identify and analyze the capabilities of collection assets. Furthermore, they can establish collection plans and monitor their execution as well.

- *All-source Collection Requirements Evaluation Manager:* Is responsible for evaluating collection operations in order to improve collection. Available sources and methods can be used in order to develop requirement strategies for collection. The collection requirements are then processed, validated and coordinated in order to be evaluated.

2. **Cyber Operation Planning**: The idea of cyber operation planning is based on the process of performing cybersecurity planning. In this process, information is gathered and specific plans are developed pertaining to requirements. Strategic planning is conducted for integration and operations. The roles of those taking on this function are as follows:

   - *Cyber Intel Planner:* Works on intelligence plans to ensure that the requirements for cyber operations are complete. Identifies, validates and collects requirements in order to perform target selection, synchronization, operation execution and validation.

   - *Cyber Operations Planner:* Enforces plans to conduct cyber operations usually by collaborating with other planners, analysts and operators. Also conducts target selection, validation, synchronization and integration of cyber operations.

   - *Partner integration planner:* Forms a bridge between cyber operation partners. Provides guidance, resources and collaborations to ensure effective cyber operations.

3. **Cyber Operation**: This refers to the operations conducted in cyberspace in order to collect information from networks and devices. These could be schemes that collect information or actions that lead to cyberattacks. The role that deals with such issues is described as follows:

   - *Cyber Operator:* Collects information and carries out processes in a system for exploiting and tracing targets. Part of their work is to perform network navigation, forensic analysis and specific network operations.

Investigate: The process of investigation deals with exploring cybersecurity issues, attacks or events in cyberspace and related devices. The different spheres of investigation and their corresponding roles described as follows:

1. **Cyber Investigation**: The cyber investigation process is relied on by law enforcement officers for tracking criminals in cyberspace through computer devices. The role associated with cyber investigation is as follows:

   - *Cybercrime Investigator*: Is responsible for identifying, collecting, analyzing and preserving evidence related to cybercrimes. Investigations must be performed by maintaining proper documentation and adopting specific investigating techniques.

2. **Digital Forensics**: The work of digital forensics is to investigate crimes that have taken place through computers or digital devices. The aim is to find evidence that

could be produced in court. It is used to recover evidence that might have been destroyed deliberately or inadvertently in civil and criminal investigations. Those that take on this responsibility and their duties are as follows:

- *Forensics Analyst:* Performs investigations on crimes that have been propagated via computers. Forensics analysts must support their investigation in a well-documented manner along with physical evidence, digital media, logs and other resources that form a part of the crime committed.

- *Cyber Defense Forensics Analyst:* Scrutinizes digital evidence and takes into account incidents propagated through computers and digital devices in order to deduce any useful information related to the cybercrimes that have taken place.

1.5 Cybercrimes

1.5.1 Overview

Cyberspace takes into account communication over computer networks. The information traveling over networks could be sensitive, thus attracting adversaries who steal information. Hence, it is important to ensure that not only the network is secured, but so is the information being transmitted. The need for cybersecurity arises because cyberspace is not free from attacks. Any criminal activity which involves a computer, network or digital tools is called a cybercrime. Activities like hacking, spamming, phishing, identity theft, unauthorized access, etc., are called cybercrimes, whereas computers, laptops, mobile devices or any digital devices which perpetuate cybercrimes are called objects of crime. Any individual, group or organization that commits cybercrimes is called a cyber criminal and usually makes use of a computer as a tool or target or both. A discussion of some cybercrimes is presented below.

- *Computer as target*: These are the cybercrimes that target computers, networks or digital devices. Cyber criminals perpetuating such cybercrimes are technically insightful. Targeting a computer could lead to gaining unauthorized access to the targeted system, vandalizing the target system or using the target system to diffuse further attacks. Computer systems may be targeted by viruses and malicious codes through emails, attachments and website links and also by mere denial of service attacks.

- *Computer as tool:* A computer may be used as a tool to perpetuate cybercrime. Rather than affecting a system, the main goal is to target an individual. This technique exploits human weaknesses wherein the adversary conducts phishing attacks, scams, thefts, spams and may also propagate illegal or obscene content.

- *Cyber warfare*: Politically motivated attackers are responsible for cyber warfare. Also known as cyberwar, these kinds of cybercrimes are promoted by the internet and usually target financial and organization systems by sabotaging their websites or performing sophisticated espionage.

- *Cyber terrorism*: Cyber terrorism is also led by politically motivated attackers which target computers, information systems, data and programs, usually resulting in violence among different groups. They may be caused by advanced persistent threats (APT), viruses, worms, malware, denial-of-service (DoS) attacks, phishing and hacking techniques.

As we know, computers and digital devices are information portals and stimulate information exchange all over the world. They are also responsible for communication and data reserves. Using a computer for committing a crime is easy, quick, inexpensive and sometimes untraceable, thus making cybercrime one of the simplest ways to commit crime. To commit a crime in cyberspace, the cyber criminal has to consider some measures, which are discussed below.

1. Step 1 - Know the target: In order to launch an attack, an adversary must know the target system being considered. Knowing a target system refers to collecting data about the target system involving the machines, components and how secure the system and the network is. Performing research on a target system may take a few weeks to a few months and it provides information as to how secure the system is so that the adversary can prepare an attack.

2. Step 2 Secure their system: In this step, the adversary tries to identify vulnerabilities in his own system and network and tries to secure his own system. By now he has enough knowledge about the security of the target system.

3. Step 3 Set up test network: Before launching an attack on the target, the adversary will build a test network and try to test the target by trying to access it remotely or pinging it to see if its active.

4. Step 4 Hammer the target system: In this step the target system is hammered. The hacker of the system creates a backdoor to get into the system, gain remote access, gain unauthorized access, crack passwords and get superuser privileges.

5. Step 5 Cover their tracks: This is the final step of the attack where the adversary has to cover his tracks so that the administrator is not aware of the system being attacked. The activities performed by the adversary may be saved in the form of logs and other files. The adversary needs to make sure that the activities are not registered and may have to delete files or reset certain configurations.

1.5.2   Traditional Computer Crime and Contemporary Computer Crime

In the previous section, we highlighted how cyber criminals offend a computer system or components in order to carry out a cybercrime. It is believed that the first cybercrime took place in the 1820s. Eventually, with the expansion of computing, sophisticated cybercrimes started making their appearance. Cybercrimes can range from basic scripting attacks to substantial malware attacks. There is also a variation in attack strategies. In this section we will take into account the evolution of cybercrimes, i.e., how cybercrimes have grown from the last few years (*traditional cybercrimes*) to where they are right now (*contemporary cybercrimes*). Although different cybercrimes were conducted all throughout the given following timeline, we consider the crimes that were paramount in the respective years [7].

- 1820, Series Repetition: The trivial cybercrime involved repetition of a series of steps for weaving a special fabric, which in turn threatened the livelihoods of people involved in the textile industry. It was believed to be an act of sabotage [8].

- 1867, Interception: The act of interception causes information sent by a sender to be intercepted by an unauthorized user who may modify the contents of the information to another form. The user may also exploit the information for malicious processes.

- 1920, Organized Crime: These crimes are defined as illegal activities that are administered and chalked out by powerful groups. Cybercriminals may use anonymization, encryption and virtual currencies to carry out such attacks.

- 1961, Phreaking: The act of phreaking refers to breaking into telecommunication systems. The motive is to obtain free calls by tampering with the internal operations.

- 1965, Telemarketing Scams: This is another fraudulent activity that exploits the use of telephones. Regarded as an act of deception, it involves the adversary trying to obtain private information of victims.

- 1970, Computer Hacking: This is the unauthorized invasion of a computer or network and is concerned with modification of system hardware or software in order to accomplish a goal.

- 1971, Creeper Virus: This virus is one of the earliest known viruses that happened to affect a computer system. It could potentially locate a computer in a given network, pass into the computer and print files displaying a message. It could start over again and again.

- 1980, Denial-of-Service and Extortion: A denial-of-service (DoS) attack is launched to prevent the legitimate users from accessing a service. This is the result of the adversary sending out multiple requests to the server in order to consume the server resources, which leads to the server not responding to legitimate users. Cyber extortion takes place when the adversary pressures or threatens to damage business if they are not paid a ransom. Usually, they try to look for loopholes in the security architecture of the business organization and try to exploit it.

- 1985, Funds Transfer Fraud and ATM Fraud: Funds transfer fraud takes place when money is transferred, paid or delivered due to fraudulent computer activity or manipulation of electronic data. When an ATM card is used for deception, it leads to ATM fraud. The adversary may use the card to withdraw money by virtue of PIN-based transactions.

- 1986, Espionage: Computer systems and networks can be relied upon to gain unauthorized access to sensitive information. This information may be restricted to the government or corporate organizations. Internal data, intellectual property, client information and marketing intelligence information are some types of sensitive information.

- 1990, Child Exploitation: One of the insidious uses of computers is that of child exploitation. File sharing, webcams and streaming videos often lead to exploitation. Key threats in the area of child exploitation have been identified to be peer-to-peer networks, darknet networks and live streaming technology.

- 1993, Botnets: Botnets are a cluster of private computer systems which may be controlled as a group. They are usually infected with malicious software and are used to launch attacks, flood networks, etc.

- 1995, Online Piracy, Identity Crime and Spam: Online piracy or internet piracy refers to illegal copying of software using the internet. It may lead to copyright infringement. Identity crime or identity theft refers to impersonation of someone else's identity. It is done deliberately and leads to identity fraud. Spamming refers to sending of irrelevant or unsolicited messages, usually for the purpose of marketing.

- 1997, Cyberterrorism: Computer systems and technology may be used by politically motivated cyber criminals in order to cause disruption. It is done to intimidate, harm or threaten a government or a part of the population.

- 1998, Cyberstalking: This is a crime wherein an attacker intimidates a victim by means of electronic communication. The attacker may send emails, instant messages or use social media as a platform to stalk the victim. It can also be done by monitoring, identity theft, threatening or gathering information about the victim to harass them in the future.

- 2002, Phishing: This is a fraudulent activity wherein an attacker masquerades as a trustworthy individual, but sends malicious files in the form of attachments or links, such that when clicked, the victim's system gets compromised. It could lead to the system behaving inappropriately or obtaining the login credentials of the user or system.

- 2003, Wireless Vulnerabilities: In a wireless environment, nodes are mobile, unlike in a wired environment where nodes are static. This leads to wireless environments being more vulnerable than wired environments. The threats could be in the form of rogue access points, bluetooth attacks, wireless driver attacks and configuration weaknesses.

- 2006, M-Commerce Attacks: Electronic commerce that relies on mobile phones has its own set of disadvantages. Installation of stealthy software (*rootkit*) could affect mobile phones, steal information and reroute calls. Digital certificates may be stolen. Unsecured WiFi threats, viruses and malware can further aggravate the situation. Encryption hacking can steal private information and electronic eavesdropping cannot be ruled out.

- 2009, Cloud Computing Attacks: The cloud environment also harbors certain vulnerabilities leading to cloud computing attacks. Attacks like denial-of-service (DoS), malware injection, side channel and man-in-the-middle are prevalent in cloud computing.

- 2013, RFID Attacks: These attacks are usually physical attacks. They are in the form of system jamming, radio signal blockage and RFID tag disabling. They also support eavesdropping, replay attacks, sniffing and spoofing.

- 2014, Credit Card Fraud: This involves a payment card, usually credit or debit, as an illegal source in order to conduct a purchase. The main idea behind credit card fraud is to purchase items without actually paying or gaining unauthorized funds belonging to an account. It has been known to result in huge financial losses.

- 2015, Data Breach: This refers to the act of sensitive data being accessed copied, transferred, viewed, stolen or used by unauthorized users. The sensitive information may be in the form of credit card information, social security numbers, healthcare information, etc.

- 2016, Distributed Denial-of-Service (DDoS) Attack: A DDoS attack sees to it that multiple jeopardized systems attack a target. This target could be a website, server or network resource. A denial-of-service attack is launched for the users of the target. The messages, connection requests and packets utilize the resources of the target and compel it to slow down, crash or shut down. The idea is to deny any service to the otherwise legitimate users.

1.5.3 Combating Crimes

In the previous subsection we have familiarized ourselves with several cybercrimes. We now know that cybercrimes are a result of vandalizing the system and can be performed by gaining unauthorized access into them using viruses, worms, frauds, data breaches, spams and scams. Different cybercrimes have different prevention and detection techniques. We have already discussed how timestamps and logs collectively provide information about unauthorized access. In this section we will focus on ways to combat cybercrimes. Following are some effective ways of doing this.

1.5.3.1 Securing Networks

Network security is the biggest concern when combating cybercrimes. The network may be part of a small enterprise or may be robust enough to span multiple organizations. It may be simply wired or wireless; either way it is vulnerable to cybercrimes. The easiest way to secure networks would be hardening the systems such that firewalls are installed or unnecessary ports are blocked. The firewall should be stable enough to protect services in the demilitarized zone as well as different critical servers. The wireless networks must ensure encrypted access points along with the service set identifier (SSID) being hidden or changed to a less suspicious name. Other security measures available for securing the network are in form of intrusion detection systems (IDS) and intrusion prevention systems (IPS), which can work collaboratively to ensure greater security. They can identify potential threats to the network by constantly monitoring and identifying events to log information about them. This information may be sent to the management.

1.5.3.2 Incident Response Team

The incident response team is concerned with combating cybercrimes in the sense that they receive information about data leakage, analyze the events and respond accordingly. The team may consist of security professionals like incident handlers, vulnerability handlers, penetration testers, reverse engineers, etc., who perform security operations. The cybercrimes usually handled by the incident response team mainly revolve around viruses, worms, unauthorized access, denial-of-service attacks, etc.

1.5.3.3 Detecting Malware

Malware works by using the principle of getting installed into a system and then enabling a backdoor so that confidential information may be retrieved. It is important that a malware is detected before a system is infected. Several malware classification techniques are adopted for the same. Network-based malware prevention technique analyzes the network traffic and blocks any malware that is found. Endpoint-based malware prevention technique has endpoint software that analyzes the traffic moving into and from the machine. It detects the malware and also any application that runs it.

1.5.3.4 Authentication and Authorization

Identity theft is one of the most common cybercrimes. The process of authentication may be used to validate the identity of a user. The process of authentication relies on what we know (*something like a PIN or a password*), what we have (*like an access card*) and what we are (*biometrics*). Authentication may be single factor or multifactor, keeping in mind the required security level. Authorization specifies the privileges or access rights of an individual for system resources. cybercrimes that involve masquerading or unauthorized access of data may be combatted using these techniques.

1.5.3.5 Filtering

The internet is full of malicious content ranging from websites to emails. Web filtering is important to prevent users from clicking into websites that contain malicious content or inadvertently enter their personal information. Phishing and spamming emails often have malware incorporated in them, which when downloaded can sabotage a system. Spam and email filtering can prevent such crimes.

1.5.3.6 Best Practices

In order to combat cybercrimes, certain best practices must be adopted. They ensure that crimes are not only detected but also prevent them to some extent. Some of the best practices are as follows:

- Updating the current version of software. This process leads to elimination of bugs present in the code and performs the required patchwork.

- Using antivirus blacklisting and malware based on signature detection technique.

- Updating the password once every few months, but not very frequently. The idea is that an attacker may hack into a system, hash the password and perform a brute-force attack to gain access to the system and install a backdoor.

- Not using the same password across multiple platforms. Many applications are connected these days. Using the same password can encourage a hacker to break into all the applications that share the same password and gain important information like banking details.

- Using a virtual private network to ensure encrypted content.

- Backing up your data can ensure that even if malware like ransomware is launched, the data is safe. However, it is important to ensure that the data is encrypted and protected.

- Using the principle of least privileges allows every new account to have least privileges, which may be escalated as desired. The idea is to not allow too many privileged users to access data. It may not only lead to insider threats but also external threats in case the account of an employee is compromised externally.

- Using multi-factor authentication based on using a combination of authentication techniques, which is difficult to crack and provides an additional layer of security.

- Cybersecurity awareness about untrustworthy websites, social engineering, malicious links and spams.

- Using passwords that contain uppercase, lowercase and special characters, which makes exhaustive search difficult.

We have observed the diverse nature of cybercrimes. Hence, it is difficult to say which method could be prioritized over the other. To ensure security, collaboration of different techniques is encouraged. Security techniques along with best practices can ensure system security and detect potential threats.

1.6   Security Models

Security models are based on the concept of confidentiality, integrity and availability. Different security models tend to different concepts and describe how security must be implemented. They also take into account what subjects can access a particular object or what objects could be accessed by subjects. Since different models have different capabilities, they could be applied to any system, keeping in mind the requirements and functioning of the system. In this section we will describe several security models [9]. They are as follows:

1. **State Machine Model**: This is the basic security model which captures the functioning of the finite state machine. The number of states, the transactions involved and the actions taken are observed by this model. The idea is to monitor the status of the system so that it does not transit to an insecure state. A particular state will have the permission of all the subjects accessing the objects. The security feature preserves is integrity. This is ensured by the fact that each state transition function is tested to verify that the current state will not be compromised in order to maintain the integrity of the system.

2. **Information Flow Model**: The state machine model extends to the information flow model and further to the Bell-LaPadula and Biba models. The model incorporates objects, transition and lattice states. This model is adopted to prevent any unauthorized information flow, thereby preserving the security feature availability. The model is capable of blocking restricted information flow between subjects and objects. However, information flow in the same classification level is highly encouraged.

3. **Non-Interference Model:** Proposed by Goguen and Meseguer, per its name, the non-interference model ensures that subjects and objects at different classifying levels do not interfere with each other (*higher or lower*). It is impossible for data to cross security boundaries, i.e., if a subject at higher level performs an action, the state of the subject at lower level cannot be changed. An interference attack takes place when an entity has the potential to retrieve information and is capable of inferring information it is not entitled to based on the clearance level.

4. **Bell-LaPadula Model:** It is a mathematical model that follows multilevel security policy using the mandatory access control and promotes confidentiality. Different subjects may have different classification levels like top secret, secret and confidential. The subjects must be authenticated with respect to their security clearances to access an object that lies at a different classification level. The Bell-LaPadula model follows certain rules, which are as follows:

   - Simple Security Property, wherein a subject that belongs to a particular level of confidentiality cannot read information pertaining to a higher level of confidentiality, often referred to as "*no read up*."

   - Star * Security Property wherein a subject belonging to a particular level of confidentiality cannot write information pertaining to a lower level of confidentiality, often being termed as "*no write down*."

   - Strong Star * Property, wherein subject may not be allowed to read/write to an object pertaining to higher/lower sensitivity.

The Biba model has its own limitations. Security issues like covert channels are still a challenge. It is ideal for models that promote confidentiality, but cannot enforce other security features like integrity and availability.

5. **Biba Model**: The Biba model is a lattice-based model built in order to ensure integrity. It is concerned with data flow from one level to another. The rules followed by the Biba model are as follows:

   - Simple Integrity Property, wherein a subject at given level of integrity may not be allowed to read an object at lower level of integrity.

   - Star * Integrity Property, wherein a object at a given level of integrity may not be allowed to write to an object at higher level of integrity.

   - Invocation Property, wherein it is prohibited for a subject at a given level of integrity to invoke a subject at higher level of integrity.

   Although this model was developed after the Bell-LaPadula model, it only addresses the concern of integrity, without highlighting confidentiality and availability. Moreover, it does not take into consideration any kinds of internal threats, but rather focuses on the external ones.

6. **Clark-Wilson Model:** The Clark-Wilson model was developed to ensure integrity in commercial systems. It introduces the concept of separation of duties, classifying data into highly protected constrained data item (CDI) and unconstrained data item (UDI). In this model, data is accessed by subjects by means of application and requires auditing. The model incorporates user (*subjects or active agents*), transformation procedure (*read/write/modify*), CDI, UDI and integrity verification procedure. The model ensures integrity by permitting only authorized users to modify information, separation of duties and consistent transactions. The "access control triple" consists of user, transformation procedure and CDI, to ensure integrity and avert fraud. It allows modification of data only appropriately. The integrity verification procedure checks the validity of the state such that data cannot be tampered with. Moreover, it also logs all the changes.

7. **Take-Grant Model:** This model features the confidentiality aspect by introducing four basic functions-grant, revoke, create and take. The subjects with take rights are permitted to remove the take rights from other subjects. Subjects with grant rights are permitted to grant rights to other subjects. Subjects with create rights are permitted to give create rights to other subjects whereas subjects with revoke rights may revoke the rights from other subjects.

8. **Brewer-Nash Model:** This model is somewhat comparable to the Bell-LaPadua model and is often referred to as the Chinese Wall model. It is used to address the problem of conflict of interest (COI). The access controls provided by this model change as per the user's previous actions. The idea is to restrict the flow of information in such a way that it cannot flow, causing conflicts of interest. The subject is permitted to write to an object only if the subject is incapable of reading another object in a different data set.

9. **Other Models**: Following are a few other security models that have been introduced.

- *Graham-Denning Model*: This model highlights certain protection rules wherein each subject is acquainted with an owner and controller. The protection rights are as follows:

    - Securely create an object
    - Securely create a subject
    - Securely delete an object
    - Securely delete a subject
    - Provide read access rights
    - Provide grant access rights.
    - Provide delete access rights
    - Provide transfer access rights

- *Harrison-Ruzzo-Ullman Model*: This model is concerned with creation, deletion, modification and accessing of subjects and objects. It is based on the fact that a finite set of methodologies are used to modify access rights of a subject on an object.

- *Lattice Model*: In this model, a lattice structure represents security levels for objects and subjects. It is based on information flow between subjects and objects. A subject may access an object if the security level of a subject is the same or higher than that of the object. It incorporates multilevel and multilateral security.

1.7 Computer Forensics

Cybercrimes know no bounds and can range from basic data theft to cyberstalking. Forensic science involves the use of specific techniques with respect to criminal justice and highlights the collection, scrutinization and analysis of physical evidence. In computer forensics, there is investigation and analysis in order to garner and conserve physical evidence (*to avoid tampering*), such that it can be presentable in a court of law. A documented chain of evidence is maintained which specifies the issue with the computing device. Locard's exchange principle states that the entity responsible for crime will bring something to the crime scene and will also leave the crime scene with something [10]. This could be used as a forensic evidence.The investigators performing forensic analysis follow specific procedures to conduct forensics and make sure that the device is isolated so that it cannot be contaminated anymore. They also make a digital copy of the data encompassed in the device, so that if the procedure affects the device, the backup data is still available to retrieve evidence. A number of techniques are deployed by forensic experts to perform the analysis. They may seek hidden files and folders, or try to retrieve deleted, encrypted and damaged data. The evidence found, if any, is documented accordingly. Thus, conducting forensic analysis is a step-by-step procedure. The following steps are adopted for the same:

1. **Policy Procedure and Development**: Forensic data can be very sensitive. If not handled with utmost care, this data may be easily compromised. Thus, a set of policies and guidelines must be referred to in order to carry out forensic investigations. This may include information about storage, retrieval, authenticity and documentation of the forensic device. The policies may also adhere to certain laws pertaining to enforcement agencies since they involve investigative protocols for carrying out the forensic process. It is also important to handle the evidence properly once information

has been retrieved. Before carrying out any digital investigation, all details must be laid out, the case should be studied and rights, warrants and authorization should be stated clearly.

2. **Evidence Assessment**: Assessment of evidence is very important for conducting forensic analysis. Assessing potential evidences gives a clear idea about the cyber-crime and the potential steps that must be taken to gather further information about the evidence. If a person is accused of committing crime related to data theft, forensic experts will analyze hard drives, email accounts, social networking accounts, etc., to assess important information to be used as evidence. Before an investigation may be carried out, it is mandatory that the forensic investigator establishes the types of evidence retrieved. This would give an idea about how to further proceed and how to preserve such data. The source and integrity of data are then studied before it can be classified as an evidence.

3. **Evidence Acquisition**: Acquiring evidence is one of the most critical phases in the forensic analysis. It is important to document events before the process of evidence acquisition, during the process and also after the process. The documentation usually would incorporate detailed information about the process, hardware and software standards and specifications, the systems involved and investigated. Removal of storage devices, retrieving confidential data using boot disks and ensuring that the evidence has been successfully copied and transferred are all documented during the evidence acquisition process. It is important that the process is performed legally by authorized professionals. The chain of evidence includes information about the custody, analysis, control and disposition of the evidence.

4. **Evidence Examination**: Forensic analysts use a combination of techniques to perform forensic analysis on potential evidence. They may search for data, files and folders using specific keywords, or try to retrieve files that have either been hidden or deleted. They take into account the timestamps and logs of the files and folders in order to find suspicious files that may have been tampered with or encrypted. Information such as when and where the file was created, and if it was downloaded or uploaded, could give enough information to the investigators about the network activity. It could reveal information about the directories, servers and other computer systems, providing the investigators with significant information. Evidence examination is also done in collaboration with investigators, lawyers and other experts to gather enough information about the evidence.

5. **Documentation and Reporting**: Documenting and reporting all the procedures involved in forensic analysis ensures that the integrity of data is preserved throughout the process. It makes sure that proper policies and guidelines have been followed while carrying out the analysis. It is important to document the entire process, failing which the validity of the case could be compromised. An accounting of the actions performed in either digital format or archives ensures authenticity of the findings and makes it easy for security researchers to convey where and how the evidence was redeemed.

Famous Computer Forensics Case Studies: Computer forensics can be traced back to approximately four decades. During the 1980s, computer forensics was used as evidence to solve some famous crimes. Some of them are as follows:

1. **BTK Killer Dennis Lynn Rader**: The BTK killer case convicted a council president of a church, Dennis Rader, as a murderer who is believed to have killed at least ten people. His method of murder involved binding, torturing and killing, hence the acronym BTK. While committing the murders, he would send peculiar notes to the police providing the details of the murder. Sometimes the clues would be in the form of poems, puzzles and pictures. One such note was a breakthrough for the police to identify him as the murderer. Rader sent the police a floppy disk containing documents created with Microsoft Office. The document was analyzed by forensic experts using the forensic tool EnCase, and it was found that the document was last modified by someone named "Dennis" at Christ Lutheran Church. Upon investigating, it was found that the president of the church council was Dennis Rader. When a background check was performed involving the DNA of the accused, Rader was found guilty and the BTK murder mystery was finally solved after thirty years [11].

2. **Maury Troy Travis**: Maury Troy Travis was accused of killing seventeen women [12]. To identify the accused, in this case, the police did not have to perform tests or use standard forensic tools. A Post-Dispatch reporter received an anonymous letter which highlighted a murder and along with the letter was a map showing a part of West Alton, with an "X" marked to show the locus of the dead body. As the body was recovered, the map was found to have been retrieved from the Internet. The investigators looked at the records for the said map, and found that only one computer had requested the map location. The Internet Protocol (IP) address and the name of the user requesting the map traced back to Maury Troy Travis.

3. **Scott Tyree:** Internet predator Scott Tyree kidnapped a teenager named Alicia Kozakiewicz and sent her picture using Yahoo Messenger to someone in Tampa, who happened to realize that the girl was missing from her home. The man contacted the investigators and provided them the details and screenshot of the Yahoo Messenger. The name Scott Tyree chose for his messenger was " masterforteenslavegirls". The IP address of the sender was traced and then the information of the sender was obtained from the carrier Verizon. The address was that of Scott Tyree [13].

4. **Corey Melton**: The home computer of Corey Melton seemed to be infected with malware, which made him approach a Best Buy technology expert. It was found that certain malware had the capability to reattach itself to movies incorporating child pornography. Melton was sentenced to prison [14].

1.8 Cyber Insurance

Technology these days solely relies on the use of computer systems. This perpetuates cybersecurity issues across all domains like the hardware, software, network, cloud, etc. To get work done ranging from minute data entry to complicated simulations, people depend on computer systems. This puts the devices at cybersecurity-related risks. Organizations across the entire globe store sensitive data, which if breached could cause prodigious losses, questioning the reputation of the organizations. Thus, organizations rely on something called cyber insurance. Cyber insurance is also known as cyber risk insurance or cyber liability. The main idea behind cyber insurance is to assist an organization reduce cyber risks by neutralizing costs pertaining to recovery of a cyber attack that resulted in a breach. It may also cover expenses for primary parties and any claims by third parties. Following are some of the reimbursable charges:

1. *Investigation*: It is important to conduct a forensic investigation to gain insight into how the breach or attack occurred, rectification of the same and exploring ways that could aid in prevention of such breaches in the future. The services may be provided by security firms, law enforcement or the Federal Bureau of Investigation (FBI).

2. *Business Losses*: Some policies may have errors or omissions in them or technical faults like network downtime. There could be business-related issues like business interruption, cost and recovery of the lost data. The cyber insurance policy will cover all such losses.

3. *Privacy and Notification*: It is important to convey data breach notifications to the affected customers and clients. This is usually handled by the law in many jurisdictions.

4. *Lawsuits and Extortion*: Confidential information and intellectual property are worth monetary expenses. Regulatory fines and legal settlements may also be required. Such issues are also handled by cyber risk insurance.

Thus, cyber insurance may be defined as an insurance product that may aid in protecting businesses and users from technology-related risks [15]. It covers liabilities related to data breach which incorporate sensitive information in the form of social security numbers, credit card numbers, health records, etc.

The process of redeeming cyber insurance is fairly similar to obtaining other insurances. Usually the life cycle follows three phases, which are discussed below [16].

1. *Acquiring a Policy*: This phase constitutes filling out application forms that cover topics related to the present security approach, protection, vulnerability and if the industry the user belongs to is targeted by cyber criminals. Based on the responses, interviews are conducted and policy terms are negotiated.

2. *Claim Submission*: Claims are submitted when losses take place. The policy is responsible for the applicable reimbursement.

3. *Policy Renewal*: Once the risk profile is reevaluated a new policy may be offered. If the offered policy is unacceptable, the process could be restarted by a different insurer.

Despite being one of the defensive techniques, cyber insurance has certain limitations, which are as follows:

1. Unavailability of advanced technology.

2. It is difficult to find solutions and map them according to network attacks.

3. Improper information flow between network users, vendors and authorities does not contribute to proper network protection.

4. It is not practically possible to measure all risks and mitigate them.

5. Product vendors often play liability shell games.

6. Information asymmetry may lead to difficulty in identifying users of different types (adverse selection problem).

When placing a cyber insurance policy, some practices could be considered, which are as follows:

1. Security investments and cyber insurance should complement each other since insurance is based on risk tolerance.

2. Engaging a well-informed broker is important since the broker can comprehend cyber risks and how they are being affected by the insurance market.

3. Going beyond the application form in order to gain sufficient risk clarity that would be beneficial in obtaining maximum coverage.

4. Focusing on fair price rather than best price to emphasize on uniformity and maturity.

5. Insurance terms may be reviewed by experienced external counsel.

6. Employ cybersecurity experts to navigate through the process better.

1.8.1 Digital Citizenship

The internet is a forum for a lot of activities which may also be part of society, politics and government, and can perpetuate cybercrimes. A digital citizen is wary of such situations and gains knowledge and skills to effectively use the internet so that cybercrimes are neither perpetuated through them, nor are they victimized by cyberattacks. A successful digital citizen has the ability to practice safe, law abiding and accountable use of the Internet by knowing their rights and responsibilities. Digital citizenship is based on the following attributes:

1. **Internet Security and Privacy**: It is important to protect one's privacy over the internet. Certain measures could be taken to ensure internet security. The most common ways of securing oneself on the internet is using passwords, not clicking on suspicious links, being wary of cyber criminals while interacting, etc. Security programs and privacy settings should be taken into consideration when using the internet.

2. **Communication with Users Online**: One of the drawbacks of communicating through the internet is lack of authenticity. Although there are many ways to ensure whether the person is actually who they claim to be, dealing with anonymous users may involve risk. Thus, a code of conduct must be followed while communicating with online users. Also, if the users seem to be suspicious, it is advisable to pull oneself back from the situation.

3. **Cyberstalking and Cyberbullying**: The internet has also been successful in dispersing crimes like cyberstalking and cyberbullying across the globe. One of the ways to tackle the issue is to educate people about it. Many times, people are not aware of the necessary steps that must be taken once they fall victim to such crimes. It is important to educate them so that necessary actions can be taken at the earliest.

4. **Footprinting**: A user of the internet must be aware of the footprints they are leaving behind. Footprints are an excellent way for cyber criminals to gain information about the users and the systems they use. The information could be the location, IP address, operating system, etc. It is not only important to be aware of the footprints one leaves behind, but also to respect the privacy of others while tagging and posting information.

5. **Identity**: Identity may be used to express oneself digitally, hence it is an important component of digital citizenship. People may use creative texts and pictures to express

themselves and this serves as an imaginative method by which people may explore themselves.

6. **Awareness**: With cybercrimes spreading at a rampant rate, it is important to educate users about the crimes that take place over the internet. Creating awareness about credibility of websites and the advertisements featured in the webpages could be one way of imparting cybersecurity awareness.

7. **Copyrights**: A lot of information available on the internet is misused. Piracy and plagiarism are easily perpetuated online. The users must be made aware of the information that is allowed to be shared with the public and the information that is not. Using unethical means to access secured information must be discouraged.

Digital citizenship in not only restricted to cybersecurity but also spans various other sectors encouraging digital access, digital commerce, digital communication, digital literacy, digital etiquette, digital law, digital rights and responsibilities and digital health [17].

The internet witnesses millions of users everyday, some of which are good digital citizens, whereas others are not. A good digital citizen performs appropriate digital security while a bad digital citizen performs inappropriate digital security. Examples of appropriate and inappropriate digital security are as follows:

1. Appropriate Digital Security

   - Using licensed software and updating it in a timely manner
   - Giving credit to sources
   - Using secure sites for communication
   - Displaying ethical behavior online
   - Not tending to unfamiliar attachments
   - Respecting the privacy of others
   - Reporting digital offenders
   - Blocking sites inappropriate for users belonging to different age groups
   - Not sharing inappropriate posts
   - Keeping up-to-date with security by regular scanning and updates

2. Inappropriate Digital Security

   - Not protecting the system (*antivirus and software*)
   - Posting information about others without permission
   - Tending to attachments from unknown sources
   - Providing information to anonymous users
   - Using devices without securing them
   - Saving passwords in plaintext
   - Accessing inappropriate sites by various means
   - Not updating software regularly
   - Downloading software that may not be available publically (*piracy*)
   - Indulging in plagiarism

1.8.2 Information Warfare and Its Countermeasures

Also referred to as cyberwarfare, electronic warfare and cyberterrorism , information warfare is the act of causing devastation by distorting computer systems involved in significant processes like stock exchange, defense operations, telecommunications, air traffic control etc. Information warfare aims at vandalizing government organizations rather than private firms or individuals. It may also involve worms, viruses and cyberattacks as a part of the mission. Cyber warriors use skills, strategies and tactics to gain sensitive information or control over computer systems. Information warfare could be launched using three techniques:

1. Gaining unauthorized access into systems to access confidential information.

2. Deploy viruses, worms and malware to perpetuate a cyber attack.

3. Considering loopholes in a network and exploiting them.

Information warfare is the new battlefield may lead to jamming or hijacking of broadcast media like television, radio and internet. In the past, the results have also been in the form of networks being disabled or spoofed and stock markets being sabotaged. With the emerging technology of drones, surveillance has become quite easy.

Information warfare incorporates a series of events that take place to cause cyberattacks. The sequence of the step-by-step procedure follows [18]:

1. Step1 Gathering information: The primary step to conduct information warfare lies in the process of gathering information about the system and the technologies involved and provides a precise model of warfare. It acts as a deciding factor since by gathering information about the target systems, cyber warriors can measure the advantages, disadvantages and outcomes of the launched attack. It also gives a rough idea about the strength and position of warriors and highlights the skills and technologies needed to hammer the target system. It is usually done by surveillance and use of sensors.

2. Step 2 Information transport: Once enough information has been collected about the target system, the next step is to transfer this information to persons who need it in a timely manner. The communication infrastructure which supports a large number of different components plays an important role here and ensures that the information is transported in real time.

3. Step 3 Information protection: The information captured must be protected. This involves two aspects of security, i.e., the physical security and the cybersecurity. Physical security ensures that the information is secured physically using bulletproof cases and locks. The idea is to prevent physical destruction or interception. The cybersecurity aspect aspect deals with protecting the information using computer technologies like passwords and encryption.

4. Step 4 Manipulating the information: Even though multiple security layers are applied to sensitive information, there may still be a slight chance that an adversary may access the information. Thus, the collected information is often manipulated. The idea is that even if the information is somehow accessed by the adversary, it will be impossible to decode the original contents of the information. Several software programs can be used to manipulate text, pictures, video, audio and other information.

5. Step 5 Extensive manipulation: This step is an extension of information manipulation and the idea is to prevent the adversary from getting the complete and correct information. The introduction of spoofing or noise into the information degrade the quality of the information, since it is difficult to tell fake messages and real messages apart, and also hard to remove noise from the original information. Jamming may lead to denial-of-service, so that information may never reach its intended destination. Moreover, techniques like overloading do the same, by continuously consuming the system resources such that the system gets engaged and is unable to offer other services.

Information warfare is a serious threat. Hence ,protection against information warfare is compulsory. Countermeasures to information warfare lie in each and every step taken by the cyber warriors to conduct cyberattacks. The following process states how information warfare can be evaded at every step:

1. Step 1 Gathering information: To prevent the adversary from gaining sensitive information, it is necessary to protect against the interception of information. Extensive manipulation of information using spoofing, encryption, introduction of noise and overloading may serve the purpose.

2. Step 2 Information transport: Once the information has already been collected by the adversary, it is very difficult to prevent the process of information transport. Information is transported using infrastructure, hence the only way to prevent information transport is by disrupting the infrastructure. Attacks on infrastructure components, like substations, generators and pipelines, would halt the information transfer. Electromagnetic architecture has visible key nodes which could be easily affected. If the architecture relies on satellite communication, communication lines may be jammed.

3. Step 3 Information protection: The countermeasure for the adversary protecting their information is quite tedious. With sophisticated cryptographic techniques, it is easier to protect information. However, the information is not likely to be protected forever since high computing systems are known to break codes. If the systems are password protected, attacks like brute force and dictionary attacks could still be effective.

4. Step 4 Manipulating the information: Only two countermeasures have proven to be successful in a situation where an adversary manipulates information and one is supposed to get the original information. The first and easiest way would be to intercept the information before the adversary has manipulated it. The second would be to prevent the modified data from being reintroduced to legitimate information. This information may be collected by different redundant sources with the hope that once in a while the correct information would be introduced to legitimate information flow. One can easily detect bad data from the rest of the data.

5. Step 5 Extensive manipulation: A combination of certain skills and techniques may be needed as a countermeasure to such situations. If the communication channel relies on frequency hopping, spread spectrum and code division multiple access (CDMA) techniques, it may be tedious to intercept or jam. Certain digital compression techniques when combined with redundancy lead to recovery of bit streams, despite large parts being destroyed.

1.8.3   Network Neutrality

Internet service over the world differs in terms of charges, websites, methods of communication, etc. Network neutrality is the principle of treating data all over the internet the same. This would ensure that the internet is available to users across the world irrespective of the content, platform, websites, method of communication, etc. The network traffic in this case is treated impartially. The idea is that operation of service at a given layer is not affected by external data and must follow protocols specific to that layer. The service providers may not be allowed to make special arrangements for certain services and websites, unlike some organizations who are beneficiaries of network access and speed.

The concept of network neutrality is supported by many users and opposed by some. This is due to the fact that it carries some advantages and disadvantages, which are stated below.

Advantages of Net Neutrality

1. It incorporates freedom of expression by allowing all blogs, services and websites to users across the world. Sometimes service providers block certain websites. Net neutrality evades that limitation.

2. It leads to an innovative and competitive environment by allowing similar access (*traffic and speed*). Usually companies and organizations benefit by customizing the internet features (*traffic, speed*) and emerge powerful. Fast delivery to all end users will encourage competition.

3. It prevents the end users from being charged an extra amount to access certain services like banking, entertainment, gaming, etc.

4. It is impossible for the internet service providers (ISPs) to modify the upload and download transfers irrespective of the contents being accessed by users.

5. There is no restriction on the amount of content that can be downloaded by a particular user at a given time.

6. Net neutrality allows startups to access potential customers easily.

Disadvantages of Net Neutrality

1. Video streaming and downloads consume a lot of resources. Thus, maintaining and upgrading the network becomes difficult.

2. With websites and blogs being open to all, objectionable content may be accessed by anyone and everyone. This could lead to illegal downloads and piracy practices.

3. Certain services like making calls are available on social media. This evades the need for telecom companies.

4. Network neutrality will affect the bandwidth since it is a limited commodity.

5. Anything, ranging from cruel to harassing posts, can be posted over the internet, making it a very toxic environment.

6. Consumers may not be able to compete against large corporations.

1.8.4 Good Practices and Policies

Information technology has brought about certain changes. The age of digital transformation ensures convenience but also invites several security risks. These security risks have the potential to harm organizations both at the highest as well as the lowest levels. Thus, it is mandatory that organizations introduce certain good practices and policies to ensure security in the work environment. Over the years a lot of good practices and policies have proven to be beneficial. Some of the good practices are as follows:

1. Preparedness, prevention, detection and correction should be the security goals of any organization.

2. Run security strategies from time to time, so that it is easier to choose tools when required.

3. Introduce access controls for data throughout the organization, to offer selective privileges to employees for data access. This could prevent insider attacks.

4. Monitoring activities (*network traffic, resources consumption and usage*) leads to transparency in an organization. Firewalls, intrusion prevention systems and intrusion detection systems may prove to be highly beneficial. They not only raise alerts but also function accordingly.

5. Always have backup. A distributed environment, ensures replicated data so that affecting one of the data centers does not mean that data is lost. In a situation when malware like Ransomware strike, it may be difficult to recover data, hence backup is a must.

6. Cybersecurity Awareness and Training should be encouraged in organizations. People who may not be aware of the consequences cyberattacks, may fall victim to attacks like social engineering.

7. Automating of systems should be done whenever updates are required. The updates should not depend on the approval of the user.

8. Organizations should have their sites protected using Secure Sockets Layer certificates and Hypertext Transfer Protocol Secure (HTTPS).

9. Insider threats should be investigated as soon as possible. Checking data logs is one way to do that.

10. Information assets should be physically secure and not only in the form of replicated data over the systems and network.

11. Using multi-factor authentication to access a particular account confirms the identity of the person. A combination of what we have, what we are and what we know could prevent a lot of security issues.

12. Incident response plans should be devised for all organizations. In the case of security breaches, organizations can rely on these plans to detect, respond and restrict the repercussions of the cyber incidents.

Cybersecurity policies are designed to protect the physical and technology assets of an organization. Some of the cybersecurity policies highlighted in the last decade are as follows:

1. Confidential data, such as financial information, patents, formulae for new technology, client data, etc., is covert and holds value.

2. Personal and organization devices must be secured. Using passwords, antiviruses, software updates and private networks are some ways to protect such devices.

3. Emails often carry with them malware and viruses in the form of links and attachments. Employees must be made aware of such bait.

4. Password management is very crucial. Passwords should not be easy to guess, hence it is advisable to include special characters, numbers, uppercase and lowercase letters. They should not be written, rather remembered. If saved in a file, the file must be encrypted. Passwords should be changed once every few months.

5. When data is transferred, security risks might be introduced. Sensitive data should not be transmitted over insecure channel. It is important to ensure that the recipients are authenticated and authorized before data is transmitted.

6. Devices should be locked or turned off when unattended.

7. Illegal software must not be downloaded.

1.8.5 Cybersecurity and Human Rights

Cybersecurity laws and policies influence human rights, since the concept deals with privacy, freedom of expression and the free flow of information. In the previous section we have seen how organizations rely on practices and policies to enhance security in their institutions. Although introducing policies is one of the effective ways to enhance security, many policies do not produce the desired result owing to their poor definitions and lack of clear checks. This may affect their accountability, balance and mechanism, thereby violating human rights. Monitoring data is one such policy, which invades the privacy of people. Thus, the need to enhance security arises along with preserving human rights.

Certain human rights pertaining to cybersecurity are assured by the United Nations' Universal Declaration of Human Rights (UDHR) and the International Covenant on Civil and Political Rights (ICCPR) [19, 20]. They highlight human rights in form of the following:

1. *Freedom of Expression*: Freedom of expression as a human right in cybersecurity allows individuals to share their ideas through different forms of communication. It may be in the form of blogs, webpages, articles, etc. This human right may be misused if people post inappropriate content over the network.

2. *Freedom of Speech*: Similar to freedom of expression, freedom of speech supports the freedom of an individual or a community, so that they can express their ideas without retaliation from by others. This human right may be misused if such groups encourage conflicts or terrorism.

3. *Right to Privacy*: Among an individual's legal rights, the right to privacy ensures that a person is free from intrusion. It is possible to communicate anonymously, keeping in mind that cybersecurity threats may prevail over the internet. Criminals could misuse the right such that it would be impossible to trace what they have been upto.

Hence, the United States Constitution does not allow the right to privacy pertaining to cybersecurity.

4. *Freedom of Association*: This is the right of individuals to come together to form societies, clubs and other groups to meet other individuals such that they are not interrupted by the government. They may express, promote and defend ideas forming unions. Over the internet, people sign petitions, join social media, etc., and form associations. As long as it does not abuse public interest, this human right is acceptable.

Technological development is always ahead of human rights laws, and poses a challenge to several institutions which have fewer protections in law. Technology also provides the platform to broadcast human rights. It can bring people together, encourage freedom of expression and increase access to information over the network. Keeping in mind the human aspects, it is important that human rights and technology go hand in hand.

1.9 Future of Cybersecurity

As we know, cybersecurity happens to be one of the biggest global challenges. Recent trends have highlighted how attacks are becoming more and more sophisticated with the growth of technology. Vandalizing systems and patching them are red team-blue team exercises which go hand in hand. There is no way to attain 100 percent security. However, it is possible to prevent security issues to a certain extent and recover the lost data. Most of the patchwork methods proposed in the past have been degraded by further advanced attacks. Be it the physical systems, or the networks, the cloud infrastructure, cybersecurity finds its use in almost all the domains. Several concepts like machine learning, artificial intelligence and cyberpsychology are the latest additions to cybersecurity. All the stated concepts are prone to cyberattacks, thus making cybersecurity an enormous issue. Another concept which is relevant to the future of cybersecurity is the concept of blockchain, which we will be taking a look at in a later chapter.

1.10 Conclusion

In conclusion, we have taken a look at the concept of cybersecurity at a fairly deep level. We have addressed the objectives, infrastructure and architecture pertaining to cybersecurity. Along with that, we have acquainted ourselves with the idea of various roles in the field of cybersecurity. The need for cybersecurity has arisen due to an increase in cybercrimes. We have discussed traditional and contemporary cybercrimes and also specified the ways to deal with those crimes. To ensure cybersecurity in an organization, security models must be followed. We have discussed several security models, their advantages and disadvantages. Other cybersecurity concepts, like computer forensics, digital citizenship and cyber insurance, have also been introduced in this chapter. Furthermore, we imparted knowledge about network neutrality and information warfare. The good practices and policies that play a major role in securing an enterprise have been highlighted. Since cybersecurity deals with certain aspects like freedom of expression, opinions, etc., the idea of human rights expression, opinions, has also been considered.

References

1. Kissel, R. (Ed.). (2011). Glossary of key information security terms. Diane Publishing.

2. Wang, E. K., Ye, Y., Xu, X., Yiu, S. M., Hui, L. C. K., & Chow, K. P. (2010, December). Security issues and challenges for cyber physical system. In Green Computing and Communications (GreenCom), 2010 IEEE/ACM Int'l Conference on & Int'l Conference on Cyber, Physical and Social Computing (CPSCom) (pp. 733-738). IEEE.

3. WaterISAC, 10 Basic Cybersecurity Measures Best Practices to Reduce Exploitable Weaknesses and Attacks, WaterISAC Security Information Center, June 2015, pp.01-06

4. Framework, P. C. Improving Critical Infrastructure Cybersecurity Executive Order 13636.

5. Newhouse, W., Keith, S., Scribner, B., & Witte, G. (2017). National Initiative for Cybersecurity Education (NICE) Cybersecurity Workforce Framework. NIST Special Publication, 800, 181.

6. Kuusisto, R., & Kurkinen, E. (2013). Information Warfare and Security.

7. Russel G Smith (2014), The development of cybercrime Past, present and future, ECPR General Conference, Australian Government.

8. Arshi Khan, The First Recorded cybercrime Took Place in the Year 1820, Retrieved from https://www.scribd.com/doc/71120466/The-First-Recorded-Cyber-Crime-Took-Place-in-the-Year-1820,

9. Security Architecture and Design/Security Models, Retrieved from https://en.wikibooks.org/wiki/Security_Architecture_and_Design/Security_Models

10. Locard, E. (2008). Locard's Exchange Principle.

11. Digital Forensics Hall of Fame, Episode 1: The BTK, Retrieved from https://eforensicsmag.com/digital-forensics-hall-of-fame-episode-1-the-btk/, 2015

12. Maury Troy Travis, Retrieved from http://murderpedia.org/male.T/t/travis-maury.htm

13. Scott Tyree, retrieved from https://en.wikipedia.org/wiki/Alicia_Kozakiewicz

14. Kashmir Hill, Child Porn Found by the Geek Squad Can and Will Be Used Against You in a Court of Law Retrieved from https://abovethelaw.com/2010/10/child-porn-found-by-the-geek-squad-can-and-will-be-used-against-you-in-a-court-of-law/, 2010.

15. Cyber Insurance, Retrieved from https://en.wikipedia.org/wiki/Cyber_insurance

16. FireEye, Cyber Insurance: A growing Imperative What is it and why you should consider it' Retrieved from White Paper https://www.fireeye.com/content/dam/fireeye-www/current-threats/pdfs/wp-cyber-insurance.pdf , 2016, pp. 07.

17. Digital Citizen definition, Retrieved from https://en.wikipedia.org/wiki/Digital_citizen

18. Megan Burns, Information Warfare: What and How?, Retrieved from https://www.cs.cmu.edu/ burnsm/InfoWarfare.html, 1999

19. Moise, A. C. (2016). Cybersecurity and Human Rights. Rev. Universul Juridic, 160.

20. Le, D. N., Van, V. N., & Giang, T. T. T. (2016). A New Private Security Policy Approach for DDoS Attack Defense in NGNs. In Information Systems Design and Intelligent Applications (pp. 1-10). Springer, New Delhi.

Steganography and Steganalysis

HO THI HUONG THOM, NGUYEN KIM ANH

Faculty of Information Technology, Vietnam Maritime University, Haiphong, Vietnam
Email: thomhth@vimaru.edu.vn, kimanhnguyen@vimaru.edu.vn

Abstract

Steganography is the art and science of concealed communication. The basic concept is to hide the very existence of a secret message. Digital objects, such as a text, image, video, or audio, can be used as the cover data. Steganalysis is the counterpart of steganography. The goal of steganalysis is to detect the hidden message, equivalently, to discriminate the stego-object from the non-stego-object. In addition, it has the scientific significance of enhancing the hidden ability of hidden techniques. In this chapter, we will present an overview of the research and solutions for the problem of hidden image detection.

Keywords: Cover image, stego image, hiding information, steganography, steganalysis, watermarking

Dac-Nhuong Le et al. (eds.), Cyber Security in Parallel and Distributed Computing, (39–262)
© 2019 Scrivener Publishing LLC

2.1 Introduction

Hiding information refers to the problem of hiding important information in other objects. History shows that hiding information began thousands of years ago. From stories of the ancient Greeks, we know that they devised a way to exchange information between allies by shaving the heads of slaves, carving secret information into their scalps, waiting for their hair to grow back and sending them to meet allies. We also know of a method of writing secret information with animal milk, fresh lemon juice or vinegar on white paper; after the ink dries no trace of the script is seen on the paper but when heated over a flame, the letters are readable. In China, people thought of a way to carve secret information on the inside of an egg or on a wooden board, which was then waxed to hide the inscription. In addition, watermarks on foreign currency are also a form of hiding information to prevent money from being counterfeited.

Nowadays, as science and technology are rapidly developing and the internet is growing globally, hidden information is also being digitized for use in areas of modern life. Digital information is divided into two main groups for the following purposes:

- *Steganography*: This is a form of hiding confidential information on another object for the purpose of exchanging it between allies.

- *Watermarking*: This is a form of embedding important information into an object to protect the object by marking it as license, copyright, fake, etc.

In principle, hiding information in multimedia data or digital image data is not much different. But as hiding information in pictures is easier, more information is being hidden in that way. The use of digital pictures is quite popular on the Internet today, with the technique of hiding information in images accounting for the largest proportion of multimedia data types, with 56.1% images, 14.8% audio and 2.8% video [1].

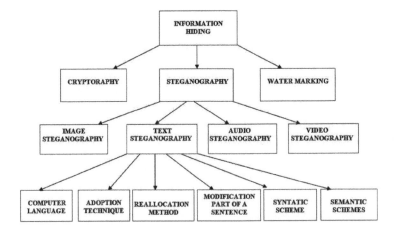

Figure 2.1 Classification of Steganography.

Cryptography hides messages by converting them into hidden texts. On the other hand, cryptanalysis uses developed cryptographic techniques in order to decipher the ciphertext obtained to understand original content of the ciphertext. In contrast to steganography, which hides information in various types of files, image steganalysis is a technique that detects any images that have hidden information. Other than the scientific sense, the research on revealing hidden images has two practical applications: First, to effectively serve the information security field; second, to improve and promote the development of hidden information technology in pictures. This leads to two different research directions: The first approach is to try to build a blind steganalysis algorithm for hidden images using any hidden technique; the second approach constructs a consistent detection algorithm (*constraint steganalysis*) based on a known hiding technique.

There are many published studies in the world that are successful using both directions. However, more sophisticated techniques of hiding information which require hidden image detectors are constantly finding the appropriate detection method to keep pace with the trend of hidden technology. Especially with the rapid development of the Internet, the demand for image-based information exchange is increasing. Ensuring security and defense or supporting upgrades and improving the safety of hidden techniques is a critical issue for researchers in the field of information security today.

Within the scope of this chapter, we provide an overview of hidden information in images, hidden image detection and detection solutions for some typical hidden methods in a manner that may give readers an approach to other hidden image detection problems.

2.2 Steganography

Steganography can be divided into two main groups as follows:

Concealing information on LSB (*least significant bit*): This is a method of replacing bits of information with LSB bits of pixels [2-4, 5-12]. In one pixel of 8-bit color image, the last bit (the 8th bit) is called the LSB bit. Therefore, changing the value of this bit (from 0 to 1 or from 1 to 0) does not affect the visual quality of the image. Information can be hidden on the LSB of coefficients transformation of the pixel such as cosine, wavelet, Fourier...

Additionally, there are several other methods of concealment in the form of interference jamming SS [14-16], and adjusting the quantization factor QIM [17-19]. Reversible data hiding technique (*after separation of information we can also restore the original image*) opens a new direction in the field of concealment with a series of reverse hiding techniques being announced [19, 20, 32].

2.2.1 Method for Evaluating Hidden Information Schema Security

We provide some symbols that will be used throughout this report. The symbol $\mathcal{C}$ is the set of all original images C, $\mathcal{M}$ is the set of cryptographic information M, $\mathcal{K}$ is the set of hidden keys K, $\mathcal{S}$ is the set of all images stego S (*hidden image*). A hidden schema (*algorithm*) is a pair of (S_E, S_X), with

- $S_E : \mathcal{C} \times \mathcal{M} \times \mathcal{K} \to \mathcal{S}$ is the information embedding function.

- $S_X : \mathcal{SK} \to \mathcal{M}$ is the information separation function.

S_E function creates an object S belonging to $\mathcal{S}$ from each $C \in \mathcal{C}$, $M \in \mathcal{M}$ and $K \in \mathcal{K}$ while S_X function separates M from S by key K.

Assume P_C is the probability distribution function of $C \in \mathcal{C}$. If the key $K \in \mathcal{K}$ and $M \in \mathcal{M}$ are randomly selected, the schema (S_E, S_X) with the P_C function will create the probability distribution function P_S of $S \in \mathcal{S}$. Then, according to Cachin's concept of concealment [32], we arrive at the following definition:

Theorem 2.1 *A hidden schema is called safe if Kullback - Leibler differential between probability distribution function of P_C and P_S in (1) equals 0.*

$$D_{KL}(P_C||P_S) = \sum_{C \in \mathcal{C}} P_C(C)log\frac{P_C(C)}{P_S(C)} \qquad (2.1)$$

when $D_{KL}(P_C||P_S) < \epsilon$, the hidden schema is ϵ secure, where ϵ is a positive real number sufficiently small.

This concept is from a theoretical standpoint, which is very difficult to implement in practice because the image space is too large (*infinite*). On the other hand, a hidden schema to ensure $D_{KL}(P_C||P_S) = 0$ is not possible because this means there are no changes in the original image, i.e., $P_C = P_S$ (*the basic lemma in Theory information*). Thus, people often hide information in order to achieve secure ϵ, ensuring that the change on the image is the smallest and barely visible to the human eye.

2.2.2 Peak Signal-to-Noise Ratio

Another method for post-processing an image after concealing information is based on the peak signal-to-noise ratio (PSNR) of the image before and after hiding information. PSNR is a method of assessing safety based on a subjective approach. According to this approach, human feelings are divided into five different levels. On each level, the quality of the image will be calculated by the PSNR, then depending on the calculated value the image will be judged as to which threshold it belongs to.

The PSNR quality is mapped according to the mean opinion score (MOS), as shown in Table 2.1. There are many stego schemes [2-20] that primarily measure human sensibility based on PSNR.

Table 2.1   Relationship between PSNR and MOS values.

PSNR [dB]	MOS
> 37	5 (Very good)
31-37	4 (Good)
25-31	3 (Medium)
20-25	2 (Bad)
< 20	1 (Very bad)

2.3 Steganalysis

Steganalysis can be defined as a classification problem based on statistical hypothesis testing. This depends on our understanding of the hidden schema; thus, steganalysis is spoken of either as a simple hypothesis test or composite hypothesis test problem.

If we do not have any information about the hidden schema, the stega method is called blind steganalysis. The classification problem can be expressed based on the composite hypothesis test as:

- H_0: X is derived from the probability distribution function P_S.

- H_1: X is not derived from the probability distribution function P_S.

Where X is the sample image data to be considered.

In a case in which information about the hidden schema is known, the stega method is called constraint steganalysis. Assuming we know the probability distribution of the P_C, the hidden schema (S_E, S_X) and the distribution of the information of M, we can calculate the P_S. From this we can provide a method of detection based on a simple hypothesis test as:

- H_0: X has a probability distribution of P_S.

- H_1: X has a probability distribution of P_C.

To solve the statistical hypothesis test, we need to find a conditional domain or features to classify so that the error rate is minimal.

There are many ways to do this division. But the problem is that any division leads to two errors that are:

- Type I error with probability $\alpha(0 < \alpha < 1)$ *(false positive)*.

- Type II error with probability $\beta(0 < \beta < 1)$ *(false negative)*.

The probability α and β with the detector F can be expressed mathematically as follows:

$$\alpha = P(F(X) = 1|X\ P_C) = \int_\omega P_C(X)dx \tag{2.2}$$

$$\beta = P(F(X) = 0|X\ P_S) = \int_{\Omega\omega} P_S(X)dx \tag{2.3}$$

A detector is acceptable if satisfied (2.4)

$$(1 - \alpha)log\frac{1 - \alpha}{\beta} + \alpha log\frac{\alpha}{1 - \beta} \leq D_{KL}(P_C||P_S) \tag{2.4}$$

There are no division algorithms that minimize both error types.

As mentioned above, steganalysis research methods focus on two main directions:

- The first direction tries to build blind detection for any steganography techniques.

- The second direction tries to detect stego images when knowing the steganography technique.

Many authors have investigated blind steganalysis for hidden images on LSBs and constraint steganalysis for some known hiding techniques. Now we will summarize the published research in the two directions mentioned above.

2.3.1 Blind Detection Based on LSB

There are many approaches to blind steganalysis for LSB such as in the spatial domain [21-25] and the frequency domain [26], for hidden images using SS technology [27], QIM *(quantization index modulation)* factor [28-30] or blind detecting of JPEG images [31].

Authors have also proposed four blind steganalysis techniques for hidden images on the LSB, three of which are are in the spatial domain and include standard deviation analysis [37], the statistical method χ^2 with a degree of freedom (χ_1^2) [34], the estimating method of information concealed in the image [38]; and a technique in the frequency domain by gray-scale analysis [33]. The specific methods are as follows:

2.3.1.1   Standard Deviation Analysis

This method is supposed to detect better than χ^2 statistics with n degrees of freedom of Westfeld and Pfitzmann [24]. In their method an 8-bit gray-scale digital image was used to test an image with hidden LSB; they made a frequency statistic of pixels into the vector $C = \{c_i, i = 0...256\}$ where c_i is the frequency of the pixel with the value i in the image. They found that for hidden image, the pairs of values c_{2j}, $c_{2j+1}(j = 0...127)$ (*called the PoV pair* pair of values) in vector C has approximate value while this rarely happens in the original image. Thus, Westfeld and Pfitzmann use the statistical method χ^2 with $n - 1$ degrees of freedom to classify (*n* is defined by the number of PoV pairs with non-zero values).

This method is only effective when the number of hidden messages is large and when the order of hidden messages is in the raster direction (*from left to right, top to bottom*), the opposite is true. Thus, to improve the above problem, in our the thesis we proposed the method of steganalysis by mapping frequency of the image pixels into two-dimensional matrix $S = \{s_{ij}, i = 0...26, j = 0...9\}$, in our s_{ij} is the frequency of the pixel that has the value $i \times 10 + j$ in the image. Then, using standard deviation analysis to classify by the thresholds t_0 (based on the "*standard deviation*" table) will result in better detection in the case where information is hidden with a small amount of information and scattered across the pixels.

2.3.1.2   Statistical Method χ^2 with a Degree of Freedom

This is a better method of detecting hidden information than standard deviation. From the observation on a sample image set (600 images) with a large amount of hidden message (from 50% LSB of the image), we find that the steganography technique on LSB will change primarily on pixels having a high frequency, so it makes the pixel frequency value here approximately equal.

So, also by using the statistical method of the frequency of the pixel into the two-dimensional matrix $S = \{s_{ij}, i = 0, ..., 26, j = 0, ..., 9\}$ as above, find the row at the largest s_{ij} of S, then use χ^2 with a degree of freedom for pairs of sum even and sum odd values at the highest value row to classify by the threshold t_0 and found in the statistics table χ^2_n the probability α of the specific Type I error.

2.3.1.3   Analyzing the Gray Ratio between Any Image and Image Set Up as \Landmark"

This method results in better detection than the two above methods in terms of classification results and execution time. It is based on the Neyman-Pearson lemma which uses the given probability α (*Type I error*) to minimize the probability β (*Type II error*). Sullivan also applied this lemma to detect hidden images with LLRT technique, which has good detection with a small message count of 5% [32].

However, the classification is not good on the original image as the author gives an approximate estimation of the original image from any image that needs to be checked by the FIR filter [32]. Thus, this thesis presents a separate case of Neyman-Pearson lemma with another method of image estimation, which can be well classified for both the original and the hidden image.

2.3.1.4   Estimating Information Concealed in an Image

This method estimates concealed information on the LSB of the image space using the "*coincidence*" theory. Initially, we estimate based on an original C image, then hide the amount of information on image C that is image S, then estimating the information on the image S based on the image C will give the approximate amount of information that has been hidden in the image. However, in reality we do not have the original image, so we have to build an image to make a *"landmark,"* so that we can estimate the information hidden in any image by the theory of coincidence built from the case having an original image to compare. Based on empirical estimates, the *"matched"* estimation method can estimate the information on the image equivalent to other estimation approaches such as RS and DI [32], but better in terms of time taken.

2.3.2   Constraint Steganalysis

Along with constraint steganalysis, there are some public steganographic programs such as OutGuess [40], Attack F5 [13], Attack HKC [42], Attack RCM [43], Attack MBNS [44].

Contributing to this research, the author has proposed four constraint steganalysis techniques for hidden images using known hiding techniques.

2.3.2.1   *HKC Hiding Technique*

This hiding technique is based on shifting pixel frequency columns. The shifting creates an abnormal signal around the frequency band with the greatest value of the pixel frequency graph, so Wen-Chung Kuo and Yan-Hung Lin provide a method of detection [42] based on the relationship between the maximum frequency column called Peak and the four adjacent frequency bands of Peak to detect hidden images using the HKC technique. However, Kuo and Lin's detection techniques are not effective in the case of low or hidden bits, so the authors propose Kuo and Lin's advanced method for higher reliability [39]. The thesis also builds a generally simpler taxonomy than that of Kuo and Lin. Based on this new expression, we can estimate the information hidden in the image using the HKC technique.

2.3.2.2   *DIH Technique*

This technique is based on the coefficient of difference of the image. This technique loses the naturalness of the histogram of different coefficients d_{ij}, which in an unhidden image that is distributed according to the Gaussian histogram but in a hidden image does not have this distribution. This is the main reason why the author proposes a method for detecting hidden images using the DIH technique [35].

2.3.2.3   *IWH Hiding Technique*

This is a reverse hiding technique based on shifting the frequency columns of the wavelet frequency histogram of LL, LH, HL bands. This is a unique case of the LSB hiding technique, but the amount of hidden message with the highest hiding ability may still be very low compared to the conventional LSB technique. Using blind steganalysis on LSB of wavelet frequency domain (χ_n^2 [13], "gray scale" of the thesis) usually results in low classification.

However, when analyzing the wavelet frequency histogram, we get the abnormal state of the histogram when we hide the information. Thus, the author gives the corresponding detection method and that can approximate the bit rate of information concealed in the image [35].

2.3.2.4   *RVH Hiding Technique (Hiding in Two Phases)*

This technique uses multiple concealment strategies to improve image quality and hiding capacity. Information to hide M is classified into M_1 and M_2. The hiding process consists of two main phases: a horizontal hiding phase to hide M_1 and a vertical hiding phase to hide M_2. This is a unique case of LSB hiding technique, but this method can be by detecting with some statistical detecting methods such as χ_1^2, "standard deviation," LLRT, etc. Because of using two-phases to hide information, it avoids balancing the pairs of value (PoV) that are normally caused by LSB technique.

Therefore, to detect hidden information, the author analyzes the frequency of bit "0" and bit "1" of the LSB on the pixel columns in even positions or on the pixel rows at the odd position of the image vector. With unhidden images, the frequency of bit 0 and bit 1 are approximately equal, but after hiding the message using RVH this rule is broken. The author has built up the expression of calculating the probability of bits 0 and 1 after each concealed phase of RVH so that the above statement can be verified. Then, we provide an algorithm for detecting and estimating the approximate number of bits of information for hidden images using the RVH hiding technique [36].

2.4   Conclusion

Steganography is still an urgent problem in the field of information protection in general, and security, politics and defense in particular. Steganography requires a comprehensive study of problems of hidden information in the image. Continuing research in this area is not only scientifically significant; it is also significant in promoting the development of the information security field.

New techniques for steganography are constantly being introduced. Each new technique has many advantages and is more difficult to detect. Analyzing and finding out the distinctive features of the image before and after hiding a message are important for the technique to detect hidden images using this technique. In this direction, in the future, we will continue to study the following issues:

- Improve algorithm to increase the accuracy of existing detection techniques.

- Provide a method of extracting information.

- Find a detection method for the m LSBs domain.

- Study methods of detecting hidden information in other multimedia environment such as video, audio, etc.

References

1. Jessica Fridrich (2009), Steganography in digital media: principles, algorithms, and applications, Cambridge University Press.

2. C.K. Chan, L.M. Cheng (2001), Improved hiding data in images by optimal moderately-significant-bit replacement, IEEE Electronics Letters, Vol. 37 (16), pp. 10171018.

3. C.K. Chan, L.M. Cheng (2004), Hiding data in images by simple LSB substitution, Pattern Recognition 37, pp. 469-474.

4. C.C. Chang, J.Y. Hsiao, C.S. Chan (2003), Finding optimal least-significant-bit substitution in image hiding by dynamic programming strategy, Pattern Recognition 36, pp. 15831595.

5. Xiaolong Li, Bin Yang, Daofang Cheng and Tieyong Zeng (2009), A Generalization of LSB Matching, IEEE signal processing letters, Vol. 16 (2), pp. 69 72.

6. W.N. Lie, L.C. Chang (1999), Data hiding in images with adaptive numbers of least significant bits based on the human visual system, in: Proceedings of IEEE International Conference on Image Processing, Taipei, Taiwan, vol. 1, pp. 286-290.

7. Ching-Chiuan Lin, Nien-Lin Hsueh (2008), Alossless data hiding scheme based on three-pixel block differences, Pattern Recognition 41, pp. 1415-1425.

8. S. H. Liu, T. H. Chen, H. X. Yao and W. Gao (2004), A variable depth LSB data hiding technique in images, Machine Learning and Cybernetics 2004, pp. 3990-3994.

9. Z. M. Lu, J. S. Pan, and S. H. Sun (2000), VQ-based digital image watermarking method, Electron. Lett, Vol. 36 (14), pp. 1201-1202.

10. F. A. P. Petitcolas, R. J. Anderson, and M.G. Kuhn (1999), Information hiding - A survey, Proc. IEEE, vol. 87 (7), pp. 1062-1078.

11. C. I. Podilchuk and E. J. Delp (2001), Digital watermarking: Algorithms and applications, IEEE Signal Process. Mag., vol. 18 (4), pp. 33-34.

12. Niesl Provos, Peter Honeyman (2003), Hide and seek: An introduction to steganography, Published by The IEEE computer society.

13. Westfeld A. (2001), High Capacity Despite Better Steganalysis (F5A Steganographic Algorithm), In: Moskowitz, I.S. (eds.): Information Hiding. 4th International Workshop. Lecture Notes in Computer Science, Vol.2137. Springer-Verlag, Berlin Heidelberg New York (2001), pp. 289-302.

14. J. K I. Cox, J. Kilian, T. Leighton, and T. Shamoon (1997), Secure spread spectrum watermarking for multimedia, IEEE Trans. on Image Processing, 6(12):1673-1687.

15. Ingemar Cox, Jeffrey Bloom, Matthew Miller, Ton Kalker, Jessica Fridrich (2008), Digital Watermarking and Steganography, Second Edition, Morgan Kaufmann Press, USA.

16. Li, Bin; Fang, Yanmei; Huang, Jiwu, (2008), Steganalysis of Multiple-Base Notational System Steganography, IEEE Signal Processing Letters, vol. 15, pp. 493-496.

17. B. Chen and G. Wornell (2001), Quantization index modulation: A class of provably good methods for digital watermarking and information embedding, IEEE Trans. Info. Theary, Vol. 47 (4), pp. 1423-1443.

18. Takayuki Ishida, Kazumi Yamawaki, Hideki Noda, Michiharu (2009), Performance improvement of JPEG2000 steganography using QIM, Journal of Communication and Computer, Volume 6 (1), USA.

19. M.U. Celik, G. Sharma, A.M. Tekalp., and E. Saber (2002), Reversible Data Hiding, In Proc. of International Conference on Image Processing, Rochester, NY, USA, Vol. 2, pp. 157-160

20. Yeh-Shun Chen, Ran-Zan Wang, Yeuan-Kuen Lee, Shih-Yu Huang (2008), Steganalysis of reversible contrast mapping water marking, Proceedings of the world congress on Engineering 2008, Vol I, WCE2008, London, U.K., pp. 555-557.

21. Fridrich, J., Goljan, M., and Du, R. (2001), Reliable Detection of LSB Steganography in Grayscale and Color Images, Proc. of ACM: Special Session on Multimedia Security and Watermarking, Ottawa, Canada, pp. 27-30.

22. S. P. Hivrale, S. D. Sawarkar, Vijay Bhosale, and Seema Koregaonkar (2008), Statistical Method for Hiding Detection in LSB of Digital Images: An Overview, Proceedings of World Academy of Science, Engineering and Technology, Volume 32, ISSN 2070-3740, pp. 658-661.

23. K. M. Sullivan (2005), Image steganalysis: Hunting and Escaping, Ph. D Thesis in Electrical and computer Engineering, University of California.

24. A. Westfeld and A. Pfitzmann (1999), Attacks on steganographic systems, In Lecture notes in computer science: 3rd International Workshop on Information Hiding.

25. T. Zhang and X. Ping (2003), Reliable detection of LSB steganography based on the difference image histogram, IEEE International Conferenceon Acoustics, Speech, and Signal Processing, Volume 3, pp.545-548.

26. N. Provos and Peter Honeyman (2001), Detecting Steganographic Content on the Internet, CITI Technical Report 01-11, submitted for publication.

27. K. Sullivan, U. Madhow, S. Chandrasekaran and B. S. Manjunath (2005), S eganalysis of Spread Spectrum Data Hiding Exploiting Cover Memory, In Proc. IS&T/SPIE's 17th Annual Symposium on Electronic Imaging Science and Technology, San Jose, CA.

28. H. Malik (2008), Steganalysis of QIM Steganography Using Irregularity Measure, MM&Sec'08, Oxford, United Kingdom.

29. K. Sullivan, Z. Bi, U. Madhow, S. Chandrasekaran and B.S. Manjunath (2004), Steganalysis of quantization index modulation data hiding, In Proc. IEEE International Conference on Image Processing (ICIP), Singapore, pp. 11651168.

30. K. Sullivan, U. Madhow, B. S. Manjunath, and S. Chandrasekaran (2005), Steganalysis for Markov Cover Data with Applications to Images, Submitted to IEEE Transactions on Information Forensics and Security.

31. Toms Pevn (2008), Kernel Methods in Steganalysis, Ph. D Thesis, Binghamton University, State University of New York.

32. Ho Thi Huong Thom (2012), Research hidden image identification, Ph.D Thesis, University of Technology, Hanoi National University.

33. Ho Thi Huong Thom, Canh Ho Van, Tien Trinh Nhat (2009), Statistical Methods to Steganalysis of Color or Grayscale Images, Proc. of IEEE-RIVF 2009 on Doctoral Symposium, Da Nang University of Technology, pp. 1-5.

34. Ho Thi Huong Thom, Ho Van Canh, Trinh Nhat Tien (2009), Novel Algorithms to Steganalysis of Uncompressed and Compressed Images, Proceedings of KSE 2009 on Knowledge and Systems Engineering, College of Technology, IEEE Computer Society, Vietnam National University, Ha Noi, pp. 87-92.

35. Ho Thi Huong Thom, Ho Van Canh, Trinh Nhat Tien (2009), Steganalysis to Reversible Data Hiding, Proceedings of FGIT 2009 on Database Theory and Application, Springer-Verlag, Jeju, Korea, pp. 1-6.

36. Ho Thi Huong Thom, Canh Ho Van, Tien Trinh Nhat (2010), Steganalysis of Reversible Vertical Horizontal Data Hiding Technique, International Journal of Computer Science and Information Security (IJCSIS), Vol. 8 (6), pp. 7-12.

37. Ho Thi Huong Thom, Canh Ho Van, Tien Trinh Nhat (2009), Detect hidden images using standard deviation analysis, Proceedings of the National Conference Selected Issues in Information and Communication Technology, No. 11, Hue City, Vietnam, pp. 284-291.

38. Ho Thi Huong Thom, Canh Ho Van, Tien Trinh Nhat (2010), Estimate the length of the message hidden on the LSB domain of the image, Proceedings of the National Conference Selected Issues in Information and Communication Technology, No. 12, Dong Nai city, Vietnam, pp. 488 495.

39. Ho Thi Huong Thom, Canh Ho Van, Tien Trinh Nhat (2010), Detection of hiding image using reversible technique based on histogram shift, Journal of Science of Ha Noi national university, Natural Science & Technology, Vol. 26 (4), pp. 261-267.

40. J. Fridrich, M. Goljan and D. Hogea (2002), Attacking the OutGuess, Proc. of the ACM Workshop on Multimedia and Security 2002, Juan-les-Pins, France.

41. Jessica Fridrich, Miroslav Goljan, Dorin Hogea (2006), Steganalysis of JPEG Images: Breaking the F5 Algorithm, Pattern Recognition, ICPR 2006 18th International Conference, Volume 2, pp. 267-270.

42. Wen-Chung Kuo, Yan-Hung Lin (2008), On the Security of Reversible Data Hiding Based-on Histogram Shift, ICICIC 2008, pp. 174-177.

43. Yeh-Shun Chen, Ran-Zan Wang, Yeuan-Kuen Lee, Shih-Yu Huang (2008), Steganalysis of reversible contrast mapping water marking, Proceedings of the world congress on Engineering 2008, Vol I, WCE2008, London, U.K., pp. 555-557.

44. L. Bin, F. Yanmei, H. Jiwu, (2008), Steganalysis of Multiple-Base Notational System Steganography, IEEE Signal Processing Letters, vol. 15, pp. 493 - 496.

3

Security Threats and Vulnerabilities in E-business

SATYA NARAYAN TRIPATHY, SISIRA KUMAR KAPAT, SUSANTA KUMAR DAS

Department of Computer Science, Berhampur University, Odisha, India
Email: snt.cs@buodisha.edu.in, skk.rs.cs@buodisha.edu.in, skd.cs@buodisha.edu.in

Abstract

The explosive growth of business, science and other areas has lead to abundant data. We are drowning in data, but starving for knowledge, which has brought about the concept known as data mining. Data mining is extraction of implicit, potentially useful and unknown knowledge from huge amount of data. Data mining techniques can be very effectively used used for security applications. The permission to access data may cause a threat to the privacy and security of user's information. This chapter deeply focuses on the security aspects of data mining and possible solution techniques. Moreover, we also highlight some privacy issues due to data mining, like intrusion detection.

Keywords: Security threat, e-business, malware analysis, vulnerability, e-business attacks

Dac-Nhuong Le et al. (eds.), Cyber Security in Parallel and Distributed Computing, (51–262)
© 2019 Scrivener Publishing LLC

3.1   Introduction to e-Business

As the engineering for information and communication technology (ICT) develops, the requirement of more sophisticated business environment is needed. The revolution in traditional business methods has resulted in e-business. Traditional business is concerned with buying and selling of goods by direct mode only, but later on, the labor and effort involved in the customer going to the shop was increasingly no longer required, simultaneously enhancing the business process. e-Business is the process of buying or selling goods and services electronically. The clients no longer need to go to the shop to purchase items physically, rather they can browse many items from different shops worldwide using their fingertips. There are different types of markets like stock market, capital market, money market etc.; but all these markets have some similarities in their business process, as they have some sellers and some buyers.

Most of the e-business is carried out via internet nowadays. e-Business is a more generic term as compared to e-commerce. It refers not only to information exchanges related to buying and selling but also to servicing customers; and collaborating with business partners, distributors and suppliers [4]. e-Business can have different subcategories such as e-learning, e-commerce, e-banking, e-governance. e-Business encompasses sophisticated business-to-business interactions and collaboration activities at a level of enterprise applications and business processes. e-Business processes are integrated end-to-end across the company with key partners, suppliers and customers and can respond with flexibility and speed to customer demands and market opportunities.

3.1.1   Benefits of e-Business

Sometimes the user wants a product which is at some far distance apart. Consider, for example, a consumer and product which are in different countries. In this case, the user has to go abroad to purchase the particular product, which is a time-consuming job, which also requires a lot of money and a lot of strength. This problem is resolved by e-business. The major benefits of e-business are:

1. Maintaining the consumer data is easier. This data can be used to enhance the business process by using data mining.

2. Shopping malls can use consumer demands and habits, to rearrange the products inside the shopping mall by using association mining technique.

3. Globalization of goods and services is possible. The user can get the goods or services across the world apart from the location.

4. Time is saved compared to visiting shops door to door, and simultaneously surfing for the product and service is possible from various parts of the globe.

5. Users can compare prices for the same product from various locations at the same time.

6. Users have more options when choosing a product or service. In traditional business the user has a limited choice of some hundred to thousand products; but in the e-business system, user can choose among some thousands to millions products worldwide. This is known as "surf more, choose one."

7. Online shopping can be done in less time compared to shopping physically. For example, if someone from India wants a product from Africa, they need not go to Africa, which is more time consuming, but rather can get the product within one or two weeks online.

8. No need to carry money all the time, which is quite risky. The user can pay online.

3.1.2   Business Revolution

Prior to e-business, people used several marketing approaches, to sell their products and services such as sales promotions, brochures, etc. The general business approach is described as follows:

The first category of business involves direct transactions from manufacturer to consumer or employer to workers. Here the business is small enough that the number of employees in the total business was no larger than a family and the manufacturer and the seller was the same person.

In the second category of business, there is one seller between the manufacturer and the consumer. The job of manufacturer is to produce the products whereas sellers deal directly with the customers. Also, in this process the business is a small-scale business and the manufacturer is barely able to satisfy a small number of customers.

The concept of wholesaler and retailer are involved in the third category of business. The manufacturer produced the products and sold it to the wholesaler. The wholesaler then sell the products to the retailers, the retailers sell their products to the sellers, and finally the sellers deal with the customer. Next, the distributor came into existence, who only carries the non-competing goods.

This type of business is not applicable to the modern era where there is increasing demand for a variety of products. The customers want speedy delivery of goods to their doorsteps; low (*reliable*) price across the globe; good product; good customer support. The manufacturers also use much more money to sustain an advantage in the marketplace due to their many competitors. A complex business process is one, which includes manufacturing the products, market research, promotion of the products in print and online media, etc. The business structure must be scalable and reliable in order to satisfy customers.

A schematic diagram of traditional business structure is shown in Figure 3.1.

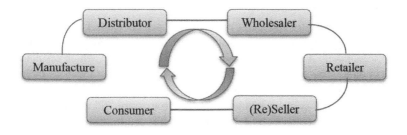

Figure 3.1   Product flow structure in traditional business.

e-Business is the common mode of business nowadays. Though the traditional approach exists, in this digitized era, the system of business is almost automated through internet. Customers can choose products online from any business store like Amazon or Flipkart. The price of the product is also paid online by using online banking, debit card, credit card, etc. Then the product will be shipped to the consumer to their doorstep. A schematic diagram of the general process of e-business is shown in Figure 3.2.

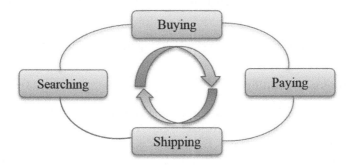

Figure 3.2   Communication cycle in e-business, from manufacturer to customer

3.2   Security Issues in e-Business

There are four types of business systems: B2B (*business-to-business*), B2C (*business-to-consumer*), C2B (*consumer-to-business*), C2C (*consumer-to-consumer*), C2G (*consumer to consumer*). These e-business systems have common components like consumer, payment option, system information, customer information, product information, etc. The business system must provide security for each of its components. There are two types of security issues present in the business system such as security threats and vulnerabilities.

Data mining is the key area in the 21st century, which is applied in almost every field of the technology. According to Steve Morgan [6], there is more investment in cybersecurity than health care. It is the case that health care providers are more careful about protecting patient data. Similarly, in e-business the data repository must be safe, because data sometimes much more precious than economy.

According to Richardson [6] attacks by means of bots, DNS attack, password sniffing, and data stolen from mobile devices are increasing tremendously. Denial of service, financial fraud, and malware threats constantly exist in the network. According to Identity Theft Resource Center (ITRC) [7], data breaches increased by 45% from 2016 to 2017, which is more than in any previous years.

e-Business has some strategies and processes [2] which relate to the transmission of goods and services from supplier to consumer via internet. There are many threats like disclosure of confidential information to modify the information, which results in loss of data and economy. The malicious user always tries to find new methods to bypass the security and privacy of the e-business system.

For example, when a consumer buys a product from store "S" and tries to pay for it, some inauthentic person collects the debit card or credit card information of the consumer. Now the inauthentic person can use the consumer data for personal use.

Similarly, there are many threats to the e-business system, which are described below.

3.2.1   Vulnerabilities

Vulnerabilities are the weaknesses of the normal functioning of the system that could be misused to impair the system or in worst case can shut down the e-business system. The vulnerabilities may create some open ports through which it is possible to attack the system. Some of the vulnerabilities are, accounts with weak passwords which can be easily guessed; programs with unnecessary privileges like administrative privilege; weak firewall configuration, etc. The vulnerabilities are discussed in Section 3.3.

3.2.2   Security Attacks

A security attack attach is any action which disrupts the security of information or intellectual property. Security attacks in the flow of e-business are a major problem. The attacks can be divided mainly into two categories: active attacks and passive attacks. Passive attacks will not modify the data which is sent from sender to receiver but rather sense the pattern of data, which is unsafe in e-business system. Active attacks are associated with the modification of message content. Release of message content and traffic analysis are known as passive attack; whereas masquerade, replay, message modification and denial-of-service attacks are known as active attacks.

Masquerade: Masquerade is a type of attack where the attacker pretends to be the authorized user. The attacker sends a message while pretending to be the authorized user. By pretending to be the authorized user, it is possible for the attacker to access all the authorized user's data.

Replay: This involves the repeat or delay of data by the malicious attacker. A detailed study of a replay attack and its prevention mechanism is discussed by Malladi *et al.* [8]. This type of attack can access all the personal information of a user when provided to a third party.

Message Modification: The unauthorized user modifies or reorders the legitimate message from the sender, and sends it to the receiver as if the sender sent the message directly to the receiver.

Denial-of-Service: This attack implies the disruption of the particular services, resulting in abnormal or unusual behavior of the system.

Some other types of attacks exist in network security which are applicable to the e-business system, such as spoofing, fabrication, sinkhole, etc., which are well explained by Pawar and Anuradha [4].

3.2.3   Malware as a Threat

The vulnerabilities in the e-business process include some malicious programs which are a proper concern of the user. Malware is considered to be a serious issue for the e-business system. Many anti-malware programs exist that protect the system against malware. Although they work quite well, malware is still able to evade them in many cases. Most of the anti-malware engines use signature-based detection. Now many researchers use data mining approaches for malware detection, which provide much greater accuracy. Some of the malware is discussed in Section 3.4.

3.3   Common Vulnerabilities in e-Business

3.3.1   Phishing

Generally a phishing attack is done by spoofed emails, which claims to be an original email message from the authorized person or organization. If the user enters any sensitive information in the location provided by the unauthorized person, the information is sent to the unauthorized person, who can misuse it.

3.3.2   Cross-Site Scripting (XSS)

Cross-site scripting [9] is possible, if the input-output validation is not checked for the user, along with the trust level of the user on any website. Cross-site scripting provides a webform, to enter the sensitive information of the end user. The sensitive information includes the credit card or debit card number, the card expiration date, pin (*password*), etc. If the user enters the details in the web-form, then the information is carried to the third party or the designer of the page. This type of attack is hard to be detected.

3.4   Threats in e-Business

There are many threats which can affect the e-business system. Malware is the common mode of disrupting the smooth functioning of the e-business system. The e-business system has two parts, one is the electronic money and the other is the information. This is an NP-hard problem to provide security to the e-business system. Some of the malware is discussed below.

3.4.1   Ransomware

Ransomware is a sinister malware, which encrypts user data from the user system and asks for money (*ransom*) to get the data back. The attacker uses the bitcoin mechanism in order to evade detection. Ransomeware was the foremost threat to e-business in 2017 because several infections were pointed out that year. According to the key findings in a report by Dick O'Brien [1], the WannaCry and Petya ransomware infections for organizations rose 29%, 30% and 42% in the years 2015, 2016 and the first half of 2017 respectively. The report states that, "The drop-off in 2017 may indicate that the 'gold rush' mentality among cyber criminals is beginning to abate somewhat, leaving the market to be dominated by professional ransomware gangs." In 2016, 470,000 infections were blocked, whereas in the first half of 2017, a total of 319,000 ransomware attacks were blocked.

3.4.2   Spyware

Spyware is a malicious computer program which works without the knowledge and consent of the user. Spyware programs are usually hidden among other programs or can be unwittingly downloaded to the user system when certain websites are visited; this concept is known as drive-by download. The user is unaware of the workings of the spyware. Spyware was created to collect sensitive information from the user. The sensitive information may be the user's credentials, debit card and credit card information, banking details, user browsing habits, etc.

In modern computing it is noticed that, the spyware targets the Windows as well as android environment. People commonly use mobile phones with an android operating system. Most of those using mobile phones are not expert in information security, so they are unaware of the spyware.

There are various types of spyware like adware, keylogger, botnet, dialer, spam, rootkit, etc. The categorization is done on the basis of the function of the families. These types of spyware are used to hamper the e-business system.

Adware: As the name suggests, adware is especially designed for the purpose of advertising. Adware is not only meant for advertising, but can also be misused to act like a spyware. Very often it pops up on some sorts of ads, but in some instances, it can steal the user information like a spyware.

Keylogger: Keylogger is also a dangerous threat in e-business because it has the capability to collect the key strokes entered on the user interface. Hence, it can collect the username and password of the user.

Botnet: Botnet creates a network of bots, which affect the e-business system in terms of collecting user information and sometimes uses user resources like memory and processor. Botnets work by means of the remote command of the botmaster.

Internet URL Logger and Screen Recorder: URL loggers track websites and pages which are visited online by the user. A screen recorder can take a small gray-scale image of the screen of the user's computer every time it changes. The images then can be stored or transmitted to a third party without user consent.

This type of spyware starts when the system starts. If the user is connected to the internet, then it starts recording all the screen shots and stores them in a specific memory area which is normally unseen by the user. By using this technique, the third party can collect most of the valuable information of the user like their password. Sometimes it acts as a keylogger, as a user may use an onscreen keyboard to type a password. Each time, when the user clicks on the onscreen keyboard, the screen is recorded and sent to the controller of the spyware.

3.4.3 Worms

Worms are self-propagating and self-replicating malware. A worm is not considered to be dangerous, but it can use the resources of the user like memory and bandwidth. This may lead to failure in the business system.

3.4.4 Trojan Horse

According to the traditional definition of Trojan Horse, it may seem to be a harmless or legitimate program, but actually it is not. It is sinister in the sense that it is hard to identify. It can create a backdoor to the user computing system or it can steal the user's personal data as per the program.

3.5 Prevention Mechanism

The e-business system is a sensitive environment in which the data is given more priority than economy. So some prevention mechanisms are needed to handle security threats, vulnerabilities and attacks. These prevention mechanisms can be categorized according to the perspective of the user and that of security personnel.

Prevention mechanisms pertaining to user:

- Strong firewall configuration must exist

- If possible, data must be encrypted before sending over the network

▪ Strong password must be used

▪ Anti-malware software should be used with updated malware definition

Prevention mechanisms pertaining to security personnel:

▪ Physical protection of computers

▪ Network system management and security

▪ Email control security

▪ Set proper access control

▪ Use data encryption techniques

▪ Digital certificate

▪ Backup the data, which can be recovered when required

▪ Wireless communication security must be there

3.6   Conclusion

Though e-business has the ability to digitize the payment and communication system, which is quite easy and speedy, it still has some flaws. Security must be maintained in the communication system as well as the standalone system. Precautions and safety measures need to be maintained in order to maintain security. Even though there is a lot of ongoing research to detect malware threats and mitigate vulnerabilities in the communication system, it is still considered to be an NP-hard problem. Data mining and machine learning methods have proven to be successful in handling the e-business system. But the business system is not still fully automated, but should be fully automated in the future.

References

1. Dick O'Brien (2017, July). An ISTR special report on ransomware 2017. Retrieved from https://www.symantec.com/content/dam/symantec/docs/security-center/whitepapers/istr-ransomware-2017-en.pdf

2. Bernard Kohan. e-Business Strategy and Proces. retrieved from http://www.comentum.com/e-business-strategy-process.html

3. Mihai DOINEA (2009). E-Business Security Architecture. Informatica Economica, Vol. 13, No. 1, pp 137-145

4. Pawar, M. V., & Anuradha, J. (2015). Network security and types of attacks in network. Procedia Computer Science, 48, 503-506.

5. Steve Morgan (2017), 2017 Cybercrime Report. Cybersecurity Ventures

6. Robert Richardson (2008). 2008 CSI Computer Crime & Security Survey. retrieved from http://www.kwell.net/doc/FBI2008.pdf

7. ACC Foundations (2018). ACC Foundation: The state of cybersecurity report an inhouse perspective. Retrieved from http://www.acc-foundation.com/foundation/sr/upload/2018-The-State-of-Cybersecurity-Summary.pdf

8. Malladi, S., Alves-Foss, J., & Heckendorn, R. B. (2002). On preventing replay attacks on security protocols. IDAHO UNIV MOSCOW DEPT OF COMPUTER SCIENCE. https://www.cse.iitb.ac.in/m̃adhumita/research_topics/authentication/replay02.pdf

9. K. K. Mookhey (2004). Common Security Vulnerabilities in e-commerce Systems. retrieved from https://www.symantec.com/connect/articles/common-security-vulnerabilities-e-commerce-systems

CHAPTER

4

e-Commerce Security:
Threats, Issues, and Methods

PRERNA SHARMA, DEEPAK GUPTA, ASHISH KHANNA

Maharaja Agrasen Institute of Technology, New Delhi, India
Email: prernasharma@mait.ac.in, deepakgupta@mait.ac.in, ashishkhanna@mait.ac.in

Abstract In the era of the demonetization and promotion of a cashless economy, e-commerce has taken center stage. An amalgam of fast internet and advanced processors is acting as a catalyst in the development of multiple e-commerce applications and their usability. Credit for the popularity of e-commerce also goes to the convenience provided by seller and buyer transactions from anywhere at any time. Furthermore, scalable high-speed transactions with lower operating costs have led to e-commerce acceptability worldwide, thus helping to expand businesses and promoting a new form of economy via e-commerce. However, traditional practitioners of business are going to leave no stone unturned to stop this flood of e-commerce transactions in the shadow of secure and authentic transactions. Therefore, in order to create a fearless environment for buying and selling over the internet, highly secure, reliable, and authentic e-commerce applications are needed. The above discussion demonstrates the importance of security for the successful implementation of e-commerce. This chapter explains the issues and problems associated with the security of worldly goods and transactions in e-commerce components and activities. Since a large amount of public money is involved in the transactions, the role of information security and privacy is not exaggerated in this kind of business. Many issues like identity theft and cyber fraud are obstacles that discourage customers from getting involved in e-commerce. Education of the public on e-commerce security issues has taken a back seat until now; it should be encouraged as trust and security are huge challenges to be addressed so that one can insulate the e-commerce system from prevailing attacks. In this chapter we will

Dac-Nhuong Le et al. (eds.), Cyber Security in Parallel and Distributed Computing, (61–262)
© 2019 Scrivener Publishing LLC

address different types of application-specific security threats, security challenges, and vulnerability issues at various levels of the system. Furthermore, we will throw light on how to deal with various security threats, issues, and present a comparative analysis of various methods used in e-commerce security in order to perform secure payment transactions in an efficient manner.

Keywords: e-Commerce security, e-commerce threats, e-commerce issues, e-commerce methods, e-commerce architecture, e-commerce life cycle

4.1   Introduction

In the era of demonetization and promotion of cashless economy, the internet has given a distributed platform to expand businesses, thus giving birth to a new form of economy known as e-economy via e-commerce. In the new economy, the internet has grown into an influential and universal communication mechanism to assist in the consummation and dispensation of business transactions [17]. Whereas, e-commerce can be explained as buying and selling of goods and services online by using user interactive GUI platforms. It has revolutionized the way trade is carried out and today e-commerce has attained center stage in commerce transactions. In other words, an amalgam of fast internet and advanced processors is acting as a catalyst in the development of multiple e-commerce applications and their usability. The credit for the popularity of e-commerce also goes to the convenience provided to the seller and buyer of transacting from anywhere and at any moment. Furthermore, scalable high-speed transactions with lower operating costs have led to the acceptability of e-commerce worldwide. Thus, helping to expand businesses and promoting a new form of economy via e-commerce [1].

However, the traditional practitioners of business are going to leave no stone unturned to stop this flood of e-commerce transactions in the shadow of secure and authentic transactions, and this lack of trust can severely affect buyers and sellers, who may choose to refrain from the use of the internet and recrudesce to traditional methods of doing business; as this aspect can turn technology into a curse in spite of a boon [2]. Therefore, in order to create a fearless environment for buying and selling on the internet, to oppose the above-mentioned misconception and insecurity among the clients, and to create a conducive environment for e-commerce security threats, the security issues should be properly reviewed and addressed by highly secure, reliable, and authentic e-commerce applications. Countermeasures must be implemented so that it does not discourage use of e-commerce operations.

The above discussion demonstrates the importance of security in e-commerce in order for its implementation to be successful. This chapter explains the issues and problems associated with the security of worldly goods and transactions in the e-commerce components and activities. Since a large amount of public money is involved in the transactions, the role of information security and privacy is not exaggerated in this kind of business. Many issues, like identity theft and cyber fraud, are obstacles that discourage customers from getting involved in e-commerce. Awareness of e-commerce security issues has taken a back seat until now, although it should be encouraged, as trust and security are huge challenges to be addressed to insulate the e-commerce system from a set of prevailing attacks. In this chapter we will address different types of application-specific security threats, security challenges, and vulnerability issues at various levels of the system. This chapter also aims to study an e-commerce security life-cycle model and proposes comparative analysis of various methods of e-commerce security. Furthermore, it throws light on to how to deal with various security threats and issues, and presents a comparative analysis of various methods used in e-commerce security in order to perform secure payment transactions in an efficient manner.

4.2 Literature Review

In the domain of e-commerce, secure transaction is one of the key issues that restrict consumers and establishments engaging in commerce. A lot of research is going on in the direction of secure and authentic transactions. Some of the work done in the past is discussed below.

Dieter Gollmann *et al.* [1] have talked about colossal growth of the internet and its services, and its active role in commerce territory apart from the academic one. Sengupta *et al.* [3] have put forward an e-commerce security life-cycle approach, and significant standards and laws in e-commerce security. Also, various security requirements to protect the e-commerce system from threats have been identified. Ladan [5] has presented an overview of the architectural framework of e-commerce and also elucidated various e-commerce security issues and security measures at different levels of e-commerce system.

Gautam and Singh [6] discuss online security for proficient payment transactions, which acts as an indispensable management and technical tool. Jarnail Singh [9] has provided guidelines for the security of e-commerce in order to enhance customer confidence in online transactions. He finds that low level security on the web servers of e-commerce and on customers' sites is the issue to be addressed.

Ahmad and Alam [15] have proposed a model of e-transaction on the basis of PGP and ECC. This chapter signifies how PGP efficiently handles customer order of information and security of payment using dual digital signature. Kraft and Kakar [16] have explored latest market trends for e-business and the vital role played by e-commerce in the retail market. The modern practices of e-commerce and development of e-commerce have been researched and acknowledged.

4.3 e-Commerce

e-Commerce is extensively used for the purchasing and retailing of goods online. However, only transactions made through digital online fund transfers measures can be considered e-commerce transactions. With each passing day, m-commerce and e-commerce are playing a more important role in internet-based retail marketing. The number of people worldwide using this technology is increasing day-by-day. To understand e-commerce security issues an understanding of the following key characteristics of e-commerce is essential.

4.3.1 Characteristics of e-Commerce Technology

Some of the key characteristics of e-commerce are as follows [3]:

1. *Automated processing*: The generation and processing of multiple payments has been automated by the payer with little effort and cost involved.

2. *Immediacy of result*: Real-time payments because of automation results in payment immediacy.

3. *Improved accessibility*: Accelerated usage of computing and communication technology with suitable software empowers access of payment services even to small enterprises that earlier could only be accessed by large organizations via dedicated network.

4. *Global reach*: The new payment system curtails geographical factors; allows business transactions on a cross-country basis. It affects certain thrust areas such as extent of payment market place, adaptation of payment schemes to regulatory regimes and many more.

5. *Ubiquity*: e-Commerce can be operated from anywhere whereas the traditional business market is defined by a physical place.

6. *Loss of collateral information*: Earlier transacting parties used to validate individual payments on the basis of collateral information that they relied upon. Whereas these days new technology waives off or alters collateral information with transactions.

7. *Interactivity*: In the 21st century the two-way communication mode is acknowledged between businesses and consumers.

8. *New business model*: They are in place to make use of new payment technologies for disintermediation of customers from banks.

4.3.2   Architectural Framework of e-Commerce

Client-server architecture is the base of e-commerce architecture. Client is basically an application which makes use of GUI to send a request to a server for certain services; the server in turn provides the requested services to the client.

In this architectural framework, client denotes customer and server denotes business application. This business application is set up on a web server (*computer program*) which provides services to the customer in the form of HTML pages or files.

The two different types of client-server architecture of e-commerce are [4]: two-tier architecture (Figure 4.1) and three-tier architecture (Figure 4.2).

4.3.2.1   Two-Tier Architecture

In this architecture data rests on the server whereas business application/logic and user interface rests on the client. The client process makes user interface available, which collects and presents the data on the customer's computer. Thus, this part of the application is known as the *presentation layer*.

The server process makes sure of the availability of interface that frames the data stored/database. Thus, this application is known as the *data layer*.

Although the business logic/application mostly resides on the client side, it can also reside on the server side. Business logic performs various functions of validating data and monitoring security and permissions.

4.3.2.2   Three-Tier Architecture

To address the limitation of two-tier architecture, three-tier architecture emerged in the 1990s. In this architecture, business logic is separated from user interface and from data access. Hence, all three are maintained as independent modules. Thus, in this architecture there are three tiers involved:

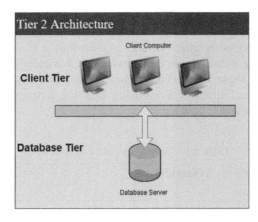

Figure 4.1   Two-tier e-commerce architecture.

- *Top tier*: User interface services; Text input session; Dialog management: Display management

- *Middle tier*: Process management services; Process development and process monitoring; Process resourcing

- *Third tier*: Database management services; Data consistency; Centralized process logic; Localizing the system functionality.

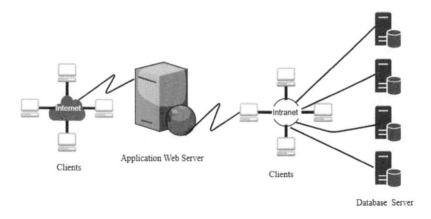

Figure 4.2   Three-tier e-commerce architecture.

Operation: In the e-commerce system, a client sends a request via the internet, which passes a firewall that filters the packets destined for wrong address or wrong ports. The web server treats the request by calling an application which accesses a database server in order to modify, update or read a record or records stored in the database and further replies with an HTML page or file. These servers are in addition connected to huge networks [5].

4.3.3   Advantages and Disadvantages of e-Commerce

We have discussed many of the characteristics of e-commerce in the section above. The internet aids in forming virtual communities, which are basically groups of people having common interests. These virtual communities become ideal target markets. There are various advantages of performing business online from the perspective of different stakeholders, as shown in Table 4.1.

Table 4.1   Advantages of e-commerce.

S.No	e-Commerce Stakeholders	Advantages
1	Organization	Low cost
		Fewer employees involved
		Global reach, even to remote areas
		Easier management of inventory
2	Client/Customer	Customized experience
		Can compare prices easily of same products/services
		Products/Services available at a mouse click
		Wider range of choices available
3	Society	Promotes cashless economy, which in turn curbs black money
		Provides online services in various sectors
		Prices of products are kept in check as no middlemen,
		such as wholesalers, retailers, etc., are involved.

If we look at e-commerce operations from the point of view of various stakeholders, there are many drawbacks associated with them, as shown in Table 4.2.

Table 4.2   Disadvantages of e-commerce

S.No	e-Commerce Stakeholders	Disadvantages
1	Organization	Data privacy issues
		Not everything can be sold, such as perishable products or,
		expensive luxury items
		Highly competitive
		Problem of adherence to legal standards
2	Client/Customer	Look and feel not available before buying
		Internet connectivity required
		Product delivery not instantaneous
		Products not available when server is down
		When delivered, product may not be as expected
3	Society	Security of data like leakage of data
		Knowledge of using internet is limited

4.4   Security Overview in e-Commerce

Security is the need of the hour when operating online, as the network's vulnerability to attack is manifold. Information is one of the most vital enterprise assets. For any organization, information should be valued and suitably secured [18]. Hence, we will discuss the purpose of security in e-commerce and different levels of the system where security is a prerequisite.

4.4.1   Purpose of Security in e-Commerce

1. *Authentication*: This ensures that only the right user has access to data [6].

2. *Non-repudiation*: This is a form of confirmation from the user that they have indeed performed an action, so that they have cannot deny performing that action in the future.

3. *Privacy*: This gives control to the user on how much of their data can be given/distributed to third parties.

4. *Confidentiality*: This is the state of keeping data private so that it cannot be accessed by any unauthorized person/party.

5. *Availability*: This means that all the data is available to a user that they are entitled to or have the right to access.

6. *Integrity*: This ensures that data received by a user is the same that was transmitted by sender, that is, no change or manipulation of data has occurred while transmitting data.

7. *Encryption*: This means encoding data in such a way that it cannot be understood directly by reading it.

4.4.2   Security Element at Different Levels of e-Commerce System

Security of the e-commerce system is of immense significance, thus it must be ensured at various component levels, i.e., hardware, software and environment. The pervasiveness of computing systems has placed computer devices everywhere, and they have become so prevalent as to blend into the background. They are also part of the emerging wireless environment [11].

4.4.2.1   Hardware

The devices that make up the system, such as web servers, network devices, and database servers, are critical points of the system and are susceptible to various network attacks. Thus, measures like a properly configured firewall must be taken. Web servers and database servers should be insulated from various other networks by using DMZ (*demilitarized zone*), which is a network that stands between a protected network and an external network. Thus, an additional layer of security is introduced in the network.

4.4.2.2   Software

The smooth operation of an e-commerce software security system requires a security OS, web server software, database software and web browser. The operating system should be configured properly, as it is quite vulnerable. In order to fix holes in security, there should be a regular updating of software and routinely released patches.

4.4.2.3   Environment

Environmental security refers to securing physical access to the network by using a manual guard, CCTV, various logs or other methods.

4.5   Security Issues in e-Commerce

We have already discussed security elements at different levels of the e-commerce system, now let's talk further about various security and vulnerability issues at these levels [5].

4.5.1   Client Level

These days customers tend to get their hands on an e-commerce system in different ways, such as wireless networks, mobile devices, etc. These modes are vulnerable to security hazards, as an outsider can eavesdrop on wireless communication. Thus, there is a need for password protection so that an outsider cannot intervene and access sensitive information. In addition, there is always a chance of misplacing the mobile device.

Security issues with respect to mobile devices and wireless networks which further affect e-business are:

- *Captured and retransmitted messages*: This refers to an attacker getting hold of a message of a legitimate user and replaying it by altering the message to the same receiver or a different one so that the attacker can gain unauthorized access to important information [7].

- *Eavesdropping*: This attack happens on unsecured network and also when the information being transmitted is not encrypted. Thus, an outsider can eavesdrop on a vulnerable network and can easily gain access to sensitive data.

- *Mobile device pull attack*: In this type of attack, the attacker controls the mobile device as a source of propriety data and control information. Data can be obtained from the device itself through the data export interfaces, a synchronized desktop, mobile applications running on the device or the internet servers [8].

- *Mobile device push attack*: In this type of attack, the attacker uses the mobile device to plant a malicious code and spread it to infect other elements of the network. Once the mobile device inside a secure network is compromised, it can be used for attacks against other devices or servers in the network [8].

- *Lost device*: A mobile device should always be protected with a password as there is always a chance of its getting lost or stolen and an unauthorized user can access it.

4.5.2   Front-End Servers and Software Application Level

It is observed that in a software system there is always a chance of bugs/faults being left by low-skilled software developers. The e-commerce security system is expected to be flexible, standards based and interoperable with other systems.

Keeping security advisories and patches updated is quite difficult, as communication network standards and protocols keep on changing. Hackers are opportunistic and make the most of these vulnerabilities by using viruses and malicious software to infect the e-business system and steal customer information.

4.5.3   Network and Server Level

Most of the networks are dependent on other networks which are privately owned and managed, whose security measures are not known to us; therefore, its control is also not available to us. Encryption is used to secure data moving across a network. The network operator is responsible for transporting information securely.

- *DoS*: Whenever hackers launch a denial-of-service attack, it turns out to be one of the most bothersome security issues faced by e-business today. It is characterized as a categorical effort by attackers to prevent users from using an e-business system.

- *Session interception and message modification*: The attacker can transmit altered messages by hijacking a session. They can also add a malicious host between client host and server host, which is popularly known as man-in-the-middle. In this case, data communication passes through the attackers' host.

- *Firewall loophole*: A firewall is a software or hardware device installed between back-end server and corporate network. It is usually implemented at network protocol layer and fails to protect the system at higher protocols. Hackers sense unfixed firewall loopholes and try to access price lists, email lists, catalogs, etc.

4.6   Security Threats in e-Commerce

e-Commerce has a tendency to be at a higher stratum for risk and attacks. In e-commerce, data are the key to track consumer shopping behavior to personalize offers, which are collected over time using consumer browsing and transactional points [19]. Server level is the physical place where all of these transactions happen. The server is regarded as the central repository for one's e-commerce business abode that entails a definite website which displays one's products and services, the database of the customer and the mechanism of payment. If any attack takes place on the server, then it proves to be a huge setback as there is a potential of losing everything. Thus, taking the initiative when it comes to security should be done to a much greater extent. Now, let us discuss various e-commerce security threats in detail [9].

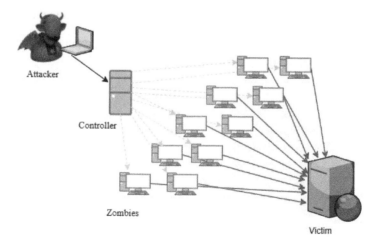

Figure 4.3   DDOS attack.

Distributed Denial-of-Service (DDos): In this type of attack the availability of a target system (e-commerce) comes into question, as millions of customers are unable to access an online system which is overwhelmed with traffic from multiple sources. In this type of attack a botnet is formed in which multiple devices are connected online; these devices tend to generate fake traffic flooding the target system, which results in the service being denied to legitimate customers. This attack affects not only the target site but also creates a congestion problem over the entire network (Internet), as shown in Figure 4.3.

It becomes difficult to control or stop the attack as one cannot differentiate between genuine traffic and attack traffic. An attacker may restrain you from getting your hands on email, websites, and online accounts that the affected computer depends on [10].

A DDoS attack consists of four elements [11]:

- *Victim*: The target host who is going to deal with the burden of the attack.

- *Attack daemon agent*: This is an agent program that performs the attack on the victim. It is set up mostly on the host computer but tends to affect both host and target computer. These daemons tend to gain access and infiltrate the host computer.

- *Control master program*: Coordinates the attack.

- *Real attacker*: Although being the mastermind of the attack, it stays in the background by using the control master program.

SQL Injection: As the name of the attack suggests, there must be an SQL query which has been inserted while the user inputs the data; as the query gets executed at the client end, the attack comes into operation. This is one of the most common web hacking techniques in which code is injected that might create havoc in the database, as shown in Figure 4.4.

The causes of SQL injection are as follows [12]:

- Running of software applications that welcome data from inauthentic internet users.

- Unable to validate the data.

- This data is further used in dynamic SQL query to database backing the application.

SQL injection results in: in identity spoofing, alteration of existing data, revealing all the data on the system, making data unavailable by destroying the data.

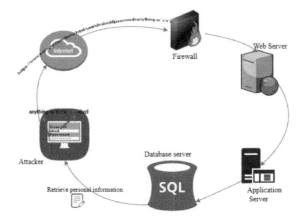

Figure 4.4   SQL injection attack.

Price Manipulation: As the name suggests, the original price is manipulated to different value. This type of attack, which is depicted in Figure 4.5, is very common in online shopping cart platforms and payment gateways. In this attack the final payable price is manipulated by the attacker at will. In coding, the programmer makes use of hidden fields in order to store value of total item cost; a hacker can tamper with a value stored on their browser, thus the total amount that is payable is modified by the attacker. Supposedly, the value of an item is modified from Rs.2000/- to Rs.200/-, then it becomes exciting for the customer but unfortunate for the seller.

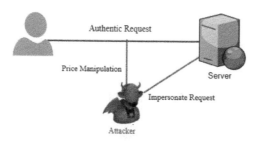

Figure 4.5   Price manipulation.

Session Hijacking: A session is a sequence of interactions maintained over a single connection between two nodes or end points, as shown in Figure 4.6. As the name of the attack suggests, the session control is taken over by the hijacker as they steal a valid session ID which allows them to enter or keep an eye on data or extract it. By changing the route of packets with their system an attacker can take part in the conversation of other users [14]. It is a combination of sniffing and spoofing.

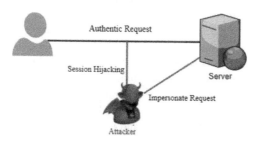

Figure 4.6   Session hijacking attack.

Cross-Site Scripting (XSS): In this type of attack a malicious script is attached to trusted websites from a compromised site. On adding malicious script the attacker gains access to sensitive information, session cookies, etc. It is a special case of code injection. Here, the end user's browser has no clue whether it is a trustworthy script or not. Thus, it goes goes ahead and executes this script. These scripts change and rewrite the HTML page content. This process is schematically shown in Figure 4.7.

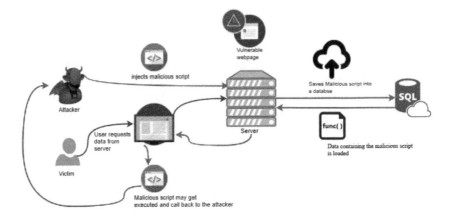

Figure 4.7   Cross-site scripting attack.

4.7   Security Approaches in e-Commerce

The security of the most crucial information of a customer, such as credit card data, should be of highest priority when transactions are carried out online. Security measures that should be ensured in e-commerce architecture are DMZ, firewalls, SSL, SET, data encryption, intrusion detection, digital signature and certificates [5].

Demilitarized Zone (DMZ): This is a special local network that holds sensitive data which is to be saved from unauthorized access. It lies between the internet and an internal network. It consists of external facing servers (*front-end servers, back-end servers*) and firewalls. The job of a firewall is not only to protect the front-end server but also to filter traffic between the corporate network and back-end servers. It provides an additional level of security as access to internal servers and data via internet in the internal LAN remains unreachable. An external node has access to what is available in the DMZ.

Firewalls: When a computer gets connected to the internet it becomes open to attack. A firewall, which is either hardware- or software-based, monitors and controls the traffic that either comes in or goes out of a computer based on predetermined security rules. It can be configured to let packets from specific IP addresses and ports enter or block them. Thus, it acts as a barrier between a trusted network and untrusted network.

Data Encryption: Encryption technology converts plain text into unreadable format, which prevents a third party from viewing the text. Hence, crucial information, such as credit card numbers, financial transactions and personal data, can be protected. It offers a technique to find out whether any alteration/modification of data has occurred over an unsecured network when the data is received. Data is transmitted over a secure network such as SSL, using secure protocol such as HTTPS.

There are two types of encryption techniques:

- Symmetric key encryption

- Asymmetric key encryption

Intrusion Detection System (IDS): IDS evenly monitors real-time network traffic. When it come across an attack signature or suspicious activity it becomes attentive and generates an alarm to alert the system or network administrator. Sometimes it responds to the malicious traffic by simply blocking the user from accessing the network. It can also prevent denial-of-service attacks. It should be installed in front of a firewall.

Digital Signature and Certificate: This supports e-commerce security features authentication and integrity. A *digital signature certificate* (DSC) is a secure digital key that certifies the identity of the holder, which is issued by a *certifying authority* (CA). It typically contains your identity (*name, email, country, APNIC account name and your public key*). Digital certificates use public key infrastructure, meaning that data that has been digitally signed or encrypted by a private key can only be decrypted by its corresponding public key. A digital certificate is an electronic "credit card" that establishes your credentials when doing business or other transactions on the Web [13].

4.8 Comparative Analysis of Various Security Threats in e-Commerce

Table 4.3 Comparative analysis of various security threats in e-commerce.

No.	Threats	Security Features Affected	Site/Assets	Severity	Protecting Threat Methods	Network Affected
1	DDoS	Availability	Server	High	Access control, firewall	Loss of access to system
2	SQL Injection	Integrity Confidentiality Non-repudiation	Client	High	Blocking, Digital certificate verification antivirus	Attacker can become administrator of database
3	Price Manipulation	Authorization Modification Encryption	Communication Network	Moderate	Encryption Digital Signature	Attacker modifies the price value
4	Session Hijacking	Authentication Confidentiality	Communication Network	Moderate to High	Encryption Digital Signature	Session is hijacked after gaining authentication
5	XSS	Integrity Confidentiality Authorization	Client	Moderate to high	Firewall	Attacker gets access to sensitive data abuse of credentials

4.9 e-Commerce Security Life-Cycle Model

e-Commerce security is a continuous process, which cannot be viewed in modular form as one-time provided service. It has become an integral part of e-commerce transactions where data is of utmost value, as it includes personal information of individuals' credit card numbers, financial transactions, etc. Electronic word-of-mouth has been framed by digital technologies which in turn proposes potential for eliciting credible information that influences consumer behavior [20]. It is the responsibility of the security system designer to ensure that system properties are not affected by various security attacks [3].

The steps to designing system security are [14]:

1. Model the system.

2. Identify the properties of the system that are to be safeguarded when met with an attack.

3. Model the adversary.

4. Ensure that the properties are safeguarded when under attack.

Security Requirement Specification and Risk Analysis: At the initial stage, information needs to be gathered that answers the following questions:

a) What are the assets of the organization that are to be protected?

b) What are the threats associated with those assets?

c) What are the access control policies?

d) What is the operational infrastructure?

e) What are the services required to access the asset?

f) What is the access control mechanism for the services?

Security attributes that are to be protected are authentication, privacy, authorization, and integrity.

Security Policy Specification: Security requirement specification and risk analysis report is input at this phase; e-commerce security policy is generated as output. Policies are basically high-level rule-based statements.

Questions that need to be answered regarding security policy issues are:

a) What types of services can users access?

b) What are the information classes present in the organization that are required to be encrypted before transmitting?

c) How can sensitive client data be protected?

d) Corporate network remote access is associated with which class of employees?

e) How are security breaches to be dealt with?

Security Infrastructure Specification: Analysis of security requirement specification and security policy specification takes place at this stage of the life cycle. In this phase one finds a list of security tools needed to protect assets. It is basically the implementation of the security policy. Some instances are:

a) Applying password aging and expiration.

b) Demanding complex passwords.

c) Recording in a written log all physical access made to servers.

d) Giving physical access to building via badges.

Testing e-Commerce Security: Several tests are conducted on the system to answer the following questions:

a) How effective is the security infrastructure?

b) What are the functions of the access control mechanism?

c) What operational context is specified?

d) How vulnerable is the infrastructure to new threats and exploits?

The main objectives of this phase are verification of the following aspects:

a) Security requirements specification

b) Configuration of security tools

c) Gap between proposed security infrastructure and the implemented infrastructure

d) Limitation of the proposed security infrastructure

Requirement Validation: This phase analyzes the extent to which security requirements of the e-commerce organization is fulfilled in accordance with security policy and implemented security infrastructure. The entire process/cycle starts again if change is incorporated into the business goal, operational environment and technology. A new set of security requirements comes into play which stimulates the new cycle of the software engineering life cycle shown in Figure 4.8.

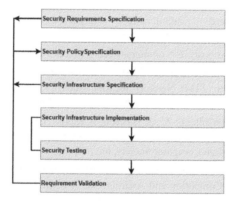

Figure 4.8   Security engineering life cycle.

4.10 Conclusion

e-Commerce is growing at an immense pace. Many technologies have come together to assist propagation of e-commerce these days. This industry is vulnerable to many threats and issues are being addressed slowly and steadily. To protect one's place of business being proactive is the first line of defense against security threats. Educating consumers on security issues is a vital element of e-commerce security architecture which is still in its infancy. Becoming familiar with threats, issues and protection methods will help in avoiding network vulnerability to outside elements. Ignorance is itself a threat, as fraudsters are on the lookout for online shoppers committing novice errors that they can take advantage of. In this chapter, we discussed e-commerce architecture, security issues, security threats, protection methods for safe and secure online shopping and security engineering life cycle that helps to familiarize us with various safeguards.

Future Scope: This paper can be used by research practitioners as a base for e-commerce security issues, threats and protection methods detailed in this chapter. Susceptibility of network to attacks and advancement in technology needs customers to be aware of e-commerce security issues so that the e-commerce industry can be insulated from fraud. Privacy concerns of consumers can be entertained by shielding huge amounts of personal information posted on the internet and also by stressing usable security to aid individuals with security controls that make sense to them and can be easily put to use [21].

References

1. Gollmann, D. (2010). Computer security. Wiley Interdisciplinary Reviews: Computational Statistics, 2(5), 544-554.

2. Marchany, R. C., & Tront, J. G. (2002). E-commerce security issues. In System Sciences, 2002. HICSS. Proceedings of the 35th Annual Hawaii International Conference on (pp. 2500-2508). IEEE.

3. Sengupta, A., Mazumdar, C., & Barik, M. S. (2005). e-Commerce securityA life cycle approach. Sadhana, 30(2-3), 119-140.

4. Thiru,   "E-commerce   architecture".   http://www.myreadingroom.co.in/notes-and-studymaterial/66-e-commerce/517-e-commerce-architecture.html

5. Ladan, M. I. (2014, August). E-Commerce security issues. In Future Internet of Things and Cloud (FiCloud), 2014 International Conference on (pp. 197-201). IEEE.

6. Gautam, R., & Singh, S. (2014). Network Security issues in E-commerce. International Journal of Advanced Research in Computer Science and Software Engineering, 4(3), 130-132.

7. Pham, Q., Reid, J., McCullagh, A., & Dawson, E. (2008). Commitment issues in delegation process. In Proceedings of the sixth Australasian conference on Information security-Volume 81 (pp. 27-38). Australian Computer Society, Inc..

8. Doukas, C., Pliakas, T., & Maglogiannis, I. (2010). Mobile healthcare information management utilizing Cloud Computing and Android OS. In Engineering in Medicine and Biology Society (EMBC), 2010 Annual International Conference of the IEEE (pp. 1037-1040). IEEE.

9. Jarnail Singh (2014). Review of e-commerce security challenges. International Journal of Innovative Research in Computer and Communication Engineering (An ISO 3297: 2007 Certified Organization) Vol. 2, Issue 2, ISSN(Online): 2320-9801 ISSN (Print): 2320-9798.

10. Kumar, P. A. R., & Selvakumar, S. (2011). Distributed denial of service attack detection using an ensemble of neural classifier. Computer Communications, 34(11), 1328-1341.

11. Kulkarni, A., & Bush, S. (2006). Detecting distributed denial-of-service attacks using kolmogorov complexity metrics. Journal of Network and Systems Management, 14(1), 69-80.

12. Dougherty, C. (2012). Practical identification of SQL injection vulnerabilities. United States Computer Emergency Readiness Team (US-CERT).

13. Digital Certificate https://www.emudhradigital.com/

14. Baitha, A. K., & Vinod, S. (2018). Session Hijacking and Prevention Technique. International Journal of Engineering & Technology, 7(2.6), 193-198.

15. Ahmad, K., & Alam, M. S. (2016). E-commerce Security through Elliptic Curve Cryptography. Procedia Computer Science, 78, 867-873.

16. Kraft, T. A., & Kakar, R. (2009). E-commerce security. In Proceedings of the Conference on Information Systems Applied Research, Washington DC, USA.

17. Delone, W. H., & Mclean, E. R. (2004). Measuring e-commerce success: Applying the DeLone & McLean information systems success model. International Journal of Electronic Commerce, 9(1), 31-47.

18. Hong, K. S., Chi, Y. P., Chao, L. R., & Tang, J. H. (2003). An integrated system theory of information security management. Information Management & Computer Security, 11(5), 243-248.

19. Akter, S., & Wamba, S. F. (2016). Big data analytics in E-commerce: a systematic review and agenda for future research. Electronic Markets, 26(2), 173-194.

20. Flanagin, A. J., Metzger, M. J., Pure, R., Markov, A., & Hartsell, E. (2014). Mitigating risk in ecommerce transactions: perceptions of information credibility and the role of user-generated ratings in product quality and purchase intention. Electronic Commerce Research, 14(1), 1-23.

21. Jang-Jaccard, J., & Nepal, S. (2014). A survey of emerging threats in cybersecurity. Journal of Computer and System Sciences, 80(5), 973-993.

5

Cyberwar is Coming

T. Manikandan[1], B. Balamurugan[2], C. Senthilkumar[1], R. Rajesh Alias Harinarayan[3], R. Raja Subramanian[3]

[1] APCSE, CSE Department, Thiagarajar College of Engineering, Madurai, Tamil Nadu, India

[2] PCSE, Galgotias University, Uttar Pradesh, India

[3] Research Scholar, CSE Department, Thiagarajar College of Engineering, Madurai, Tamil Nadu, India

Email: tmcse@tce.edu

Abstract

"War" is the most dangerous game played by humans when their resources are threat, which has then continuously evolved throughout history due to greed. After the huge losses incurred in the world wars, humanity was restored with diplomacy. War is initiated when emotions like fear and greed encroach upon the minds of people in a society. Basically, fear is triggered due to the lack of resources necessary for living a peaceful life, and questions begin to arise in the minds of people as to what would happen if these resources were to be threatened by those of a faster-growing society with more money and arms which might be used to enslave their own society. Greed happens after a nation reaches a stable state and wants to to become. Armed warfare in today's world has been reduced due to diplomatic efforts, but the fear of reduced resources and greed for money are still visible, and the resources are now becoming digital all over the world with the development of technologies like 5G, the internet of things, smartphones, smarter cities, etc., but so are cyberattacks with ransomware such as WannaCry, NotPetya, BadRabbit, etc. With everything connected to the Internet, it has become a battlefield connected to the civilians of all nations, placing them on the battlefield unknowingly. This connectivity is a bigger threat as it can cause massive devastation in rising digital economies and in everyone and everything, even our brains, which, along with the internet's ever-encroaching war on people's emotions, is evidence that a war is coming-a cyber war!

Keywords: Cyberwar, ransomware

Dac-Nhuong Le et al. (eds.), Cyber Security in Parallel and Distributed Computing, (79–262)
© 2019 Scrivener Publishing LLC

5.1 Introduction

Ever since the computer revolution first began with cheap and powerful personal computers reaching each and every household in the world, the risk of the computation tool being misused according to the whims of bad people also increased. This has led to significant cyberattacks in the time period so far and is continuing with new connections extending the cyber battlefield.

The very first generation of threatening viruses was released by Bob Thomas of BBN Technologies in 1971, which was called Creeper [1]. The originator was not self-replicating initially. It was injected into a system which, once infected, would display the message "I'M CREEPER: CATCH ME IF YOU CAN." It corrupted DEC PDP-10 computers, the reputed mainframe computers in 1968, operating on TENEX operating system. Creeper led to the development of its adversary named Reaper, one of the world's first anti-virus softwares. Early definitions of so-called viruses began displaying a sentence in a third party personal computer without the attackers own presence.

Figure 5.1 Virus alert!

The act of displaying a message turned out to display a poem with the evolution of Rich Skrenta's Elk Cloner in 1981. Elk Cloner [1] set Apple II computers as its target. It is actually a boot sector virus spread via floppy disk as a game. The game, when booted the 50th time, closes it and displays the poem of Elk Cloner. Elk Cloner actually didn't create any harm to the victim but it corrupted the disk. Skrenta added a signature byte to the disks memory to point out that it is already corrupted. The computer needed to be rebooted every time to get rid of cloner.

Furthermore, Skrenta decided to spread cloner without the use of floppy disks by creating a boot sector virus that would display a message automatically in an Apple II computer. The cloner was spread via a hard drive which modified the boot sector codes. When the computer was booted the next time, Elk Cloner made its presence in the system even without starting any application or game explicitly.

After being used to display messages as a prank in other's computers, viruses came to play a role in business. In 1986, Basit Farooq Alvi and Ajmad Farooq Alvi, two brothers from Pakistan, worked to prevent customers of their computer store from using illegal copies of their medical software. The evolution of the boot sector virus from Skrenta, led them to create the Brain boot sector virus [2], the name Brain being the name of their computer store. It became the first virus threat to MS-DOS. The Brain boot sector virus was injected into the machines which used illegal copies of their software. It placed the 5KB virus in the boot sector of floppy disks, which slowed down the system. It cannot be detected as it does not harm the system. Rather, it displayed a message which warned against using pirated software and provided their contact information to get rid of the infection.

In 1988, an experiment conducted by Robert Tappan Morris from Cornell University to determine the size of the Internet led to the creation of the first worm distributed over the Internet. The worm was released from MIT as an experiment. Once downloaded into a system, the worm infected the system by slowing it down. The actual exertion of determining internetgauge changed to a virus affecting system because of the nature, the Morris worm [3] spread over the systems. The worm is more likely to be run in the same system many times, slowing it down every time and finally making it unusable. Hence, self-replicating worms are more harmful even today. The unintended results of the graduate student's experiment was responsible for about $10 million of damage, as stated by the U.S. Government Accountability Office.

The worm was washed out by Clifford Stall, whose survey noted that the Morris worm infected about two thousand computers in just fifteen hours. He also stated that the disinfection took about two days. Colleagues of Morris stated that the survey was cooked up. Robert Morris was sentenced to three years probation and fined $10,500 plus the cost of his supervision. The Morris worm was actually the impetus for security personnel to concentrate on Internet security

With the slow relief from the accidental worm of Morris in the Internet, there entered an intentional injection of a worm named Michelangelo [4] in 1991. The attacker was Roger Riordan, an anti-virus expert from Australia. Although the impact of the Michelangelo virus was expected to be great, in reality only a few thousand computers were found to be infected by it. Yet another boot sector virus, it actually did little harm to the systems.

Michelangelo has been considered one of the threatening viruses of the 1990s mainly because of its media hype. The Michelangelo virus works by infecting the first 17 sectors of every track in the infected hard disk on March 6th of each year. As seen so far, boot sector viruses seem to be more threatening. A boot sector virus affects the master boot sector (MBR), which runs every time the computer starts. The MBR controls the boot sequence and also determines the partition in which the computer boots into. Once the virus can successfully infect the MBR, then the computer boot will fail and the contents inside the memory will be lost. Boot sector viruses are hard to remove; hence, the better solution is to prevent them by appropriate verification of external drives for viruses before being injected into the system. Good anti-virus software does the job.

After a decade of Michalangelo's hype, in January 2003, a huge computer worm threatening the internet world by causing a denial-of-service attack was discovered. The attack requires prerequisite knowledge of the loophole in ancient Microsoft SQL. IP address spoofing over a particular UDP port can cause buffer overflow and destruct normal service of the SQL server [5]. David Litchfield from Microsoft conducted a proof of concept and fixed the issue of this SQL Slammer attack. The issue was submitted to the Microsoft Security Response Center and a patch was developed to counterfeit it. In the next Black Hat, Microsoft released the patch and requested every SQL user to add the patch for security. The POC was studied by researcher Michael Bacarella released publicly during Black Hat. The attacker implemented it and released it over the Internet. About 75,000 servers that were not patched were affected in just 10 minutes. It was thought that the victims did not report the virus attack because it resulted from their mistake of not adding the patch.

After the era of using viruses to threaten and demolish computers passed, the era of destroying targeted computer sources using viruses evolved. The dot product was named Stuxnet [6], which has the capability of attacking the programmable logic controller (PLC) of industrial control systems. The PLC is responsible for making logical decisions by monitoring input and producing appropriate output in an automated machine. Stuxnet was born in 2009 at Kaspersky Lab. Stuxnet attacks systems running Windows, which actually is not a kind of PLC. As PLC is a proprietary machine-language-based device, the virus initially captures the system running the PLC. Then it infects Siemens SIMATIC WinCC[1], a supervisory control and data acquisition (SCADA) and human-machine interface (HMI) system. As these program the PLC, infecting them destroys the proper programming of PLC. This results in an improper automation process by PLC, disrupting the industrial process on a large scale. Stuxnet initially spreads in three systems, each of which has the capability of infecting another three and so on.

Stuxnet has a record of causing substantial damage to Iran's nuclear program. The worm can be wiped out by a suitable anti-virus program.

Once Stuxnet reached its supremacy, a so-called extended version of Stuxnet was developed, not with the same notion of destroying industrial control systems, but with the aim of gaining information from and deleting recent information in those systems [7]. The attack was created by Unit 8200 of the Israeli Intelligence Corps in 2009. The unit captures sensitive information that is encrypted and transferred as signals.

The worm creates a file, with a prefix ˜DQ, in the infected system. Hence, the model is named Duqu. Duqu also targeted the Iran nuclear deal, but with the goal of gathering sensitive information, instead of demolishing it. Unlike Stuxnet, the worm is very difficult to predict because of its passive nature. This behavior let it prevail in Kaspersky Lab for a long time without being detected. Once the threat was discovered in 2010, the worm program codes were kept and added in antivirus software.

The recent attackers started concentrating on espionage rather than sabotage. The result was the development of a modular computer worm named Flame [7] in 2012. The worm, also known as Skywiper, has the ability to wipe away the contents in the infected system. Kaspersky Lab[2] and CrySyS Lab[3] called it the most tedious malware they had ever seen. The wiper acquires the system in a similar way as its ancestors, Stuxnet and Duqu, by affecting the rootkit functionality. Flame is capable of spreading over a LAN or via a USB stick. It can capture user activities by recording audio and capturing screenshots, keystrokes and network traffic. Skype conversations also find a place on the list. The collected data and other files can be sent to the control server for analysis by attackers. The worm targeted sources in Iran, Syria and Israel. Kaspersky entered into a program with its competitors as yet another precaution against the espionage worm.

5.2   Ransomware Attacks

Ransomware continues to be the most threatening form of modern cybercrime [8]. Ransomware acquires data from an entire computer through email attachments, drive-by downloads, malicious pdfs and exploit kits, and then openly blackmails the owners by asking them to pay to restore the computer to its original state. The malware may be locker, where the entire system is locked and not able to be used, or it may be crypto, where some dedicated, sensitive files are locked and access is denied. The lock or access denial is released only after the demand is met for mammoth amounts of bitcoins to be transferred to the hackers as a fine, owing to the innocence of the owner. Also, ransomware makes no assertions that the key will decrypt the lock on files or the system even after the fine is

[1]https://w3.siemens.com/
[2]https://www.kaspersky.com/
[3]https://www.crysys.hu/

paid. Listed below are the siblings of ransomware, each becoming more threatening and blackmailable.

5.2.1 Petya

One of the family members of encrypting ransomware is Petya. The malware was discovered in March 2016. Petya infects the master boot record (MBR) of Windows-based systems. The propagation is via email attachments to victims. Once Petya corrupts the MBR, it prompts a restart of the system. Upon restart, the corrupted boot sector encrypts the Master File Table of the computer. Petya then bids for a fine amount that must be paid as bitcoins to get back the old state of the system (Figure 5.2 shows a screenshot of the ransom note left on an infected system). Several patches came from Microsoft for the victims' sake. But the overfitting, makes the next worm version cleverer. The new version of Petya, named NotPetya [8] by Kaspersky, pretended to be a Ukraine tax software update and infected thousands of systems throughout around 100 countries. Pharmaceutical giant Merck paid a ransom of $300 million to NotPetya for its information.

Figure 5.2   Petya ransomware.

5.2.2 WannaCry

Undisputably, the most devastating attack in history, which infected several thousand banking, law and government agencies, was perpetrated by WannaCry ransomware in May 2017 [8, 9]. The attack exploited a vulnerability in Microsoft's implementation of the Server Message Block (SMB) protocol. The SMB, which is responsible for authentic interprocess communications and message transfer, was developed by the U.S. National Security Agency. The loopholes in the protocol were released as EternalBlue by some brokers. This led to the implementation of WannaCry (WannaCrypt). Once WannaCry reaches a computer, it searches for the kill switch if not found. This option is used to shut down the computer immediately, if it is not possible to do so in the usual way. Then it encrypts the computer in its usual fashion, as was done in Petya.

WannaCry also attempts to exploit the SMB vulnerability to spread to random systems on the internet. The modern versions, instead of encrypting computers as a whole, encrypt dedicated files and then demand bitcoins for a decryption key. The demand proposed is $300 in bitcoins within 3 days or $600 in bitcoins within 7 days. A screenshot of the ransom note left on an infected system is shown in Figure 5.3.

Marcus Hutchins discovered the hardcoded "kill switch" step of WannaCry, which severely reduces the spread of the worm. Several variants of the worm came with distributed attacks with the intention of spreading offline. Research was carried out on the encryption process of WannaCry. The Windows operating systems were updated to get rid of unauthorized encryptions.

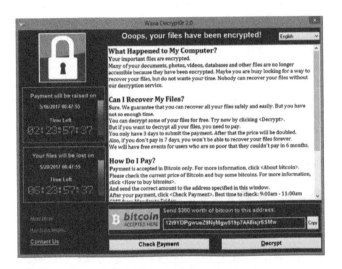

Figure 5.3   WannaCry ransomware.

5.2.3 Locky

The Locky worm was discovered in March 2016 but became much more insidious in 2017 by spreading via emails with an attachment containing malicious macros as Word document. It used a social engineering technique by using the sentence "Enable macro if data encoding is incorrect". If a user enables the macros, then the malicious macros get installed. It is followed by encryption of files with a particular extension and the demand for bitcoins for a key. Hollywood Presbyterian Medical Center lost their patient data due to Locky [10]. The data were recovered at a cost of $17,000 ransom.

Several ransomware attacks came in 2017 with similar encryptions and demands. The attacks targeted government agencies and industries having potential data. Even though ransomware is responsible for some of the biggest cyberattacks in history, it is not part of technology as a whole. It evolved with many shadow brokers and insiders leaking bugs in software.

As depicted in Figure 5.4, initially worms were intended to threaten others or show off the attacker's technical competency to others. Later, they were formulated for business computers business to punish those involved in illegal activities. Then, the worm began to be used for illegal purposes. The aim was to make money by stealing/destroying data. Today, cyberattacks have become a money-making business. Both millionaires and criminals are using the technology for an ill-intentioned purpose. The attackers seem to count on the innocence of the victims, as researchers coming up with patches and anti-versions to restrain from most of the worms are not reaching users immediately. This reachability deficiency is used by most of the attackers. In the future, cyberattacks are expected to create life risks for users. Blakmailing someone for money now can lead to threatening their lives later.

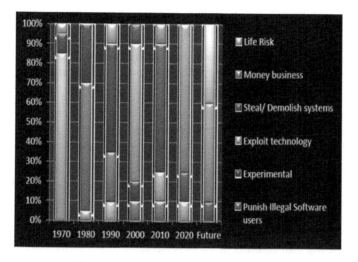

Figure 5.4   Motives of the attackers over the years.

5.3   Are Nations Ready?

As the world nations are moving towards a digital economy evolution, the army that protects the citizens of a nation on land, air and water now has to move to digital medium as a cyber army to protect the netizens as well. The number of warriors on the digital battlefield has been increasing over the years. Cyber warriors are no longer just those employed by the nation's military, but rather include rogue cyber hacktivist groups with an agenda for hacking other nations or their own. Let's look at the state of preparedness for some nations in the world.

India: Some of the different intelligent agencies and government agencies in India regarding cybersecurity are:

- Department of Electronics and Information Technology (DeitY), which includes the Indian Computer Emergency Response Team (ICERT)

- Intelligence Bureau or Central Bureau of Intelligence

- National Intelligence Agency

- National Technical Research Organization

- Defense Research and Development Organization (DRDO)

Apart from these, there are private agencies or NGOs regarding cybersecurity, like the Indian Cyber Army [11], which is an autonomous association with ethical hackers in it, and also acts as a resource center for the Indian national police and other intelligence agencies.

Bangladesh: Even though Bangladesh is a smaller country, the ideas put forth in the National Cybersecurity Strategy of Bangladesh document [12] show how effectively the nation is equipping itself for maintaining the cybersecurity of their country. The strategy to improve the cybersecurity of the nation includes:

- Improving the cybercrime laws through globalized laws and authorizing government entities.

- Improving national infrastructure on cybersecurity through a national security framework, spreading of awareness, preventive measures, tracking and fixing vulnerabilities.

- Improving organizational structures to respond to attacks through collaboration of stakeholders, National Cybersecurity Council, incidence management at the national level, collaborating with private sectors, skill training for citizens.

Apart from legal government entities, there are hacktivist groups in Bangladesh like Bangladesh Cyber Army, and news has been reported online about their hacking activities, such as attacks on Indian websites and making demands on Indian officials [13].

United States of America: The United States of America is one of the most powerful nations in the world with the largest army, which is supported by the largest military budget in the world. It has also invested in the cybersecurity of the nation. As per the world economic forum, the Pentagon has announced an increase in cybersecurity staff, and U.S. Cyber Command has also been involved in launching attacks against the Islamic State [14].

In 2007 the United States launched the Stuxnet worm to advert Iran's nuclear program, which shows the power of a network security breach. But what if this attack was more malicious and was used to launch an attack on another country unilaterally? This case shows the importance of security in the army sector, as weapons are connected to the cyber world and the probability of any countries weapon system being compromised has increased.

Privacy has also been a big concern in the cyber world. Tensions around the world rose when Edward Snowden, a former contractor for the United States government, exposed the surveillance activities of the US intelligence NSA and also global intelligence agency [15], which created awareness and panic in people all around the world.

Russia: As per the world economic forum, it is believed that many military cyberattacks on Georgia and Ukraine originated from Russia. Russia has been involved in many cybersecurity controversies, including the controversy over the 2016 U.S. elections results, which the intelligence experts suspect Russian hackers were involved in [16].

Many of the attacks that have happened in the cyber world were traced backed to Russian IP addresses, which puts Russia in an uncomfortable position in the cybersecurity world [17]. Attacks on Estonia, France, Germany, Kyrgyzstan, and Ukraine were suspected to be done from Russia.

Pakistan: Pakistan has also been honing its cyberwarfare capabilities for years, and has been suspected of various attacks like Operation Arachnophobia and Operation Hangover [18]. Operation Arachnophobia is the name of the investigation done by the FireEye cybersecurity company to study a a Bitterbug malware that was targeting Indian computers. Operation Hangover was an attack from India that targeted Pakistan; the response from Pakistan was Operation Arachnophobia, which targeted Indian computers.

China: China is the world's most populous nation with a population count of 1.4 billion. China has one of the biggest armies in Asia.

There have always been tensions over China's cyberattacks; even google has closed their search engine facility in China. Because of the size of its population, the number of internet users is large, but so is the growth in the number of hackers in the nation. Its been reported by Symantec that a third of the malicious software in the world originates from China. Many of the Chinese hackers are driven by patriotism and call themselves "Honker". When Baidu, the biggest search engine in China, was hacked and the Iranian Cyber Army left a message saying that it had done it, the Honker Union retaliated by hacking Iranian websites. There are also other hacktivist groups such as the Red Hacker Alliance.

There have been multiple accusations made against China about hacking other nations like Australia, Canada, India and the United States of America.

Germany: The German Government is developing a major program to protect its computer networks and supply systems. A new institution the National Cyberdefence Centre (*Nationales Cyber-Abwehrzentrum*) will be responsible for detecting potential threats, analyzing them and coordinating the necessary measures to disable the threat. In addition, a National cybersecurity Council will be established [19].

Iran: Iranian hackers attack on a Saudi oil company is a notable influence of Iran in the cyberwarfare domain. There are different Iranian hacker groups, like Rocket Kitten, which are acting aggressively in attacking, which in turn creates tensions within cyber radar.

Israel: There have been alleged reports that Israel has hacked Russia's Kaspersky Lab to get intel about nation state attacks research conducted in it. In the 2006 war against Hezbollah, Israel alleges that cyberwarfare was part of the conflict, where the Israel Defense Forces (IDF) intelligence estimates several countries in the Middle East used Russian hackers and scientists to operate on their behalf. As a result, Israel attached growing importance to cyber-tactics, and became, along with the U.S., France and a couple of other nations, involved in cyberwar planning [20].

In the war between Israel and Syria, an air attack dubbed Operation Orchard was launched by Israel on Syria. U.S. industry and military sources speculated that the Israelis may have used cyberwarfare to allow their planes to pass undetected by radar into Syria.

United Kingdom: It's been reported in sites like Wired that the United Kingdom has hacked undersea cables of Yahoo and Google to decipher the data traffic [5], and also a hack organized by United Kingdom government on Belgacom for data monitoring of traffic.

In the UK, the National cybersecurity Centre, part of the signals intelligence agency GCHQ, has been taking steps to protect public bodies and companies. It has been advising them on how to deal with these lower-level criminal attacks that, it says, "affect the majority of people, the majority of the time." Ian Levy, NCSC's technical director, says that "there is much hyperbole about the capabilities of cyber actors." "Certainly, some nation states invest huge sums of money and significant highly skilled resources in their cyber programmes and use those for various things that are detrimental to the interests of the UK" [16].

North Korea: North Korea is believed to be the source of various cyberattacks on the United States and South Korea. CNN news reported the direct involvement of North Korea's hacker army attacking banks worldwide. The hackers, who stole 81 million dollars from Bangladesh banks, were traced back to North Korean IPs. Experts have speculated that this money could be used for the country's military budget. The security groups found similarities in the malware attack on Bangladesh banks and the attack that happened in Sony, which was also suspected to be done by North Korean hackers.

There are already tensions resulting from the nuclear tests being done by North Korea, and with their development in cyberwarfare, they are the ones to watch out for in the future.

5.4   Conclusion

History has shown us that there have always been disputes between various nations of the world. The only difference is that the nature of weapons has changed from stones, swords and guns to computers. In the first section of this chapter, we have seen how various malicious attacks can impact organizations and countries on a large scale. Some attacks are done for fun, some for money, and some for vengeance. These attacks are done by a single person on a small scale and also by a country on another country. So, in the next section of the chapter we compiled information on how various nations are progressing in the development of cyberwarfare capabilities. It is evident that each nation is key to building their cyber army to protect themselves and to compromise other nation's security system. It is essential that the international intelligence and peace agencies must form treaties in order to avoid any catastrophic cyberattacks. Because in the future a coordinated massive cyberattack might destroy the world due to everything being connected.

References

1. Touchette, F. (2016). The evolution of malware. Network Security, 2016(1), 11-14.

2. https://home.mcafee.com/virusinfo/virusprofile.aspx?key=221, Retrieved 2018-03-30.

3. https://www.cisco.com/c/en/us/about/press/internet-protocol-journal/back-issues/table-contents-25/virus-trends.html, Retrieved 2018-03-30.

4. https://home.mcafee.com/virusinfo/virusprofile.aspx?key=1446, Retrieved 2018-03-30.

5. Schultz, E., Mellander, J., & Peterson, D. (2003). The MS-SQL Slammer Worm. Network Security, 2003(3), 10-14.

6. Shakarian, P., Shakarian, J., & Ruef, A. (2013). Attacking Iranian Nuclear Facilities: Stuxnet. Introduction to cyber-warfare: A multidisciplinary approach, 223-239.

7. Shakarian, P., Shakarian, J., & Ruef, A. (2013). Introduction to cyber-warfare: A multidisciplinary approach. Newnes. Paulo Shakarian, Jana Shakarian, Andrew Ruef, Chapter 8 Duqu, Flame, Gauss, the Next Generation of Cyber Exploitation, pp. 159-170.

8. Mansfield-Devine, S. (2017). Ransomware: the most popular form of attack. Computer Fraud & Security, 2017(10), 15-20.

9. "Player 3 Has Entered the Game: Say Hello to 'WannaCry'", blog.talosintelligence.com. Retrieved 2018-03-30.

10. Winton, R. (2016). Hollywood hospital pays $17,000 in bitcoin to hackers; FBI investigating. Los Angeles Times, 18.

11. Indian Cyber Army (https://www.ica.in)

12. National Cybersecurity Strategy of Bangladesh (https://www.unodc.org/cld/lessons-learned/bgd/the_national_cybersecurity_strategy_of_bangladesh.html?&tmpl=cyb)

13. Bangladesh Cyber Army(https://www.hackread.com/indian-government-and-and-30-websites-hacked-by-bangladesh-cyber-army/)

14. Breene, K. (2016, May). Who are the cyberwar superpowers. In World Economic Forum. Retrieved October (Vol. 27, p. 2017). (https://www.weforum.org/agenda/2016/05/who-are-the-cyberwar-superpowers/)

15. Edward Snowden Leaks (https://en.wikipedia.org/wiki/Edward_Snowden)

16. More countries are learning form Russia's Cyber Tactics (https://www.ft.com/content/b7dbc0de-1b04-11e8-aaca-4574d7dabfb6)

17. Cyberwarfare by Russia (https://en.wikipedia.org/wiki/Cyberwarfare_by_Russia)

18. Pakistan Cyber war capabilities (https://defence.pk/pdf/threads/has-pakistan-developed-cyber-attack-and-defense-capabilities.482614/)

19. Germany prepares for Cyberwar (http://www.newsecuritylearning.com/index.php/feature/88-germany-prepares-for-a-cyber-war)

20. Cyberwarfare(https://en.wikipedia.org/wiki/Cyberwarfare)

21. North Korea Cyberwarfare CNN report (https://edition.cnn.com/2017/10/11/asia/north-korea-technological-capabilities/index.html)

PART II

Cybersecurity in Parallel and Distributed Computing Techniques

---

6

Introduction to Blockchain Technology

ISHAANI PRIYADARSHINI

University of Delaware, Newark, Delaware, USA
Email: IshaaniPriyadarshini@udel.edu

Abstract

Data is one of the most valuable assets. With cyber criminals becoming increasingly skillful in their attempts to steal valuable data, cybersecurity tends to be one of the greatest global concerns, making cyber defense mandatory. In the past, various techniques have been proposed owing to the security needs of various institutions; however, security assaults know no bounds, hence resulting in either the techniques being weakened or futile. The latest approach to protect valuable data is blockchain technology. In this chapter we will be taking a look at the concept of blockchain technology and how it is crucial to the security industry. As we delve a bit more into the details, we will be taking a look at the characteristics of blockchain technology, its structure, types, architecture and workings. Since Bitcoin is one of the most widespread applications of blockchain technology, this chapter also highlights the workings of bitcoins. Later on, we discuss a few of the challenges faced by this technology and its scope in the future.

Keywords: Blockchain, Bitcoin, cybersecurity

Dac-Nhuong Le et al. (eds.), Cyber Security in Parallel and Distributed Computing, (93–262)
© 2019 Scrivener Publishing LLC

6.1 Introduction

One of the biggest cybersecurity issues faced by individual computer users as well as corporate firms is data theft, not only because it threatens an individual's privacy, but also because it defeats one of the primary purposes of cybersecurity, i.e., confidentiality. Over the last few decades, several techniques have been proposed to deal with the issue, and many of them have been short lived, the reason being highly skilled cyber criminals. The latest addition is blockchain technology. Data dispersed over the network is prone to pilferage and plagiarism and often it is impossible to trace back to the cyber criminal. Blockchain technology eliminates the issue on many levels. A blockchain may be defined as a distributed database incorporating information or a book that marks all the events and transactions, executed and shared among concerned parties. The transactions are verified and information entered can never be erased. Every transaction made has a verifiable record. Blockchain technology finds its use in financial as well as non-financial sectors.

Blockchains are public registers such that all transactions are accumulated in a list of blocks [1]. When several blocks keep being added on, it leads to a chain-like formation. Blockchain technology is primarily based on the concepts of cryptography and distributed systems. Encryption techniques have been known to obscure content, such that it is available only to the intended users. But certain information needs to be available to specific groups of people, and it invites additional risk of the information getting manipulated. Blockchains tackle the issue. When data is accessed and updated, any change made is recorded and verified. Thereafter, it is encrypted so that further changes cannot be made. These changes are then updated into the main records. It is a repetitive process and every time a change is made, the information is preserved in a new block. It is fascinating to note that the first version of the information is well connected to the latest one. Thus, the changes made could be seen by everyone, but only the latest block can be modified. Blockchain imitates a distributed database by incorporating information duplicated across the network in real time. This means that the database has multiple locations and the records are public and easily verifiable. Since there is not a centralized version, data corruption is futile. Modifying records is tedious, thus making it easier to detect if someone is trying to do so. Thus, a blockchain could be thought of as a piece of data that has the following properties:

1. It is constantly updated. This makes it easier for the users to access and modify data anytime.

2. It is a distributed system in the sense that duplicated copies of data are stored and span the network. Updating one record updates every other copy in real time.

3. It has verified data. When data is modified, it has to be verified by users using cryptographic techniques.

4. The data is secure because cryptographic techniques and distributed systems do not allow tampering of data and security techniques.

One way of classifying blockchains is as permissionless blockchains and permissioned blockchains. Permissionless blockchains are open, they can be connected and abandoned by any peer as a reader or writer. They are decentralized and the information is readable by users. Permissioned blockchains authorize limited readers and writers. They are managed by a central entity which decides which individuals can read or write [2].

6.2   Need for Blockchain Security

Blockchain technology offers a way to share data and ensure transparency. The parties involved are guaranteed that the data they are dealing with is error free and cannot be changed. This feature is not only beneficial in the technical domain, but also finds its use beyond that. The following are a few reasons that make blockchain technology a favorite in many domains:

- It ensures transparency. Blockchain technology is an open source technology, such that other users cannot modify it. Logged data within a blockchain is difficult to alter, which makes it a relatively secure technology.

- It reduces transaction costs significantly. A blockchain does not need a third party to complete peer-to-peer and business transactions. Since no middlemen are involved in the transaction, the process is faster.

- Transaction settlements are quicker for blockchain technology as compared to traditional banks which rely on working hours and protocols. The location at different parts of the world further contributes to the delay. But blockchain does not have any such restrictions, thereby allowing faster transaction settlements.

- It promotes decentralization since there is not central data hub. This allows individual transactions to be authenticated. When information is updated to different servers, even if the information comes across adversaries, a trivial amount of data will be compromised.

- Since third parties are not involved in the transactions any more, users and developers take the initiative, thus introducing user controlled networks.

- It tracks the movement of goods, hence leading to transparency. This also simplifies several other management processes.

- In the case of irregularities being detected, one can always trace back to the point of origin, which makes investigations easy for executing required actions. This leads to quality assurance.

- Blockchain technology eliminates human error since it records data and protects it from being altered. Since records are verified everytime they pass from one node to the next, accuracy is guaranteed. This ultimately leads to accountability.

- Smart and sophisticated contracts can be easily validated, singed and enforced using blockchain technology.

- Blockchain technology eliminates electoral fraud, thus leading to clarity in voting.

- Reliability of blockchain technology is contemplated for stock exchanges.

- Energy supply can be accurately tracked.

- Blockchain technology encourages peer-to-peer global transactions. Cryptocurrency transactions are fast, secure and cheap.

- Blockchain technology leads to data objectivity. It not only preserves integrity of data but can also alert users if data is modified. Even if data is breached for an organization, it cannot be used, thus a balance is maintained between security and governance.

- Blockchain technology is used to authenticate devices. It may soon replace passwords, thus eliminating human intervention. This is because it does not promote centralized architecture.

- Since every transaction is time stamped and signed digitally, it highlights non-repudiation. Even with the system's new iteration, previous records will be stored in the history log. This leads to traceability.

6.3   Characteristics of Blockchain Technology

In the previous sections, we have familiarized ourselves with the concept of blockchain technology. We now know that blockchains serve multiple purposes. The purposes are based on some characteristics, which are presented below [1, 2].

- *Decentralization:* Blockchain technology does not rely on a centralized transaction system to validate transactions. The involvement of central trusted agencies leads to cost and performance issues. Since a third party is not required for blockchains, they rely on cryptography and algorithms to maintain data consistency in distributed networks.

- *Persistence:* Validating transactions is quick in blockchain technology. Invalid transactions may be dropped off. Transactions which are already a part of the blockchain may neither be deleted nor rolled back. Data tampering could be easily realized.

- *Anonymity:* Users interacting with blockchains are assigned system-generated addresses. This masks the identity of the user.

- *Auditability:* Transactions in real time rely on previous unspent transactions. As crrent transaction gets incorporated into the blockchain, the status of unspent transactions changes to spent. This makes verifying and tracking transactions easy.

- *Public Verifiability:* The correctness of the state of system can be confirmed by any user. This is not the case in systems that rely on central trust agencies. Users need to communicate with the agencies to obtain information about the correct state.

- *Transparency:* Blockchain data is updated for public verifiability. However, the amount of information may be restricted to users depending on their privileges.

- *Privacy:* Although privacy is easier to achieve in centralized systems, blockchains with specific protocols can allow a certain level of privacy to safeguard sensitive information.

- *Integrity:* Blockchain technology protects against unauthorized modifications, leading to data integrity. Since the system allows public verifiability, data integrity can be verified by anyone.

- *Redundancy:* Blockchain technology relies on decentralized architecture. This means that data is duplicated across all writers, unlike centralized systems which rely on backups and physical servers to achieve data redundancy.

- *Trust Anchor:* The trust anchor is the entity responsible for providing read and write access to a system. They are the highest authorities and they possess grant and revoke rights.

6.4   Types of Blockchains

In the previous sections, we have taken a look at the "permissioned" and "permissionless" blockchains. However, there is another way to classify blockchains. This classification is done on the basis of blockchain networks. Blockchains have been known to be of three types, which are defined as follows:

1. Public Blockchains: These blockchains are open and transparent, implying that anyone can read, write or audit these. They can be reviewed by anyone at any given point of time. The decentralized consensus mechanism is responsible for decision-making since no one is in charge. The proof of work (POW) and proof of stake (POS) are taken into account when making decisions. These have no access restrictions and anyone can participate in transactions and validations. Some common public blockchains are Ethereum and Bitcoin [4].

2. Private Blockchains: These blockchains are confined to an individual or organization. An authority is responsible for read-write operations. This authority is also responsible for selectively giving read-write access to users. The mining rights may also be given selectively, thus making it similar to a centralized system, although it is cryptographically secured and also cost-effective. In this blockchain, not everyone can read, write, audit or make transactions. They are permissioned blockchains. A bankchain is a typical example of a private blockchain.

3. Consortium or Federated Blockchains: These blockchains have one or more in charges for decision-making. They are semi-permissioned and are represented by a group of companies or individuals. This leads to faster transactions and offers multiple points of failure, thereby preserving data. The members are responsible for making transactions/decisions. They can read, write, audit and mine data. Common examples of consortium blockchains are R3 and EWF (*Energy Web Foundation*).

6.5   The Architecture of Blockchain Technology

The single version of truth provided by blockchain makes use of digitally signed blocks and algorithms to carry out quick and real-time transactions and documentations, which are further encrypted. The idea was proposed by Satoshi Nakamoto, who wanted to create a cryptocurrency (*Bitcoin*) that does not rely on centralized architecture and intermediaries. Blockchains incorporate blocks which are based on pointers that connect data from previous blocks. These blocks may not be altered easily, thereby ensuring security. New block validations also rely on consensus algorithms.

The end-to-end transaction of blockchain follows certain mechanism. In this section we will take a look at the architecture of blockchain technology responsible for its functioning. The blockchain technology architecture is based on the following components [9]:

1. **Blockchain Platform**: The blockchain may be defined as an application that runs on a distributed network. It is a decentralized transaction system which is transparent in the sense that any node handling a blockchain software is capable of handling the entire blockchain. The corresponding data is stored in either a flat file or a relational database. Google's LevelDB is accountable for storing metadata. The installed application gets synced from server to nodes. The servers encompass transaction records

based on cryptographic protocols and consensus algorithms. Since the software is robust, it is virtually impossible to break into the applications running. The transactions do not need third parties for authentication and validation. The transactions are verified by nodes in a peer-to-peer network. When many nodes agree with respect to their blocks in individual databases, they are said to be in consensus. The three main layers of blockchain are illustrated in the diagram shown in Figure 6.1. As we can see, the clients supported are full, web and mobile. The blockchain layer is responsible for maintaining chain of blocks, whereas the protocol and client layers provide peer-to-peer protocol and consensus rules.

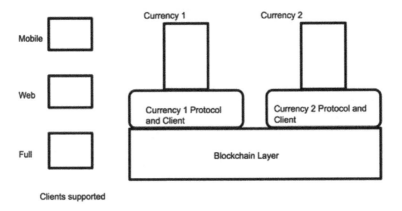

Figure 6.1   Blockchain architecture diagram.

2. **Blockchain Nodes**: Blockchain technology operates on the collaborated peer-to-peer (P2P) network and internet protocol of the internet. In a P2P network, there is no centralized node, and all nodes are capable of providing and consuming services. The nodes in a blockchain are responsible for maintaining duplicate copies of the database which contain information related to payment and ownership. Transactions lead to nodes agreeing on updates. Nodes are responsible for different functions in a blockchain. They connect to peers and validate blockchains. Full nodes contain duplicated database in order to verify transactions without relying on additional lookups. Nodes that store some part of the database verify transactions using simple payment verification (SPV). Miner nodes are used to confirm transactions so that they can become part of the blockchains. This is done by adding data into data structures (*Block*), based on cryptographic protocols. Committed blocks cannot be modified since it may lead to invalidation of all other blocks, which is done to ensure data integrity. Hence, rollbacks are unattainable.

3. **Network Protocol Stack**: Blockchain nodes can discover and contact other valid nodes. The blockchain message exchange follows the process of handshaking between nodes to exchange information over the network. The Blockchain Overlay Network is responsible for allowing different types of blockchains to synchronize and manages their operations. This layer can be used to support other applications as well. The information flow in blockchain technology is depicted in Figure 6.2, along with, the blockchain network architecture.

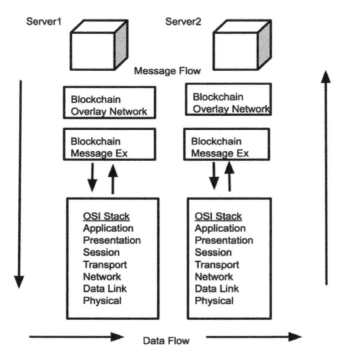

Figure 6.2   Network architecture of blockchain.

4. **Transactions**: Blockchains are used by applications to timestamp transactions. The records in a blockchain exist as transactions and blocks. Transactions may be created by clients or client applications. They have significant data that contributes to the blockchain. Sequence of transactions are stored in blocks and these blocks are created by miner nodes. In the illustration given in Figure 6.3, it is clear that when a transaction is registered in a system, a newly generated transaction is added to the blockchain node network. Minor nodes check the validity, after which it undergoes a cryptographic hashing technique to generate a unique sequence of characters. It is collaborated by other transactions and newly generated hash is stored with other metadata in a data structure header. This creates a block for which the header serves as key. This can lead to creation of the succeeding child block.

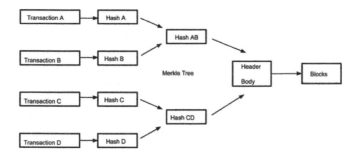

Figure 6.3   How transactions get converted to blocks.

In Figure 6.3, we can see how a number of transactions get converted into blocks, which eventually are formed into chains. The transactional data part incorporates the set of transactions. The Merkle root is a data structure which forms part of the block header. The idea is that previously recorded transactions cannot be changed unless the block recording it and the following blocks are changed. The hash value of the previous block header is also a part of block incorporation transaction records, thereby forming chains.

6.6   How Blockchain Technology Works

In the previous section, we have taken into account the architecture for blockchain technology. In this section we will be dealing with how it works. The most widespread application of blockchain technology is the digital currency Bitcoin, which is created electronically and does not need a central authority to enable payment transactions. It was coined by a software developer by the name Satoshi Nakamoto in 2008. He used mathematical proofs to come up with an electronic payment system that could lead to transactions in a secure, verifiable and and inflexible way. There are a few features of bitcoin that make it different from the traditional digital currencies across the world.

1. *Decentralization*: As blockchain technology is decentralized, bitcoins are maintained by volunteer coders and dedicated computers over the world. A lot of individuals prefer bitcoins due to the non-involvement of third parties for transactions. It eradicates the double spending problem in such a way that digital assets cannot be reused. Certain cryptographic protocols and algorithms ensure integrity of the transactions.

2. *Limited Supply*: Growing demand and constant supply lead to increase in the value of asset. Bitcoins are limited and their supply is regulated by sophisticated algorithms.

3. *Pseudonymity*: Bitcoin transactions do not require the identity of the sender. There is no third party to verify the identity. For a transaction to take place, all that is required is a transaction request. The protocols analyze previous transactions and make sure that the sender has sufficient bitcoins to send and the authority, before the transaction takes place.

4. *Immutability*: Bitcoin transactions are irreversible. This is because whenever a transaction takes place, it stores the added new information in the blocks.

5. *Divisibility*: The smallest unit of bitcoin is one part of a hundred million, roughly a hundredth of a cent. It is called as satoshi and has an edge over traditional currencies because it can also lead to microtransactions.

Traditional commerce has its own limitations ranging from financial fraud to transaction costs. Bitcoin proves to be an effective solution. Let us take a look at how blockchain technology works in relation to the popular bitcoins.

Blockchain technology eliminates the involvement of third parties for transaction validation and relies on cryptographic proof for the same [9, 10]. Transactions are secured using digital signatures. The receiver has a public key to which each of the transactions is sent. The receiver uses the private key of the sender to digitally sign the transactions. The cryptocurrency owner must prove ownership of the private key in order to spend the currency. The receiver of the digital currency must verify the signature and ownership of the private key using the sender's public key for the transaction to be successful.

Once the transaction takes place, it is communicated across all the nodes of Bitcoin, which has to be verified first and then registered. The validity of each transaction is a must before it is added to the public ledger. To record a transaction, a node must verify two things:

- The cryptocurrency is actually owned by the spender. This is done by verifying the digital signature.

- The spender is equipped with sufficient cryptocurrency to carry out the transaction. This could be done by checking every transaction recorded in the spender's account.

The illustration in Figure 6.4 exhibits the working mechanism of blockchain technology.

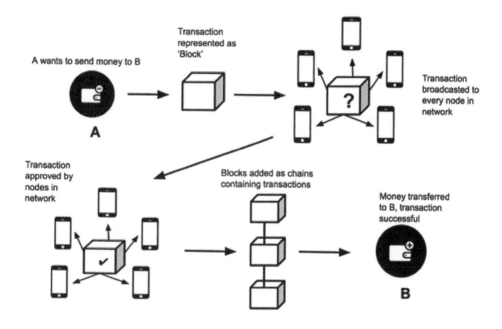

Figure 6.4   Cryptocurrency transaction using blockchain technology.

Blockchain technology was the result of developing a mechanism for Bitcoin transactions that the entire network would agree to. Initially, before blockchain technology was developed, and only bitcoins prevailed, transactions did not always come in order; thus, there was a need to eliminate double spending of the cryptocurrency. The transactions are passed from node to node in a bitcoin network; hence, the order in which the transactions are received at a node, might not be the actual order of the transactions taking place. For example, Transaction A might occur before Transaction B, but the number of nodes Transaction A has to pass could be more than that of Transaction B, thus leading to Transaction B being recorded in a node first. This was a challenge in a distributed network and Bitcoin solved this problem using blockchain technology. The transactions were then placed in blocks, thus leading to blockchains. This means that all the transactions taking place in a block have occured at the same time. The blocks are then arranged linearly in a chronological manner, in such a way that a given block is linked to the previous block by its hash value.

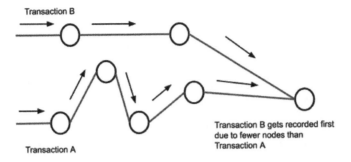

Figure 6.5   How double spending may occur.

Although the proposed method eliminated a lot of issues, one problem still remained unsolved. Multiple blocks could have been created at a given time for different nodes. Several blocks could have arrived at different nodes for different points. The problem was solved using a mathematical puzzle wherein a block could be accepted in a blockchain if it could answer a specific mathematical problem. This is referred to as proof of work, as the node which generates a block must prove that sufficient resources have been invested to solve the puzzle. This means that there is need to develop a mechanism so that the entire Bitcoin network can agree regarding the order of transactions, which is a daunting task in a distributed system in Figure 6.6.

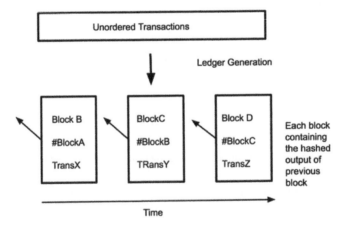

Figure 6.6   Blockchain generation from unordered transactions.

6.7   Some Other Case Studies for Blockchain Technology

As we know, Bitcoin is the most popular case study of the blockchain technology. However, blockchain technology is not only limited to working of cryptocurrencies. In this section we will take a look at a few other use cases of blockchain technology. They are as follows [2, 7]:

- *Supply Chain Management*: The supply chain management (SCM) workflow consists of a number of services ranging from manufacturing, storage, production, etc., to delivery and consumption. It involves multiple writers and the data that must be stored is huge. When a product moves from one hand to another, the transactions will be recorded, thereby reducing time delays and eliminating human error. Orders, receipts, shipment notifications, etc., could be tracked down easily. Physical goods could be linked to serial numbers, barcodes, digital tags, etc. Moreover, information can be shared between vendors and suppliers.

- *Interbank and International Financial Transactions*: Blockchain technology is being adopted by financial institutions for several reasons. Cross-border transactions become a lot more quicker and cheaper. Better trade accuracy along with shorter settlement process is the key to share trading. Smart contracts in the form of commercial transactions and agreements can be ensured. It strengthens identity management, which is required for banking. Since the transactions are transparent and traceable, it leads to better loyalty programs and rewards, thereby enhancing the overall performance.

- *Decentralized Autonomous Organization (DAO)*: A DAO relies on smart cards for functioning. There is no central management, although there are rules specified in the smart contracts, which define how the organization should behave. The organizations must be managed in a decentralized manner, hence creating the demand for permissionless blockchains. Sometimes, dedicated permissionless blockchains may also be required. These systems are usually built on top of an existing blockchain technology with its own currency.

- *Land Registry:* The data pertaining to land registry may be moved to safe and transparent infrastructure secured using cryptographic protocols. South African startup by the name of ChromaWay is already working on the same [8].

- *Proof of Ownership*: One of the most common case studies for blockchain technology is proof of ownership of intellectual property. A public blockchain at the time of stamping could be used to manifest ownership at a later time. The digital object along with the identity of the owner could be committed using a hash to provide sufficient evidence of ownership.

- *e-Voting*: One of the most important public demands for e-voting is privacy, since votes must be anonymous to avoid any sort of intimidation. However, there must also be public verifiability, so as to preserve integrity of the votes. Since a lot of parties are involved in voting who do not trust each other, one of the reasonable solutions is the use of blockchain technology.

6.8 Challenges Faced by Blockchain Technology

Blockchain technology is one of the most revolutionary technological advances in recent times. It has been adopted by industries belonging to several domains like finances, healthcare, cloud storage, etc. Despite its supremacy in the technological world, there are several concerns pertaining to blockchain technology. Following are some of the challenges faced by blockchain technology [2].

- *Scalability or Network Size*: With a large number of transactions taking place everyday, with each block storing data, and new blocks being generated, scalability becomes a challenge. If a blockchain is not supported by a robust network, there may be several system failures. Storage optimization of blockchains or redesigning the blockchains altogether may prove to be beneficial in dealing with scalability problems.

- *Privacy Leakage*: Blockchains do not guarantee transactional privacy. Bitcoin transactions may reveal personal details about users [5]. IP addresses may be traced back to user pseudonyms despite the use of firewalls and network address translators [6]. Anonymity is one way to deal with privacy issues.

- *Selfish Mining*: Selfish mining leads to insecurity of blockchains. It relies on a small amount of hashing power to make the network vulnerable. The mined blocks are kept without broadcasting and public may be able to access the private branch only if certain requirements are fulfilled. Hence selfish miners can mine private chains without the fear of losing to competitors, hence availing more revenue.

- *Initial Cost*: Initial setup of blockchain technology is expensive as it incorporates software cost and qualified personnel expertise. Huge demand and limited supply also contribute to the same.

- *Integration with Legacy Systems*: Moving to a blockchain-based system may be done by either rebuilding the entire system (*new blockchain based*) or fusing the existing system with blockchain technology. Eradicating legacy systems may not be easy, thus the feasible solution would be to make changes to an existing system that can support blockchain technology. This may require time, money and skills.

- *Energy Consumption*: Validating transactions on blockchain requires computing complex mathematical algorithms for transaction verification and network security. Computations consume a lot of power and energy.

- *Public Perception*: Since blockchain technology is recent, lot of people are unaware of it. Many find it synonymous with bitcoins. Before the technology is adopted and applied across several domains, people must be made aware of it.

- *Privacy and Security*: Initially blockchains were made visible to the public. However, in order to protect data and restrict access, blockchains are made permissible. This requires a lot of planning and exercise

- *Complexity*: Blockchain technology is based on new vocabulary which incorporates several jargons. People who are involved in work related to blockchain technology must familiarize themselves with the phrases.

- *Human Error*: The data contained in blockchain may not be reliable, thus events must be recorded accurately.

- *Unavoidable Security Flaw*: One of the remarkable security flaws in blockchains is that if more than fifty percent of the systems used as a service tell a lie, the lie becomes truth and is referred to as a "51% attack." Hence it is important to monitor mining pools.

- *Politics*: Several public disagreements have cropped up between community sectors since Bitcoin protocols can digitize governance models. There have been reports about forking of blockchains, wherein a blockchain protocol is updated.

6.9   The Future of Blockchain Technology

We know that technologies like blockchain are capable of diminishing cyber risks, which are a global concern. Apart from that, blockchain technology is being used in several industries for providing specific benefits. More and more organizations are adopting blockchain technique and hopefully blockchain technology is the future of the internet. Since cryptocurrencies are are increasingly being used and financial institutions are relying on blockchaining methods, global banking may change. In this section, we will take a look at how this technology will impact the future [2, 11-15].

- *Blockchain Testing*: Blockchain performances may be falsified to lure users for earning profit. It is important to know which blockchain would fit business requirements, thereby making blockchain testing mandatory. There are two phases to support this. In the standardization phase, blockchains are tested based on certain criteria for validation. The testing phase witnesses blockchains being tested for different criteria.

- *Eliminating the Process of Centralization*: Although blockchain technology is based on decentralization, selfish mining could easily take advantage of the 51% attack. This would defeat the purpose of decentralization, hence few methods must be proposed to handle the issue.

- *Big Data Analytics*: When big data is combined with blockchains, it may lead to data management and data analytics. Data management ensures that data is stored and secured whereas data analytics handles transactions.

- *Blockchain Miscellaneous Applications*: Blockchains could be adopted by traditional organizations for better working of their systems. The concept of smart contract could be implemented with blockchains [6].

- *Combating Crime*: Blockchain technology (*software*) has the potential to track down criminals. Apparently, it will be much cheaper than the already existing methods

- *Banking Sectors*: Central banks could be replaced by blockchains in the near future. The infrastructure costs, cross-border payments and security trading could be reduced by blockchain technology.

- *Industries*: Blockchains may create new industry opportunities and distort the existing ones. The transactions will be quick and efficient, with no third party intervening between two end parties.

- *Governments*: Finance in many nations may be influenced by cryptocurrencies.

- *Human Factor*: The human factor for authentication authentication may be eliminated completely.

6.10 Conclusion

In this chapter, we have introduced one of the most contemporary technologies. Cybersecurity happens to be the foremost priority of any nation or organization. Blockchain technology offers advanced security measures which are difficult to breach. We have taken a look at what blockchain technology is and why it has been needed in recent times. There are certain characteristics of blockchain technology that make it a favorite among cryptographers and we have discussed those characteristics. On the basis of blockchain networks, three types of blockchains are known, which we have also highlighted in this chapter. Apart from that, the architecture and working of blockchain technology is also presented. Bitcoin is one of the applications of blockchain technology, which we have emphasized in this chapter, along with some other case studies. Even though blockchain technology is modern day savior of security issues, there are still some challenges facing it, a few of which are presented in this chapter. Finally, the presumed effects of blockchain technology in the future have been listed.

References

1. Zheng, Z., Xie, S., Dai, H., Chen, X., & Wang, H. (2017, June). An overview of blockchain technology: Architecture, consensus, and future trends. In Big Data (BigData Congress), 2017 IEEE International Congress on (pp. 557-564). IEEE.

2. Wst, K., & Gervais, A. (2017). Do you need a Blockchain?. IACR Cryptology ePrint Archive, 2017, 375.

3. Types of Blockchains, retrieved from https://en.wikipedia.org/wiki/Blockchain#Types_of _blockchains

4. Barcelo, J. (2014). User privacy in the public bitcoin blockchain. URL: http://www.dtic.upf.edu/jbarcelo/papers/20140704_User_Privacy_in_the_Public_Bitcoin_Blockc hain/paper. pdf (Accessed 09/05/2016).

5. Szabo, N. (1997). The idea of smart contracts. Nick Szabo's Papers and Concise Tutorials, 6.

6. Dejan Jovanovic, Blockchain Case Studies, Retrieved from https://medium.com/@dejanjovanovic_24152/blockchain-case-studies-2271d37d3ed , 2017

7. Pete Rizzo, Sweden's Blockchain Land Registry to Begin Testing in March, Retrieved from www.coindesk.com/swedens-blockchain-land-registry-begin-testing-march/ , 2017

8. Vamsi Chemitiganti, The Architecture of Blockchain, Retrieved from http://www.vamsitalkstech.com/?p=1615 , 2016.

9. Saberi, S., Kouhizadeh, M., Sarkis, J., & Shen, L. (2018). Blockchain technology and its relationships to sustainable supply chain management. International Journal of Production Research, 1-19.

10. Scott, B. (2016). How can cryptocurrency and blockchain technology play a role in building social and solidarity finance? (No. 2016-1). UNRISD Working Paper.

11. Zheng, Z., Xie, S., Dai, H., Chen, X., & Wang, H. (2017, June). An overview of blockchain technology: Architecture, consensus, and future trends. In Big Data (BigData Congress), 2017 IEEE International Congress on (pp. 557-564). IEEE.

12. Ver, R., & Antonopoulos, A. M. (2018). Blockchain Revolution How the Technology Behind Bitcoin Is Changing Money. ADC Publishing Book.

13. Atwood, M., & Yonis, A. (2018). Blockchain Technology Explained: The Simplified Guide On Blockchain Technology (2018) Blockchain Wallet, Blockchain Explained.

14. Bhardwaj, S., & Kaushik, M. (2018). BlockchainTechnology to Drive the Future. In Smart Computing and Informatics (pp. 263-271). Springer, Singapore.

15. Anascavage, R., & Davis, N. (2018). Blockchain Technology: A Literature Review.

Cyber-Security Techniques in Distributed Systems, SLAs and other Cyber Regulations

SOUMITRA GHOSH, ANJANA MISHRA, BROJO KISHORE MISHRA

C. V. Raman College of Engineering, Bhubaneswar, Odisha, India
Email: soumitraghosh311@gmail.com, anjanamishra2184@gmail.com,
brojokishoremishra@gmail.com

Abstract

This chapter focuses on various cybersecurity techniques meant for parallel as well as distributed computing environment. The distributed systems basically are candidates for giving increased performance, extensibility, increased availability, and resource sharing. The necessities, like multi-user configuration, resource sharing, and some form of communication between the workstations, have created a new set of problems with respect to privacy, security, and protection of the system as well as the user and data. So, new age cybersecurity techniques to combat cybercrimes and protect data breaches are the need of the hour. The chapter also focuses on the need for service level agreements (SLAs) that prevail between a service provider and a client relating to certain aspects of the service such as quality, availability, and responsibilities. The Cuckoo's Egg lessons on cybersecurity by Clifford Stoll as well as various amendments to curb fraud, data breaches, dishonesty, deceit and other such cybercrimes, are also thoroughly discussed herein.

Keywords: Cybersecurity, cybercrime, threat, security, computing, computer security, risk, vulnerability, parallel, distributed

Dac-Nhuong Le et al. (eds.), Cyber Security in Parallel and Distributed Computing, (109–262)
© 2019 Scrivener Publishing LLC

7.1   Introduction

Distributed computing is a more generic term than parallel computation. More often than not, both terms are used interchangeably. Unlike parallel computing where concurrent execution of tasks is the working principle, distributed computing deals with additional capabilities like consistency, partition tolerance and availability.

A system like Hadoop or Spark is an example of distributed computing system that is highly robust and reliable in the sense that it can handle node and network failures. Such systems achieve data loss prevention through data replication over multiple nodes in the network. However, both systems are also designed to perform parallel computing. Unlike HPC systems like MPI, these new kinds of systems are able to continue with a massive calculation even if one of the computational nodes fail.

7.1.1   Primary Characteristics of a Distributed System

A distribution middleware connecting a network of autonomous computers is known as a distributed system. Any typical arrangement of a distributed system enables users to share different resources and capabilities with a solo and integrated consistent network.

- *Concurrency*: Enabling sharing of resources by various nodes in a distributed setup at the same time is the concept behind concurrency.

- *Transparency*: The perception of the system as a single unit instead of an assembly of autonomous components is the main idea behind transparency. The aim of a distributed system designer is to hide the complexity of the same as much as possible. Transparency parameters can be usage permissions, relocation, concurrency, breakdown, diligence and user resources.

- *Openness*: The objective of openness is to design the network in a way that can be easily configured and/or modified. Developers often require adding new features or modify/replace any existing feature in any distributed node, which is easily facilitated if there is proper support for interoperability based on some standard protocols. Also, well-defined interfaces smoothen the process [1].

- *Reliability*: Distributed systems are capable of being highly resistant to failures, secure and more consistent when compared to a single system.

- *Performance*: Performance wise, a distributed system also outperforms an autonomous system by a huge margin by enabling maximum utilization of resources.

- *Scalability*: Any distributed system must be designed keeping in mind that it may have to be extended or what we call scaling based on future requirement or increasing demand. A system may demand scaling on parameters like geography, size or administration [1].

- *Fault Tolerance*: Fault tolerance and reliability of a system can be considered close neighbors. A fault-tolerant system is one that provides high reliability even in the toughest of scenarios, be it subsystem failures, network failures, etc. Providing security to the system in various ways possible, like increasing redundancy of data, preventing denial-of-service (DoS) attacks, upgrading the level of resilience of the system, etc., makes a system a fault-tolerant one.

7.1.2 Major Challenges for Distributed Systems

The challenges of a distributed system is shown in Figure 7.1.

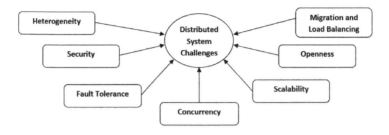

Figure 7.1   Challenges of a distributed system.

Heterogeneity: Services and applications spanning a varied group of computers and networks can be used, run, and accessed by users over the Internet.. Hardware devices of different variants (*PC, tablets, etc.*) running various operating systems (*Windows, iOS, etc.*) may need to exchange information or communicate among themselves to serve a particular purpose. Programs written in unlike languages will be able to converse with one another only when these dissimilarities are dealt with. For this to take place, like the Internet protocols, agreed upon standards also need to be required and accepted [3]. The word middleware applies to a software layer that provides a programming abstraction in addition to masquerading the heterogeneity of the core networks, programming languages and operating systems hardware.

A program code that can be relocated from one computer to a different one and executed at the destination is referred to as a mobile code. One such example of a mobile code is Java applet.

Security: While using public networks, security becomes a huge concern with respect to distributed environment. Security, which can be described in broad terms as confidentiality (*protection against revelation to illegitimate persons*), integrity (*protection against modification or dishonesty*) and availability (*protection against meddling with ways to use resources*), must be provided in DSS. Encryption procedures can be used to fight these concerns, such as those of cryptography, but they are still not infallible. Denial-of-service (DoS) attacks can still take place, where a server or service is showered with fake requests, usually by botnets (*zombie computers*). The possible threats are data leakage, integrity infringement, denial-of-service (DoS) and illegal handling.

Fault Tolerance and Handling: Fault tolerance becomes more complicated when some unreliable components become an integral part of the distributed system. Distributed systems require the fault tolerating ability of a system and function normally. Failures are unavoidable in any system; some subsystems may stop functioning whereas others go on running fine. So as you would expect, we require a means to detect failures (*by employing several techniques like issuing checksums*), mask failures (*by retransmitting upon failure to obtain acknowledgement*), recover from failures (*by rolling back to a previous safe state if a server crashes*), and build redundancy (*by replicating data to prevent data loss in case a particular system in the network crashes*).

Concurrency: Numerous clients trying to ask for a shared resource at the same moment may lead to concurrency issues. This is critical as the results of any such information may depend on the completion order and so synchronization is needed. Moreover, distributed systems do not have a global clock, hence the need for synchronization becomes more evident for proper functioning of all components in the network.

Scalability: Scalability issues arise when a system is not well equipped to handle a sudden boost of any number of resources or number of users or both. The architecture and algorithms must be efficiently used in this situation. Scalability can be thought of comprising primarily three dimensions:

- *Size*: Size represents the number of users and resources to be processed. Difficulty that arises in this scenario is overloading.

- *Geography*: Geography represents the distance linking users and resources. The difficulty that arises in this scenario is communication reliability.

- *Administration*: As the dimension of distributed systems grows, many of the nodes need to be controlled. The difficulty that arises in this scenario administrative chaos [3].

Openness and Extensibility: Interfaces should be alienated and openly obtainable to facilitate trouble-free additions to existing components and those components that are freshly put in [2]. If the well-defined interfaces for a system are available, it is easier for developers to insert fresh features or substitute components in the future. Openness issues become serious when an already published content is suddenly taken back or reversed. Besides, often than not there is no central authority in open distributed systems, as dissimilar systems may have their personal mediator. For example, organizations like Facebook, Twitter, etc., allow developers to build their own software interactively through their API [2].

Migration and Load Balancing: Some sense of independency must exist among tasks and users or applications so that when certain tasks are required to move within the system, other tasks of users or applications are not affected and in order to get to get a better performance out of the system, the load must be distributed among the available resources.

7.2   Identifying Cyber Requirements

Before putting ourselves into the world of the Internet, a few things need to be very clear in our minds if we need to distance ourselves from cyberbullies or prevent any privacy breach of our personal data. As a matter of fact, having answers to a few layman's questions would really come in handy before we start our journey in this cyber world.

- Who has a certified way in? (*Would address issues related to confidentiality*).

- Who is allowed to craft alterations to the information? (*Would address issues related to integrity*).

- When is there is a need to access the data? (*Would address issues related to availability*) [4].

Confidentiality, integrity and availability, also known as the CIA triad, is a framework of standards to provide data security to a company. It is also called the AIC triad in order to avoid any confusion with the Central Intelligence Agency.

In this context, confidentiality ensures that the information is received by the correct person for whom the information was actually intended by the sender. Integrity ensures the message or information received by the receiver is the original message that was actually sent by the sender and no sort of modification or alteration of the actual message was done during the message transmission. Availability is an assurance of the trustworthiness of the data used by authentic people.

There are other factors besides the CIA triad which have grown in importance in recent years, such as Possession or Control, Authenticity, and Non-Repudiation.

7.3   Popular security mechanisms in Distributed Systems

7.3.1   Secure Communication

Suitable adjustments are made to provide a safe medium of communication amid clients and servers so that the CIA factors are preserved. Secure channel provides a safe way of communication between a client and a receiver, preventing any intrusion of a third party from happening so that the confidentiality and/or integrity and/or authentication is not compromised. There are several protocols by which we achieve this purpose. Here we will discuss a few of the protocols that help preserve the authentication factor [5].

7.3.1.1   Authentication

Authentication and integrity are interdependent. For instance, consider a disseminated framework that supports verification in aid of a relationship, but does not provide rules for guaranteeing the integrity of the information. Alternatively, a framework that just ensures data truthfulness, while not measuring for validation. This is why the information authentication and truthfulness must be as one. In numerous conventions, this mix functions admirably. To guarantee truthfulness of information once it is exchanged subsequent to the right verification, we make use of special keys encrypted by the session keys. The session key, which is a shared secret key, applies to the encryption of information truthfulness (*integrity*) and discretion (*confidentiality*). Such a key is usable while, the set up channel exists. At the point when the channel is shut, the session key is lost. Here we will talk about the verification strategies in view of the session key [6, 7].

7.3.1.2   Shared Keys Authorship-Based Authentication

Figure 7.2 depicts an authentication protocol based on shared keys. If a person, say X, wishes to build a communication channel with another person, say Y, their communication is facilitated by sending a request message (say message1) by X to Y.

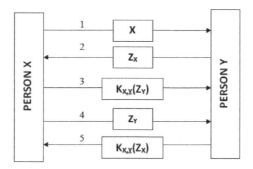

Figure 7.2   Shared secret key-based authentication.

The challenge Z_Y is sent back to X from Y through message2. This challenge can consist of any random number. X encrypts the challenge with the secret key $K_{X,Y}$, which is shared by y, and sends the encrypted challenge to Y in the form of message3. At that point, when Y gets a response from $K_{X,Y}(Z_Y)$ to its own challenge Z_Y, and to check whether Z_Y is included or not, he decrypts the message using the shared key. This way he knows X exists on the other side and figures out who else is required for encryption of Z_Y with $Z_{X,Y}$. Y exhibits that talks with X, however X still did not demonstrate talks with Y, so he sends the challenge Z_X (via message4) that it is answered with return of $K_{X,Y}(R_X)$ (via message5). X is assured speaking with Y when it decodes message5 to find $K_{X,Y}$ and Z_X. In this fashion, $(N(N-1))/2$ keys would be required to manage "N" hosts.

7.3.1.3 Key Distribution Center-Based Authentication

The key distribution center (KDC) is another technique which can be utilized as an authentication method. The key distribution center shares a secret key with each user, but no two users are required to have a shared key. With the key distribution center, it is important to deal with N keys.

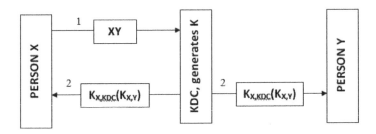

Figure 7.3   Role of KDC in authentication.

Figure 7.3 shows how this authentication works. X expresses its interest to communicate with Y by sending a message to the Key Distribution Center. A message is returned to X by the Key Distribution Center that contains secret shared keys $K_{X,Y}$ which can be used by X. Furthermore, using the shared key $K_{X,Y}$ which is encrypted by secret key K_Y, KDC is sent by the Key Distribution Center to Y. The Needham-Schroeder verification protocol is outlined in view of this model [6].

7.3.1.4 Public key encryption based authentication

Figure 7.4 depicts the use of public key cryptography as an authentication protocol. X being the first person, makes the first move of sending challenge Z_X to user Y, which is encrypted by its public key $K + Y$. A challenge must be sent to X by Y after the latter decrypts the message. X is assured of communicating to Y, in view of the fact that Y is the only user who can decrypt this message by means of the private key associated with the public key of X. When Y receives the channel establishment request from X, it returns the decrypted challenge accompanying its own challenge Z_Y to authenticate X and generate session key $K_{X,Y}$.

An encrypted message with public key $K + X$ related to X includes Y response to the challenge X, own challenge Z_Y and session key that is shown as message 2 in the figure. Only X is able to decrypt the message using the private key $K - X$ related to $K + X$.

Finally, X returns his response to the challenge Y using the session key $K_{X,Y}$ which is produced by B. Therefore, it can decode messages 3 and, in fact, Y talks to X [5].

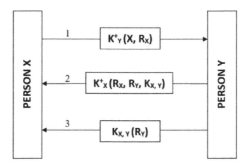

Figure 7.4   Public key encryption based on mutual authentication.

7.3.2   Message Integrity and Confidentiality

Besides authentication, a safe medium must also pledge confidentiality and integrity. Information truthfulness states that there should be no modification in the message during transmission of the same from the sender to the recipient. Confidentiality ensures that messages reach the intended receiver and not to any eavesdropper. Message encryption helps us achieve confidentiality. Cryptography can be carried out by using a shared secret key with the recipient or by means of the public key of the recipient [8, 9].

7.3.2.1   Digital Signatures

A digital signature can be thought of as the digital counterpart of a handwritten signature or printed seal that offers better security than conventional signatures. A computerized signature guarantees approval of confirmation and respectability of any message or electronic report. Uneven cryptography, which is a sort of open key cryptography, frames the premise of advanced marks. By the utilization of an open key calculation, for example, RSA, two keys can be created, one private and one open. To make an advanced mark, marking programming, such as an email program, makes a restricted hash of the electronic information to be agreed upon. The private key is then used to encode the hash.

The encrypted hash along with other data, such as the hashing algorithm is the digital signature. The purpose behind encoding the hash rather than the whole message or report is that a hash capacity can change over a discretionary contribution to a settled length hash esteem, which is generally substantially shorter, in this manner sparing time as hashing is considerably quicker than marking. Each piece of hashed information creates an interesting code. Any adjustments to the information brings about an alternate esteem. This encourages us to approve the integrity of the information by utilizing the endorser's open key to unscramble the hash. In the event that the unscrambled hash coordinates a moment of processed hash of similar information, it demonstrates that the information hasn't changed since it was agreed upon. On the off chance that the two hashes don't coordinate, the information can be thought of as being endangered. As it were, the information has either been altered somehow (*honesty*) or the mark was made with a private key that doesn't compare to the general population key displayed by the endorser (*verification*).

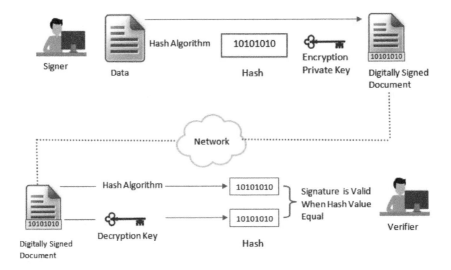

Figure 7.5   Digital signature.

7.3.2.2 Session Keys

During the formation of a protected channel, after completion of the verification stage, the users generally connect with a master session key to guarantee privacy. Another strategy is utilizing the same keys for classification and secure key settings. Assume that, the key that was utilized to build up the session is being utilized to guarantee both trustworthiness and classification of the message as well. In this situation, each time the key is imperiled, an assailant can unscramble messages transmitted during the old discourse, which isn't at all satisfactory. Be that as it may, on the off chance that we utilize the session key to meet our motivation, if there should be an occurrence of a traded off key situation, the assaulted can interrupt just a single session and transmitted messages during different sessions stay private. In this manner, the blend of the keys into long-haul session keys, which are less expensive and brief, is typically a decent decision for executing a protected channel for information trade.

7.3.3   Access Controls

In dispersed frameworks, when a customer and server make a protected channel between them, the customer more often than not produces demands for some administration from the server. Without legitimate access rights, such demands can't be dealt with. Revocation of access is a very critical thought in access control. It is imperative that when we have given a access to some resource to a party, we have the capacity to that back that access again, if or when required. Some well known access control models are talked about below [10].

7.3.3.1   Access Control Matrix

An Access Control Matrix is a table that expresses a subject's entrance rights on a resource. These rights can be of the sort read, compose, and execute. Assurance by a program called supervisory reference will apply incorporated questions on administration issues, for example, making, changing and erasing objects. A reference record subject runs errands and chooses whether or not the subject is approved to perform specific activities. The access control matrix lists all procedures and documents in a network. Each line means a procedure (*Object*) and every segment implies a document (*Subject*) [8, 11]. Every network passage is the entrance rights that a subject has for that protest. At the end of the day, each time the circumstance of S asks for an approach known as M from thing O, the supervisory reference might take a look at it, regardless of whether M exists in $M[S, O]$. In the event that m in $M[S, O]$ isn't generally to be had, the call fizzles out. An access control list (ACL) is a rundown of access control entries (ACE), where each ACE recognizes a trustee and determines the entrance rights permitted, denied, or reviewed for that trustee.

7.3.3.2 *Protection Domains*

An access control list (ACL) is able to help actualize an effective access control framework, through evacuating unfilled earnings. However, an access control list or highlight list pays little respect to other criteria. The protection domain technique decreases the utilization of access control lists. Protection domain is an arrangement of sets containing access rights and questions. Each match precisely indicates which activities are permitted to run for each protest. Solicitations for activities, are dependably issued inside the range. Along these lines, the supervisory reference first looks through its insurance area, at whatever point the subject demands a question's activity. As per space, the supervisory reference can check regardless of whether the application can be run or not. Rather than being approved to do the supervisory reference in the whole assignment, each subject could be allowed to complete a declaration to decide it has a place with which sort of gathering. One needs to convey his endorsement to supervisory reference each time they need to peruse a site page from the Internet. We secure it with digital signatures to ensure the beginning of the testament and its well-being [9].

7.3.3.3 *Trusted Code*

The ability to migrate code between hosts has been created in recent years with the development of distributed systems. Such systems can be protected by a tool known as Sandbox, which enables running programs downloaded from the Internet in separation to prevent system failures or software vulnerabilities. If while trying to set up a rule is prohibited by the host, the program will come to a halt. If one wants to build a more flexible sandbox, playground designing procedures can be downloaded from the internet.

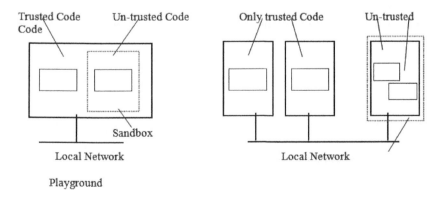

Figure 7.6   Schematic of a sandbox and a playground.

Playground is a selective machine that makes arrangements for versatile code, which can comprise neighborhood resources, organize associations with outside servers, and provide records for applications that keep running over the field. But mobile local sources of machines are alienated from playground physically and are not easily reachable by received code from the Internet. Remote procedure calls can help clients of such a machine accomplish a playground. Then again, there is no portable code for exchanging to open machines in the field. The refinement, including playground and sandbox, can be detected in Figure 7.6.

7.3.3.4 Denial of Service

The purpose of access control is to allow authentic users to have access to resources. Denial-of-service is an attack that stops authentic users from getting access to resources. Since distributed systems are open in nature, the need for protection against DoS is even more essential. It becomes very difficult to prevent or manage DoS attacks that run from a single/multiple source(s) to arrange a distributed denial-of-service (DDoS) attack. The intention usually is to install a malicious software into a victim's machine [12]. Firewall plays an important role here in restricting traffic into a internal network from the outside world based on various filters according to suitable needs of the organization [11].

7.4 Service Level Agreements

A service level agreement, abbreviated SLA, is more about providing the basis for post-incident legal combat than increasing quality, availability and responsibilities of service. It is a contract between a service supplier (*internal/external*) and the user that consists of the levels of service that a customer can expect from that service supplier. Service level agreements are output-based in that their intention is exclusively to sketch out what the end user will receive [13].

7.4.1 Types of SLAs

Service level agreements are classified into various levels:

- *Customer-Based SLA*: A customer-based SLA is a contract consisting of all services that are used by an individual group of customers. For example, a service level agreement involving a provider (*IT service provider*) and the finance section of a large company for services such as finance system, procurement/purchase system, billing system, payroll system, etc.

- *Service-Based SLA*: A service-based SLA is not restricted to any specific customer group, instead it is a contract for all clients using the services being provided by the service supplier. For example:

  - A mobile service provider provides a regular service to all its clients and offers definite repairs as a part of an offer with the general charges.

  - An email system for the whole firm. Because of varied levels of services being provided to different customers, critical situations may arise because of lack of uniformity.

- *Multilevel SLA*: A multilevel SLA is categorized into different levels to address different sets of customers for the same services within the same SLA. For example:

- Corporate-level SLA: It covers all the common service level management (*usually known as SLM*) concerns relevant to every customer throughout the entire firm. These concerns are probably less unstable and so updates (*SLA reviews*) are less commonly needed.

- Customer-level SLA: It covers all service level managementconcerns related to the particular client set, in spite of the services being used.

- Service-level SLA: It covers all service level management concerns related to the exact services, in relation to this precise client set [15].

The parameters that describe service levels for an Internet service provider are supposed to assure:

- A narrative of the service being offered: Repairs of parts such as domain name servers, active host configuration protocol servers, and network connectivity.

- Dependability: Duration of availability of service.

- Receptiveness: This implies service time inside which a request will be replied to.

- Procedure for reporting problems: How problems will be reported, who can be contacted, technique for escalation, and what other remedies are undertaken to get through the issue effectively.

- Supervising and accounting level of service: Usually concerned with who will monitor a general performance, what information will be collected and how often as well as how much right to use the client is given to performance data, what information could be collected and how often, in addition to how much access the purchaser is given to all the performance facts.

- Penalty for not meeting service commitments: May cover credit or settlement to clients, or allowing the client to end the connection.

- Get away terms or limitations: Occasions under which the service levels were assured no longer hold. For example, an exclusion from uptime provisions in situations of various natural calamities destroying the ISP's gadgets.

The content of every service level agreement varies according to different service providers but uniformly covers common topics, such as quality and volume of task (*taking into account both accuracy and correctness*), receptiveness, efficiency and speed. The document serves as a common understanding of responsibilities, services, guarantees, areas prioritized and warranties offered by the service supplier.

Commonly used technological descriptions to enumerate the service level, such as mean time between failures (MTBF) or mean time to recovery, response, or resolution (MTTR), which mention a threshold value (*average or minimum*) for service level performance are mentioned in an SLA [13].

7.4.2 Critical Areas for SLAs

The information security team and the information technology team must work hand-in-hand to develop the most important terms of service level agreements. SLAs must focus on those areas in which information technology groups have the most perceptive outcome and control in order to have a radical effect on the information security program. It is seen that the effects of such agreements are lessened if the information security teams fail to restrict the SLAs to only the most vital items. Analyzing the risks associated with an organization or assessing past events may point the way to the most vital components for a specific firm. In most cases, the following areas are proposed as important issues:

7.4.2.1 *Examining the Network*

Network scans are carried out by many information security teams to recognize susceptibilities of the network. Recognizing the problems is just the starting point of the development. How the crisis should be handled or taken care of is the second step. The third step can be thought of as how it can be integrated into a course to avoid any occurrence in the future. To automate the network scanning practice, different firms use various commercial tools. One such tool is ISS Internet Scanner, which, if used, can document vulnerabilities grouped into categories of High Risk, Medium Risk and Low Risk. Following are various risk levels defined in the Help Index of ISS Internet Scanner:

- High: This refers to any susceptibility that allows an intruder to gain immediate admittance into a system such as gaining superuser entry and access permissions or finding a way around a firewall. For example, a susceptible Sendmail 8.6.5 version permits a fraud to carry out instructions on mail servers, installations of BackOrifice, NetBus or an Admin account devoid of any password.

- Medium: Medium susceptibility may refer to intrusions providing confidential data, slowing down performance or having a high prospective of giving system admittance to an impostor. For example, recognition of active modems on the network, zone transfers, and writable FTP directories.

- Low: Low susceptibility may refer to network breaches providing confidential data that could eventually lead to a compromise. For example, all users can access Floppy Drives, limited SSL validation may be performed by IE, not enabling logon and logoff auditing.

The Internet technology groups may look for the following in a report:

- Modifications in configuration

- Installing service packs

- Setting up patches

- Modifications in ACL (*access control list*)

- Registry edits

- Stopping services

These recommendations helps the Internet technology groups by cutting short the time requirements for finding solutions to the above problems, which would further lead to quick implementations. As you would expect, the extent of the time required to resolve the shortfall will be decided based on the severity of the openness. Say, high vulnerabilities must be resolved within 48 hours, medium vulnerabilities may be resolved within a week and Low vulnerabilities may be resolved within a month.

7.4.2.2 Forensics

Forensics plays a very important role in covering many investigations. Internet security teams are regularly asked at some point in an investigation what took place, when it occurred and/or whether it should have taken place or not. Log files are very vital with respect to carrying out a forensics inquiry without which the inquiry usually results in failure.

Therefore, SLAs with respect to forensics can consist of:

- Duration of time held on to before being overwritten.

- Proxy logs, firewall logs, server logs, syslogs, DHCP logs, and client logs.

- Setting the threshold required to move the logs to any central logging server, portable media, offsite information storage, etc.

7.4.2.3 Managing Records/Documents

More often than not, an efficient IT firm will usually be associated with a properly managed information protection plan. In addition to this, the Internet technology groups should have the suitable abilities, good records of internet technology processes, gears and assets, which must be kept up-to-date for a suitable execution of an Internet security agenda. A well-documented network topology is essential while conducting risk evaluations, network scanning or responding to possibilities or analytical requirements, etc. Service Level Agreement related to network topology may address points like updating the network topology on a monthly basis by respective Internet technology groups.

Points that may be kept in mind while preparing SLAs related to document management are:

- Alterations in settings

- Modifications in network infrastructure

- Alterations in API

- System failure logs and relevant crisis resolution

- Rate of recurrence of records assessment

- Thorough task explanation

- Accountable persons for every file on paper service and preservation contracts

7.4.2.4 Backing Up Data

The basis of any strong Internet security program is data backup. Data backups allow an organization to recover its data either fully or from some recognized baseline or checkpoints in case of some unpleasant occurrence. Some fundamental issues that need to be considered when preparing a SLA include:

- Theoretical support records.

- Substantiation of the information on support for soundness.

- Credentials of which server or application are backed-up and the specific program.

- Validation of reinstatement by a planned test on a regular basis.

- Label of an offsite storage place and the pickup and/or dropoff schedule.

- Label of which backups include classified or patented data about the organization.

- Justification of the classification idea used by the Internet technology groups to trace backups.

- Backup-related documentation comprising ways to carry out, reinstate, etc.

- Verification of anti-virus before backing up.

The founding of Internet security service level agreements between the Internet technology groups and the Internet security groups is essential to give surety to the project that practical actions are employed in the project. This provides the Internet technology groups with rational prospect and offers the Internet security groups with an authoritative place anywhere in the line, except last [14].

7.5   The Cuckoo's Egg in the Context of IT Security

Even though a book on digital security from 1986 is not requested much today, the visionary ideas from 30 years ago are still relevant today. It may sound obsolete, yet amidst the sprouting Internet technology (IT) of 1986, the belief in systems offering ongoing protection from malware and hacking existed at that point. In the University of California's Lawrence Berkeley Research Center, the astronomer Clifford Stoll was given the job of tracking a 75-cent accounting error in a centralized server PC's custom records. It was discovered that nine seconds of execution time were stolen by a programmer misusing vulnerabilities in a UNIX content manager framework.

A nitty-gritty account of the digital spying war that followed was written about in the 1989 book called *The Cuckoo's Nest: Tracking a Spy Through the Maze of Computer Espionage*. It is a first-person account of Stoll's hunt for the hacker that broke into the lab's computer and how he ran test programs to expose a hidden network of spies. This genuine international mystery novel provided numerous individuals with their first exposure to digital security. It superbly mixed Cold War antagonistic vibe, processing personal data and the protection versus security face-off. The book reports Stoll's adventure as he tries to get assistance from the U.S. and German governments to take care of this genuine danger that no one wanted to claim.

The egg in *The Cuckoo's Egg* title alludes to how the programmer bargained a considerable amount casualties. The essentialness lies in the way that, in actuality, a cuckoo bird does not lay its eggs in its own nest. Rather, she waits for an unattended nest of some other bird. The mother cuckoo at that point sneaks in, lays her egg in the empty nest, and escapes, abandoning her egg to be incubated by another mother. Like the cuckoo bird, Stoll's programmers exploited security defenselessness in the effective and extensible GNU Emacs content tool framework that Berkeley had introduced on the greater part of its UNIX machines. As Stoll stated, "The survival of cuckoo chicks relies upon the numbness of different species" [16].

It is uniquely significant that the meaning of the cuckoo's egg in the book is a malware program that an aggressor uses to supplant a real program. More specifically, it was swapped for atrun, which is executed at regular intervals meaning the aggressor needed to hold back for five minutes at the most before their pernicious code was executed. Stoll alludes to this as the "hatching" of the cuckoo's egg [17].

"I watched the cuckoo lay its egg: once again, he manipulated the files in my computer to make himself super-user. His same old trick: use the Gnu-Emacs move-mail to substitute his tainted program for the system's atrun file. Five minutes later, shazam! He was system manager" [18].

The spy ring invested a considerable measure of energy endeavoring to assume control of standard client accounts so they could sign in as those clients and audit the framework without causing an alert. In one moment, subsequent to turning into a framework head with the Emacs assault, one programmer opened up the framework's secret word document. Despite everything he didn't recognize what the passwords were to every one of the clients on the framework since they were scrambled. Rather than attempting to break them, he just deleted one of them. He picked a particular client and eradicated the client's secret word. When he signed in as that client later, the framework would allow access since there was no secret key guarding the record. Inevitably, the programmer began downloading the whole secret key record to his home PC. Stoll later found that the programmer executed a splendid new assault. He scrambled each word in the lexicon with a similar calculation that encoded passwords and looked at the encoded passwords in the downloaded watchword record with the scrambled word reference words. On the off chance that he found any that coordinated, he could now sign in as a genuine client. Savage power word reference assaults are standard today, however in those days, this was another thought.

Stoll regularly kept running into government administration and spies who were anxious to take any data that Stoll had with respect to his examination but who were additionally reluctant to share anything that they knew in kind. There's also a second important issue. As Stoll is wrapping up the book, he finishes up by stating that in the wake of sliding down this Alice-in-Wonderland gap, he found that the political left and right have a common reliance on PCs. However, the right sees PC security as important to ensure privileged insights into national matters, whereas their "leftie" counterparts were stressed over an intrusion of their protection.

The Snowden case is only the last out of a progression of exchanges about protection versus security that the United States and different nations have made in the previous twenty years. As Bruce Schneier brings up, this is a false contention stating that the level-headed discussion wasn't about security versus protection, rather freedom versus control [18].

He and different distinguished scientists describe why this isn't an either-or choice. He mentioned that one can have security and at the same time protection; however, you need to work for it. In this book, arguably Stoll was the first who raised the issue. He battled with it in those days as we on the whole are doing today.

The third determinative issue is the digital spying risk. The business world truly ended up mindful of the issue with the Chinese government's information trade-off with Google toward the end of 2009. The U.S. military had been managing the Chinese digital observation danger, in those days celebrated as Titan Rain, for a decade prior to that. In any case, Stoll claims that his book depicts the main open situation where spies utilized PCs to direct secret activities, this time supported by the Russians. The occasions in *The Cuckoo's Egg* began happening in August 1986, just about 15 years before Titan Rain, and a portion of the administration characters that Stoll mentions in the book imply that they thought there were other nonpublic surveillance movements that happened sooner than that. The fact of the matter is that the digital secret activities risk has been around for somewhere in the range of 30 years and hint at not leaving at any point in the near future.

The fourth and last determinate issue is not really a digital issue at all, but rather an insight problem. All through the book, Stoll battles with whether or not to distribute his discoveries. He frames the issue this way: "If you describe how to make a pipe bomb, the next kid that finds some charcoal and saltpeter will become a terrorist. Yet if you suppress the information, people won't know the danger" [16].

7.6   Searching and Seizing Computer-Related Evidence

7.6.1   Computerized Search Warrants

A court order might be issued to look through a PC or electronic media if there is reasonable justification to trust that the media contains or is booty, confirmation of a wrong doing, products of wrong doing, or an instrumentality of a wrong doing. For more data, one can refer to Fed. R. Crim. P. 41(c).

Three critical issues concerning court orders for search warrants have been addressed below: particularity, reasonable time period for analyzing seized electronic gadgets or storage media, and the maintenance of seized information.

7.6.1.1   Particularity

Court orders should especially portray the place to be sought and the things to be seized. "At the point when electronic capacity media are to be looked in light of the fact that they store data that is proof of a wrongdoing, the things to be seized under the warrant ought to more often than not center around the substance of the applicable records as opposed to the physical stockpiling media" (Searching and Seizing Computers and Obtaining Evidence in Criminal Investigations, Computer Crime and Intellectual Property Section, Criminal Division, U.S. Division of Justice, Washington, D.C. (3rd ed 2009) at 72).

One approach is in any case an "all records" depiction; include constraining dialect expressing the wrongdoing, the suspects, and important era, if pertinent; incorporate unequivocal cases of the records to be seized; and after that show that the records might be seized in any shape, regardless of whether electronic or non-electronic (Id. at 74-77).

In a few wards, judges or justices may force particular conditions on how the pursuit is to be executed or expect police to disclose how they intend to constrain the hunt before the warrant might be conceded.

7.6.1.2   Reasonable Time Period for Examining Seized Electronic Equipment

Courts have held that the Fourth Amendment requires the measurable examination of a PC or electronic hardware to be directed inside a sensible time (United States v. Mutschelkaus, 564 F. Supp. 2d 1072, 1077 (D.N.D. 2008)).

Drawn out postponement in acquiring a court order to look through a seized electronic gadget can be held to be absurd under the Fourth Amendment. For instance, in U.S. v. Mitchell, 565 F.3d 1347, 1351 (eleventh Cir. 2009), a 21-day delay in acquiring a court order for the litigant's PC was held to be irrational.

There might be forced law authorization purposes behind deferrals, including pausing while a warrant can be secured or sitting tight for the fulfillment of all the more pressing dynamic examinations that required criminological inspector assets. So also, confounded legal investigation as a result of the volume of records or the nearness of encryption may give convincing motivations to delay.

7.6.1.3   Irrational Retention of Seized Data

In United States v. Ganias, 755 F.3d 125 (2d Cir. 2014), the United States Court of Appeals for the Second Circuit held that they consider regardless of whether the Fourth Amendment grants authorities executing a warrant for the seizure of specific information on a PC to seize and inconclusively hold each record on that PC for use in future criminal examinations. They hold that it doesn't. For instance, if police look and grab an electronic gadget for proof of one wrongdoing, hold the documents and, years after the fact, scan the records to confirm in a different criminal examination, that will disregard the Fourth Amendment, as indicated by the Second Circuit's choice in Ganais.

7.6.2 Searching and Seizing

As data and interchanging innovations have entered regular day-to-day existence, PC-related unlawful activity has drastically expanded. As PCs or other information stockpiling gadgets can provide methods for carrying out wrongdoing or be a vault of electronic data that is confirmation of a wrongdoing, the utilization of warrants to scan for and seize such gadgets is given increasing significance. The pursuit and seizure of electronic proof is in many regards the same as some other inquiry and seizure. For example, as with some other inquiry and seizure, the pursuit and seizure of PCs or other electronic stockpiling media must be conducted pursuant to a warrant which is issued by a district court if there is probable cause to believe that they contain evidence of a crime [20].

Realizing that criminals have not missed out on the PC revolution, the United States Department of Justice has published a manual committed solely to the laws of searching for and seizing PCs and electronic surveillance of the Internet. This record was composed with an end goal to help law enforcement organizations the nation over in getting electronic proof in criminal investigations.

According to James K. Robinson, Assistant Attorney General of the Criminal Division, this manual was essential for law enforcement operators and prosecutors, as well as for any American who utilizes a PC. He further stated that electronic security is essential to all of us, and the department needs everybody to recognize what their rights are. Entitled, "Searching and Seizing Computers and Obtaining Electronic Evidence in Criminal Investigations," the Criminal Division's Computer Crime and Intellectual Property Section (CCIPS) made this report. The psychological distress caused by PC-related crime requires prosecutors and law enforcement specialists to see how to get electronic confirmation put into PCs. Electronic records, for example, PC arrange logs, messages, word handling documents, and ".jpg" picture records, have progressively given the legislature vital confirmation in criminal cases.

The manual provides government law enforcement operators and prosecutors with a methodical process that can enable them to comprehend the legitimate issues that emerge when they look for electronic proof in criminal investigations. The manual diagrams how electronic observation laws apply to the Internet, and also how the courts have connected the Fourth Amendment to PCs.

This manual replaces *Federal Guidelines for Searching and Seizing Computers* (1994), and also the 1997 and 1999 supplements. Despite the fact that organizations getting together and making a game plan accomplished the objective of giving efficient control to every government specialist and lawyer in the field of PC investigation and arrest, intervening changes in the law and the rapid development of the Internet since 1994 has cultivated the need for a fresh direction. This manual is intended as an updated version of the recommended rules on seeking and seizing PCs with direction on the statutes referring to acquiring electronic confirmation in cases involving PC systems and the Internet. The manual offers help, and is not a specialist. Its examination and conclusions ponder current troublesome areas of the law, and doesn't speak to the official position of the Justice Department or other offices. It has no administrative impact.

The law overseeing electronic confirmation in criminal investigations has two essential sources: the Fourth Amendment to the U.S. Constitution, and the statutory security laws arranged at 18 U.S.C. 2510-22, 18 U.S.C. 2701-11, and 18 U.S.C. 3121-27. Although other established and statutory issues are covered now and again, most circumstances exhibit either a sacred issue under the Fourth Amendment or a statutory issue under these three statutes. The association of this handbook mirrors that division: session 1 and session 2 address the Fourth Amendment law of hunt and seizure, and session 3 and session 4 center around the statutory issues, which emerge generally in cases including PC systems and the Internet [19].

7.7 Conclusion

This chapter focused on various cybersecurity techniques meant for parallel as well as distributed computing environment. The distributed systems basically are candidates for giving increased performance, extensibility, increased availability, and resource sharing. The necessities like multiuser configuration, resource sharing, and some form of communication between the workstations have created a new set of problems with respect to privacy, security, and protection of the system as well as the user and data. So, new age cybersecurity techniques to combat cybercrimes and protect data breaches are the need of the hour. The chapter also focused on the need for service level agreements (SLA) that prevail between a service provider and a client relating to certain aspects of the service such as quality, availability, and responsibilities. The Cuckoo's Egg lessons on cybersecurity by Clifford Stoll as well as various amendments to curb fraud, data breaches, dishonesty, deceit and such other cybercrimes have also been thoroughly discussed here.

References

1. Mishra, K. S., & Tripathi, A. K. (2014). Some issues, challenges and problems of distributed software system. International Journal of Computer Science and Information Technologies. Varanasi, India, 7(3).

2. Nadiminti, K., De Assunao, M. D., & Buyya, R. (2006). Distributed systems and recent innovations: Challenges and benefits. InfoNet Magazine, 16(3), 1-5.

3. http://www.ejbtutorial.com/distributed-systems/challenges-for-a-distributed-system

4. https://www.rsaconference.com/writable/presentations/file_upload/grc-f42.pdf

5. Shahabi, Reza Nayebi. "Security Techniques in Distributed Systems." system 2: 3.

6. Liu, H., Luo, P., & Wang, D. (2008). A scalable authentication model based on public keys. Journal of Network and Computer Applications, 31(4), 375-386.

7. Wang, F., & Zhang, Y. (2008). A new provably secure authentication and key agreement mechanism for SIP using certificateless public-key cryptography. Computer Communications, 31(10), 2142-2149.

8. Malacaria, P., & Smeraldi, F. (2013). Thermodynamic aspects of confidentiality. Information and Computation, 226, 76-93.

9. Chandra, S., & Khan, R. A. (2010). Confidentiality checking an object-oriented class hierarchy. Network Security, 2010(3), 16-20.

10. Andress, J. (2014). The basics of information security: understanding the fundamentals of InfoSec in theory and practice. Syngress.

11. Prowell, S., Kraus, R., & Borkin, M. (2010). Seven deadliest network attacks. Elsevier.

12. Kumar, P. A. R., & Selvakumar, S. (2011). Distributed denial of service attack detection using an ensemble of neural classifier. Computer Communications, 34(11), 1328-1341.

13. https://www.paloaltonetworks.com/cyberpedia/what-is-a-service-level-agreement-sla

14. https://www.sans.org/reading-room/whitepapers/standards/internal-sla-service-level-agreements-information-security-548

15. Kearney, K. T., & Torelli, F. (2011). The SLA model. In Service Level Agreements for Cloud Computing (pp. 43-67). Springer, New York, NY.

16. https://researchcenter.paloaltonetworks.com/2013/12/cybersecurity-canon-cuckoos-egg/

17. https://security.stackexchange.com/questions/16889/what-is-a-cuckoos-egg/16892

18. Stoll, C. (2005). The cuckoo's egg: tracking a spy through the maze of computer espionage. Simon and Schuster.

19. https://www.govcon.com/doc/justice-department-releases-guide-to-searchin-0001

20. https://www.lexology.com/library/detail.aspx?g=13704bd6-f4e4-4157-b111-9c58ccfd9f7d

CHAPTER

8

Distributed Computing Security: Issues and Challenges

MUNMUN SAHA[1], SANJAYA KUMAR PANDA[2] AND SUVASINI PANIGRAHI[1]

[1]Department of Computer Science and Engineering, Veer Surendra Sai University of Technology, Burla, India

[2]Department of Information Technology, Veer Surendra Sai University of Technology, Burla, India

Emails: munmunsas@gmail.com, suvasini26@gmail.com, sanjayauce@gmail.com

Abstract

Distributed computing is a model in which multiple computers interact, coordinate and communicate with each other by sharing and passing messages. The computers can be connected by a wide area network that is geographically distant, or may be connected by a local area network that is physically close. The goal is to make such a network work as a single computer. Security is the most vital requirement of modern distributed computer systems as the system stores critical information, which is accessed and passed along in all types of applications. Therefore, designing a secure system is especially challenging due to the distributed nature of modern systems. Moreover, security in a large distributed information system faces complex challenges, especially where open environment is concerned. In this chapter, we study various security issues and challenges in distributed computing security along with the security issues in advanced areas like heterogeneous computing, cloud computing, fog computing, etc. Moreover, we present the methods/schemes/protocols used in various security issues along with possible methods of implementation.

Keywords: Distributed computing

Dac-Nhuong Le et al. (eds.), Cyber Security in Parallel and Distributed Computing, (129–262)

8.1 Introduction

With the advancement of technology, computing becomes one of the emerging areas in the field of computer science. The goal of computing is to provide enormous computing power to the users. The computing power ranges from a personal computer to a set of data centers. However, the computing power of a personal computer is very much limited in solving complex scientific and engineering problems. One of the possible solutions is to integrate multiple computers and utilize their computing power. Note that these computers may not be located in the same place. One such kind of computing is distributed computing, which permits the users to share processing power, information, memory, storage and many more [1]. It studies distributed systems. A distributed system may have any of the possible configurations, such as minicomputer workstation, mainframe personal computer and so on. Here, the computers are geographically distant and they are connected through a wide area network; and a large number of networks consisting of multiple hosts are connected with each other, but run as a single system. To uplift the efficiency and performance, the software system shares their components with multiple computers. The main advantage is scalability, as it can be increased by connecting more computers as and when required. At the same time, security is the main concern of distributed computing due to a large variety of resources integrated into one single unit [2, 3]. It is also a primary concern for preserving the integrity, confidentiality, availability of the information, authenticating the identity in communication, ensuring non-repudiation of data origin and delivery. Security goals are decided by the security policies and it can be achieved by various security mechanisms.

While interacting with the distributed network, there is a set of rules, which can define the constraints of the users. These rules are called security policy. Security issues of distributed computing are broadly classified into the following parts:

(1) Confidentiality, integrity and availability.

(2) Authentication and access control.

(3) Broken authentication, session and access.

(4) Other data-related issues.

Confidentiality is to keep the contents of the communication as private. Integrity is to keep the contents as it is, i.e., unaltered. Note that confidentiality and integrity are well-defined in terms of access control policies. Availability is the reliable access to the information by authorized people. There are different formal models for confidentiality and integrity such as the Bell-LaPadula model [4] and Biba model [5]. There are also policies associated with system access control, which are referred to as accessing control policy. The access control policy rules state "who," "what" and "under what condition" one can access the data. They are classified as either discretionary or nondiscretionary. There are three well-known access control policy models. They are role-based access control (RBAC), discretionary access control (DAC) and mandatory access control (MAC). In RBAC, access rights are given to the users based on their roles in the systems. In DAC, the owner of a particular object specifies the policy. In MAC, if there is an access right rule for a particular user, then it will grant the permission to the user for accessing the resource. These policies are distributed among the nodes in the distributed system. Therefore, a central monitoring system is required to continuously monitor the policies.

Threats are an unwanted bug in the network system, which invariably burn down a secure communication in the network (*especially, distributed network*). Some security threats are relevant to the entire community, without distinguishing any particular user or node. There are various attacks on security, such as distributed denial-of-service attack, reputation attack, malicious attack, damage attack, event-triggered attack, compound attack and user attack. As a result, there can be threats from mobile agent to host and there can be an insecure communication channel. Many existing models/algorithms/protocols have addressed the security issues in a distributed computing system such as cyber physical production system (CPSS) model [6], European computer manufacturer and association (ECMA) model [7], security multi-agent system model, log-based distributed security algorithm, elliptic curve Diffie-Hellman (ECDA) key exchange protocol [8], advance encryption algorithm (AES) and so on. The applications of distributed computing are cloud computing, fog computing, mobile computing and many more.

The rest of this chapter is organized as follows. Section 8.2 presents various security issues and challenges in distributed computing security. Section 8.3 focuses on the security issues and challenges in advanced areas like fog computing. Finally, concluding thoughts on the topic are presented in Section 8.4.

8.2 Security Issues and Challenges

8.2.1 Confidentiality, Integrity and Availability

Shamir [9] has proposed a cryptographic approach to maintain confidentiality in distributed computing. His scheme allows a secure communication for any user-pair by verifying their signature without disclosing the private and public keys. It also does not require a third party. His scheme assumes the existence of a key generation center, which provides a personalized smart card to the user, after joining the network for the first time. The smart card authorizes the user to sign and encrypt the sending messages, and also to verify and decrypt the receiving messages. The above process is repeated on an independent basis, without revealing the identity of another party. After all the cards are issued, the center can be closed and can continue to function for an indefinite period in a decentralized way. The third party auditor (TPA) is a third person, who has the ability and experience to perform all auditing processes. It is used to check the data integrity in the presence of various incidents and doubtful actions in the distributed system. Balusamy *et al.* [10] have presented an algorithm where the data owner has been involved in checking the integrity of the outsourced data. This scheme assures the data owner about the security and integrity of the data. The owner has all the information about the resource in the system and is involved in the auditing process. The auditing process is first performed by the TPA. If the TPA finds that there is any updating or alteration needed in the resource, then the TPA informs the owner. Subsequently, the owner checks the log of the auditing and validates those changes. If the owner identified any unusual action on the data, then the owner can assign another auditor or may personally check the data. Here, a particular threshold value is assigned to the TPA and it should not be exceeded by the TPA. Reddy and Balaraju [11] have proposed a security method in the cloud. They have used TPA to provide security and integrity in the cloud environment. Note that TPA acts as a mediator between the service provider and the user. TPA resolves the data inconsistency and data integrity issues by editing the data and managing the cloud environment. They also used some security keys to provide security.

Bowers *et al.* [12] have designed a high availability and integrity layer (HAIL) to point out the threats that are caused by an unavailable service provider. HAIL spreads the data among different service providers to make service available at any time. Moreover, HAIL regulates the service providers to provide a reliable solution for unreliable components. It leads to cost-effective components. Reliable storage made for unreliable storage (RAID) has inspired the idea of HAIL.

8.2.2 Authentication and Access Control Issue

Li *et al.* [13] have proposed an intelligent approach based on cryptography for securing distributed big data storage in cloud computing. They have focused on the problem of cloud operator abuse, and proposed a security-aware efficient distributed storage model for securing mass distributed service and providing security protection. Their approach is to store the data among the cloud servers in a distributed manner by encrypting the data without any major overhead and latency. They have classified the data as normal data and sensitive data and used alternative data distribution (AD2) algorithm to assign the data to clouds. Here, a single cloud is assigned to the normal data and two clouds are assigned to the sensitive data. Secure efficient data distribution algorithm is also accompanied by data splitting in order to prevent sensitive data. They have used an efficient data conflation algorithm to perform the decryption process for the sensitive data. This algorithm is mainly adopted by those enterprises that use STaaS and requires a very huge data storage security. Amin *et al.* [14] have proposed a lightweight protocol for authenticating Internet of things devices in distributed cloud computing architecture. Their protocol uses a smart card for authentication of the user. The user is registered using the smart card and can securely use the private information from all the private cloud server. They have used tools like automated validation of internet security protocols and applications (AVISPA) and BAN logic model for proofing the strength of the protocol. In AVISPA [15], high level protocol specification language is used to model the protocols. It has four back-ends, namely OFMC, CL-AtSe, SATMC and TA4SP, and one translator (i.e., `hlpsl2if`). This tool supports unilateral, weak and strong authentications between users. They have preferred password-based hash function for easy implementation. Here, the user gets a common secret session key after authentication. Finally, they have done the cryptanalysis and confirmed that the protocol prevents all possible threats.

Gritzalis [16] has developed a baseline policy in a distributed healthcare information system. The author has modeled the developed policy by considering some of the aspects such as local need, user requirement and expectations, and international recommendation. Moreover, the author has created a decision mapping roadmap and developed baseline security policy after identifying and analyzing various aspects. Lopriore [17] has proposed a model to protect the object in a distributed system. The author has evaluated the model by analyzing some salient viewpoints, such as network traffic, storage overhead, inter-process interaction and communication. In order to generate the access right to each object in the distributed network, the author has used symmetric key cryptography for including an encryption key with every object and password with every domain. Here, a process has to grant permission from the object pointer, which is written in a cipher text including the password of the domain, for accessing the object in the distributed network.

8.2.3 Broken Authentication, Session and Access

Broken authentication happens due to the flaws in the authentication and session management. It allows the attacker to bypass the process of authentication. The attacker may use an automated tool with a list of passwords to perform the attack. Malina *et al.* [18]

have introduced a two-factor authentication protocol, which relies on the zero-knowledge approach. The protocol is a modification of Schnorr's authentication solution and takes advantage of elliptic curves. They have discussed the security lacunas of Mifare cards and their possible attacks.

Tsai and Lo [19] have presented a scheme for the mobile users to get services from different cloud service providers by using a single private key. This scheme requires less memory space and processing time as it does not require verification tables for the smart card generator service. Note that smart card generator produces the public and private keys for both cloud service providers and users. Odelu *et al.* [20] have analyzed the scheme of Tsai and Lo [19], and reported the server impersonation attack and mutual authentication issue on their scheme. As a result, they have presented an authentication scheme, which provides session-key security in order to avoid the passive and active attacks. They have simulated the presented scheme using AVIPSA tool [15] and NS-2 simulator, and showed that the scheme is appropriate for the real-life applications.

8.3   Security Issues and Challenges in Advanced Areas

In this section, we discuss the security issues associated with some advanced areas, such as heterogeneous computing, grid computing, cloud computing, parallel and distributed computing, mobile cloud, distributed embedded system computing and fog computing. Xie and Qin [21] have proposed a model in order to overcome the security requirement problem in a heterogeneous distributed system. In their model, n heterogeneous sites connect with n number of sites in a queuing architecture and m number of users submit the independent task. The main component of the model is the SATS, which contains tack allocation decision maker, security adaptive window, execution time manager, security overhead manager and degree of security deficiency calculator. Finally, the entire task is modeled with security requirement and performance evaluation of each model is calculated. Smith *et al.* [22] have presented a solution for pointing out the threats in service-oriented on-demand grid computing. They have analyzed the security threats within service-oriented on-demand distributed environment, which are based on three levels of trust relationship and three types of grid application. They have used a sandbox-based approach using virtual machine and jailing mechanism for ensuring trust in the first two levels and used trusted computing platform alliance in the third level.

Cheng *et al.* [23] have proposed rendezvous-based trust propagation algorithm in order to overcome the trust propagation issue in a distributed network. The algorithm has three nodes, namely target, requester, provider for communication of trust information. Computed trust tickets and trust information are directed by the trust provider and trust requester, respectively, and they will meet with certain probability in some common rendezvous node. They evaluated the propagation scheme, which shows better results as compared to the previous flood-based method. Khattab *et al.* [24] have proposed a honeypot back-propagation scheme in order to overcome the distributed denial-of-service attack. This scheme follows traceback hop-by-hop mechanism in which honeypot roams around the nodes for receiving accurate attack signature. Furthermore, a hierarchical tree is formed at the autonomous system level followed by the router level. In addition, it provides a flexible pushback defense framework, which allows attack detection by tracing accurate attack signature.

Liu *et al.* [25] have proposed a swarm scheduling approach to solve the potentially intractable problem in distributed data-intensive computing. They have formulated a novel security constraint model for solving the scheduling problem by targeting workflow application. They have investigated different meta-heuristics adaptations on the scheduling workflow algorithm, and proposed a novel variable neighborhood search strategy for preventing particle swarms getting trapped in local minima. Colom *et al.* [26] have proposed a scheduling algorithm and a predictive model to handle the security requirements in parallel and distributed cybersecurity field. Their intention is to boost up the intrusion detection and increase the security perimeter. Their scheduling algorithm aims to distribute the intrusion detection system task and supports the combination of enterprise and personal computing resource. They have verified the model by a number of experiments. Firstly, an experimental DIDS is designed with the help of a number of existing IDS solutions. Secondly, a prototype implementation is built to prove the concept. Finally, singular test showing the feasibility is performed to provide a good insight into future work. Jakbik *et al.* [27] have developed a novel architecture by enforcing cloud security. It is based on non-deterministic meta-scheduler and multi-agent scheme, driven by generic heuristics. By using these schemes, denial-of-service and timing attacks can be avoided from the cloud and it can be integrated in the OpenStack platform. They have suggested two different models for satisfying user security demands. The first model schedules tasks in the virtual machines by providing the proper security level and is referred to as the scoring model. The second model calculates the time spent in the cryptographic operation for a particular task. The above scheduling system has been simulated in order to assess the effectiveness of the proposed algorithm. It increases the system security and creates resistance against attacks without hampering the overall performance of the cloud environment.

Zeng *et al.* [28] have proposed a security-aware and budget-aware workflow scheduling technique (SABA) for reducing workflow execution time without violating the security requirement of users. They have provided a secure scheduling of tasks under budget constraints, which leads to secure practical application. Moreover, they have introduced simple, effective and immoveable datasets for the proposed scheduling model, and used clustering technique and priority rank on the basis of data dependency. Note that data dependency reduces the time and the cost of accessing data. Khan and Bagchi [29] have introduced a new software architecture by targeting geo-distributed mobile computing paradigm. This architecture enables numerous services to the devices in geo-distributed mobile cloud computing systems and supports the devices to work in a dynamic environment. The main goal is to design a reliable remote procedure called framework to solve some of the issues, such as standardization and bandwidth. They have identified the frequent disconnectivity problems of mobile devices, such as network bandwidth, processing capacity and battery lifetime, in roaming, and used chained stateful servers with portable XDR format to handle this problem. Moreover, a re-transmission facility is provided in the architecture to avoid packet loss in the network. The authentications of the mobile clients are processed through the primary and secondary servers to get higher security.

Sujithra *et al.* [30] have proposed a novel cryptographic technique for storing mobile (*smart phone*) data in the remote cloud without any major performance degradation. In the case of loss or theft of the smartphone, the data may be captured by unauthorized user. Although there is a password into the files and data on the smartphone, the unauthorized user can access it by the process of eavesdropping. Therefore, the authors have introduced a three-tier cryptographic algorithm to overcome the above problem. In the first tier, they have used MD5 algorithm for encryption. It requires a key from the user. In the second tier, the encrypted data is further encrypted with the AES algorithm. In the last tier, they have used ECC or RSA algorithm to perform the last encryption of the resultant encrypted data (key) of the second tier. Finally, they have shared the key to the corresponding user.

Nam and Lysecky [31] have presented a security awareness in multi-objective optimization model for distributed reconfigurable embedded systems. They have designed a model and optimization framework by considering asymmetric multicore processor, single core processor, FPGAs and heterogeneous resources. They have used a dataflow model which integrates power, latency (*computation and communication*) and security level models. They have considered a multi-objective algorithm to improve security and energy. They have evaluated the presented work using an application, called video-based object detection and tracking.

Fog computing is a distributed computing paradigm which acts as a mediator between data centers and devices [32]. It provides various facilities, such as storage, management, control, measurement and networking, to the cloud-based services. As a result, the latency, and bandwidth limitation problems faced by cloud computing can be easily solved using fog computing. However, it faces a lot of security and trust issues due to a large number of end users, which are as follows:

1. In fog computing, each node is connected to all other nodes and they are dependent on each other [33]. If a fog node fails then it may result in a trust problem. Note that the nodes are communicated through the process of message passing.

2. A security issue may arise in fog computing due to topological rebuilding process. When an old fog node quits, and a new fog node is introduced, which may not be able to adopt the existing topology, it results in a topological disorder problem.

3. While collaborating with other fog nodes, if one of the fog nodes is stormed by a malicious attack and the corresponding node gets infected, then the infected node may attack the other running nodes. As a result, it leads to a trust crisis and security issue among the fog nodes.

Zhang *et al.* [34] have categorized security and trust issues in Fog computing into six types, namely attack, authentication and access control, privacy, secure communication, trust and others. They have discussed several open research issues on trusted execution environment, fog orchestration, access control, collusion attack, context-aware security and service trust.

Elmisery *et al.* [35] have offered an algorithm to calculate the approximate interpersonal trust between the cloud and the fog node using middleware agent. Here, the agent generally calculates the trust in a decentralized way and is done with the help of entropy. The user privacy is achieved by implementing the local concealment process. However, the fog nodes contain only global concealment agent. These two concealment processes are hidden from the cloud-based services and released when they are shared. Sun and Zhang [36] have introduced a model based on the characteristics of the human nervous system to address the special security issues in the fog architecture. They have modeled an evolutionary game-based security mechanism. They have introduced a strategy, called credible third-party dynamics penalty, which sets the attack cost spent by the malicious users higher than the profit. As a result, the malicious user is forced to stop attacking the system. They have recommended a credible third party to cope with the bandwidth and the behavior of the user. They have conducted the simulation test using MATLAB.

8.4 Conclusion

In this chapter, we have presented the security issues and challenges of distributed computing security. First, we have discussed the fundamental security issues such as confidentiality, integrity, availability, authentication, access control and many more. Here, we looked at the role of the third party auditor and briefly highlighted the AVIPSA tool. Next, we discussed the advanced areas, namely heterogeneous computing, grid computing, cloud computing, parallel and distributed computing, distributed embedded system computing and fog computing, along with their security issues and challenges. Here, we saw that the authors used well-known security algorithms, such as MD5, ECC, RSA, AES and many more.

References

1. Anita, S. (1997). Security In Distributed Computing: Did You Lock The Door?. IEEE Concurrency, 5(3), 76-77.

2. Chakrabarti, A., Damodaran, A., & Sengupta, S. (2008). Grid computing security: A taxonomy. IEEE Security & Privacy, 6(1).

3. Xiao, Y. (2007). Security in distributed, grid, mobile, and pervasive computing. CRC Press.

4. Bell, D. E., & La Padula, L. J. (1976). Secure computer system: Unified exposition and multics interpretation (No. MTR-2997-REV-1). MITRE CORP BEDFORD MA.

5. Biba, K. J. (1977). Integrity considerations for secure computer systems (No. MTR-3153-REV-1). MITRE CORP BEDFORD MA.

6. Monostori, L. (2014). Cyber-physical production systems: Roots, expectations and R&D challenges. Procedia Cirp, 17, 9-13.

7. ECMA, https://www.ecma-international.org/, Accessed on 5th May 2018.

8. Kumari, K. A., Sadasivam, G. S., & Rohini, L. (2016). An Efficient 3D Elliptic Curve DiffieHellman (ECDH) Based Two-Server Password-Only Authenticated Key Exchange Protocol with Provable Security. IETE Journal of Research, 62(6), 762-773.

9. Shamir, A. (1984, August). Identity-based cryptosystems and signature schemes. In Workshop on the theory and application of cryptographic techniques (pp. 47-53). Springer, Berlin, Heidelberg.

10. Balusamy, B., Venkatakrishna, P., Vaidhyanathan, A., Ravikumar, M., & Munisamy, N. D. (2015). Enhanced security framework for data integrity using third-party auditing in the cloud system. In Artificial Intelligence and Evolutionary Algorithms in Engineering Systems (pp. 25-31). Springer, New Delhi.

11. Reddy, K. S., & Balaraju, M. (2018). Comparative Study On Trustee Of Third Party Auditor To Provide Integrity And Security In Cloud Computing. Materials Today: Proceedings, 5(1), 557-564.

12. Bowers, K. D., Juels, A., & Oprea, A. (2009, November). HAIL: A high-availability and integrity layer for cloud storage. In Proceedings of the 16th ACM conference on Computer and communications security (pp. 187-198). ACM.

13. Li, Y., Gai, K., Qiu, L., Qiu, M., & Zhao, H. (2017). Intelligent cryptography approach for secure distributed big data storage in cloud computing. Information Sciences, 387, 103-115.

14. Amin, R., Kumar, N., Biswas, G. P., Iqbal, R., & Chang, V. (2018). A light weight authentication protocol for IoT-enabled devices in distributed Cloud Computing environment. Future Generation Computer Systems, 78, 1005-1019.

15. AVISPA: HLPSL Tutorial, A Beginner's Guide to Modelling and Analysing Internet Security Protocols, Document Version: 1.1, 2006, http://www.avispa-project.org/, Accessed on 30th April 2018.

16. Gritzalis, D. (1997). A baseline security policy for distributed healthcare information systems. Computers & Security, 16(8), 709-719.

17. Lopriore, L. (2013). Object protection in distributed systems. Journal of Parallel and Distributed Computing, 73(5), 570-579.

18. Malina, L., Dzurenda, P., Hajny, J., & Martinasek, Z. (2018). Secure and efficient two-factor zero-knowledge authentication solution for access control systems. Computers & Security, 77, 500-513.

19. Tsai, J. L., & Lo, N. W. (2015). A privacy-aware authentication scheme for distributed mobile cloud computing services. IEEE systems journal, 9(3), 805-815.

20. Odelu, V., Das, A. K., Kumari, S., Huang, X., & Wazid, M. (2017). Provably secure authenticated key agreement scheme for distributed mobile cloud computing services. Future Generation Computer Systems, 68, 74-88.

21. Xie, T., & Qin, X. (2007). Performance evaluation of a new scheduling algorithm for distributed systems with security heterogeneity. Journal of Parallel and Distributed Computing, 67(10), 1067-1081.

22. Smith, M., Friese, T., Engel, M., & Freisleben, B. (2006). Countering security threats in service-oriented on-demand grid computing using sandboxing and trusted computing techniques. Journal of Parallel and Distributed Computing, 66(9), 1189-1204.

23. Cheng, N., Govindan, K., & Mohapatra, P. (2011). Rendezvous based trust propagation to enhance distributed network security. International Journal of Security and Networks, 6(2-3), 112-122.

24. Khattab, S., Melhem, R., Moss, D., & Znati, T. (2006, April). Honeypot back-propagation for mitigating spoofing distributed denial-of-service attacks. In Parallel and Distributed Processing Symposium, 2006. IPDPS 2006. 20th International (pp. 8-pp). IEEE.

25. Liu, H., Abraham, A., Snel, V., & McLoone, S. (2012). Swarm scheduling approaches for work-flow applications with security constraints in distributed data-intensive computing environments. Information Sciences, 192, 228-243.

26. Colom, J. F., Gil, D., Mora, H., Volckaert, B., & Jimeno, A. M. (2018). Scheduling framework for distributed intrusion detection systems over heterogeneous network architectures. Journal of Network and Computer Applications, 108, 76-86.

27. Jakbik, A., Grzonka, D., & Palmieri, F. (2017). Non-deterministic security driven meta scheduler for distributed cloud organizations. Simulation Modelling Practice and Theory, 76, 67-81.

28. Zeng, L., Veeravalli, B., & Li, X. (2015). SABA: A security-aware and budget-aware workflow scheduling strategy in clouds. Journal of parallel and Distributed computing, 75, 141-151.

29. Khan, A. U., & Bagchi, S. (2018). Software architecture and algorithm for reliable RPC for geo-distributed mobile computing systems. Future Generation Computer Systems, 86, 185-198.

30. Sujithra, M., Padmavathi, G., & Narayanan, S. (2015). Mobile device data security: a cryptographic approach by outsourcing mobile data to cloud. Procedia Computer Science, 47, 480-485.

31. Nam, H., & Lysecky, R. (2018). Security-aware multi-objective optimization of distributed reconfigurable embedded systems. Journal of Parallel and Distributed Computing.

32. Mahmud, R., Kotagiri, R., & Buyya, R. (2018). Fog computing: A taxonomy, survey and future directions. In Internet of everything (pp. 103-130). Springer, Singapore.

33. Nath, S. B., Gupta, H., Chakraborty, S., & Ghosh, S. K. (2018). A Survey of Fog Computing and Communication: Current Researches and Future Directions. arXiv preprint arXiv:1804.04365.

34. Zhang, P., Zhou, M., & Fortino, G. (2018). Security and trust issues in Fog computing: A survey. Future Generation Computer Systems, 88, 16-27.

35. Elmisery, A. M., Rho, S., & Botvich, D. (2016). A fog based middleware for automated compliance with OECD privacy principles in internet of healthcare things. IEEE Access, 4, 8418-8441.

36. Y. Sun and N. Zhang (2017), Fog Computing Security Mechanism Based on Human Nervous System, Saudi Journal of Biological Sciences, Vol. 25, Issue 2.

9

Organization Assignment in Federated Cloud Environments based on Multi-Target Optimization of Security

Abhishek Kumar[1], Palvadi Srinivas Kumar[2], T.V.M. Sairam[3]

[1] Computer Science Department, Aryabhatta College of Engineering & Research Center (ACERC Ajmer), Rajasthan, India

[2] Department of Computer Science and Engineering, Sri Satya Sai University of Technology and Medical Sciences, Sehore, Madhya Pradesh, India

[3] Department of Computing Science and Engineering, Vellore Institute of Technology, Chennai, India
Emails: abhishekkmr812@gmail.com

Abstract

Cloud security alliance permits interconnected cloud computing conditions of various cloud service providers (CSPs) to share their assets and convey more proficient administration execution. In any case, each CSP gives an alternate level of security regarding expense and execution. Rather than expending the entire arrangement of cloud benefits that are required to send an application through a solitary CSP, purchasers could profit by the cloud organization by adaptively allocating the administrations to various CSPs while keeping in mind the end goal to fulfil every one of their administrations' security necessities. In this chapter, we demonstrate the administration task issue in unified cloud situations as a multi-target enhancement issue in light of security. The model enables shoppers to consider an exchange between three security factors- cost, execution, and hazard when appointing their administrations to CSPs. The cost and execution of the conveyed security administrations are assessed utilizing an arrangement of quantitative measurements which we propose. Next we address the issue of utilizing preemptive streamlining technique, the client's needs. Reproductions demonstrated that the model aids in decreasing the rate of security and execution infringement.

Keywords: Cloud computing, cloud service providers

Dac-Nhuong Le et al. (eds.), Cyber Security in Parallel and Distributed Computing, (139–262)
© 2019 Scrivener Publishing LLC

9.1 Introduction

Cloud is a sort of hybrid and appropriated architecture involving user-friendly interactions among related and virtualized PCs, which effectively serves as no less than one bound together data resource from the perspective of organization level planning and verification developed between the expert center and users. Cloud enrollment brings about another chapter of effective and economically feasible new plans for activity and sector openings. The requirement of distributed computation depends in part on prerequisites such as limiting costs, business dexterity, diminishing capital use, and removing a provisioning package. These administrations are referred to as work processes which are an accumulation of undertakings that are handled in view of administration prerequisites. In cloud, administration is given to clients or diverse clients have distinctive QoS requirements. Booking the administrations for various client prerequisites is troublesome. The planning technique ought to be created for numerous work processes with various QoS necessities. Mapping the different work processes to assets with various QoS necessities is NP hard. Booking of work processes is done by various calculations to consider numerous QoS parameters. There are numerous current calculations created for various QoS; for example, economic based, service time based or even both can be considered.

Assuming there are more than two quality of service parameters in a single target work, the issue ends up being all the more troublesome. This chapter focuses on numerous QoS parameters, such as cost and time, in addition to dependability. Whereas different framework utilized MQMCE calculations fulfill the numerous QoS parameters, such as diminishing cost and time, in addition to expanding unwavering quality and accessibility in a solitary target work. Multi-objective optimization is an area of multiple criteria decision-making that is concerned with scientific streamlining issues, including the ability to upgrade more than one target at the same time. For different target issues, the objectives are to point out conflicts and figure out the concurrent progress of every goal. Many, or even most, tried-and-true arranging issues genuinely have unique outcomes.

There are two general ways to deal with different target optimizations. The primary way is to join the independent target limits into a singular cluster limit or migrate all objects to the relevant cluster. As seen in a previous study, affirmation of a lone target is acceptable with systems, for instance, requirement theory, measured total methodology; however, the issue lies in the best possible determination of the weights or utility capacities to portray the chiefs inclinations. Moreover, it can be extremely hard to correctly and precisely select these weights, in spite of somebody being acquainted with the issue space. Aggravating this disadvantage is the fact that scaling is required among goals and little disturbances in the weights can in some cases prompt very extraordinary arrangements. In this previous instance, the requirement is to transfer objects to the basic cluster, an obliging worth has to be set up for every part of these past goals. This will be genuinely subjective. Within the two cases, a accelerated procedure could reestablish an individual plan and then a course of action for game plans that can be dissected for trade-offs. Consequently, a boss often leans towards a game plan with a good course of action that takes into consideration the various targets.

The second methodology is to add the two different modules to a unique module.while making concenation operation the two different node operations were perfomed based on operation the action of the task will be done on the particular server. The certifyable issue GA has a flexible usage and simply designed with userfriendly framework. The task was perfomed on the individuals data. In this implementation at first including more customers seek resources by then investigate the regard uninhibitedly then at the end streamline the variables capably. Finally, convey the results in an outstandingly when appeared differently in relation to past methodologies.

9.2   Background Work Related to Domain

9.2.1   Basics on Cloud computing

The basic idea of dispersed registering is to pass on computational requirements as organizations over the cloud. Buyers are not essential to place assets into a far-reaching PC to lead their business; Rather, they can obtain conveyed processing organizations in light of their solicitations [8]. The basic gear is by and large encouraged in generous DCs using complex virtualization practices to recognize anomalous state preparation, flexibility, furthermore, accessibility. As mentioned above the ease of use of servers depends on the flexibility which doesn't need money for hosting in servers. In this regard it is required to propogating the things and utilizing the things in the propogating way [13].

The servers in the cloud depends on the budget we are investing on the server with 3 different modes i.e.; Paas, Saas, Iaas [17]. For the different services of the cloud there are multiple frameworks which are providing by Amazon such as EC2, S3, etc., EC2 is a service which provides better service with best availability nature with 99.99%. Efficency.the avilbility of server depends on the budget we are investing on server and availability. Mostly such type of servers were mostly used for Private cloud services means it is used in case of specific organizations etc [1, 3-5].

9.2.2   Clouds Which are Federated

In the standard environment of the cloud the cloud service depends on the cloud service provider (CSP). The cloud service provider depends on the service provider and there service. If in the case of single cloud the overall cloud should be stored in the single cloud. The CSP should give good service, flexibility, ease of use, easy access,availability all the time, etc., the output of csp results to good quality of service (QoS). The application programing interphase (API) is the basic fundamental need for the service.

9.2.3   Cloud Resource Management

Resource management defins the minimum number of things that are needed for the development and maintaining the server. Resource management should be in such a way that it should maintain the server capacity if how many requests may have [6-9, 11-15]. Cloud resource approach depends on the modes of the services such as SaaS, PaaS, IaaS.

For the cloud server we are using we can scale up or scale down the services, storage and other based on our requirement. Auto-scaling organizations are given by PaaS providers, for instance, Google App Engine. Auto-scaling for IaaS is mind-boggling by virtue of the nonattendance of and the deficiencies in the available standards. In disseminated registering, paying little respect to whether single or joined, the assortment is capricious and visit, and brought together organization and control may be not ready to give nonstop organizations and helpful confirmations. In this way, the united organization can't reinforce adequate responses for cloud resource organization approaches (See Table 9.1).

Table 9.1   Reasons for the federation of cloud.

Reasons	Description
Sharing	True notion of sharing between parties have different organizational policies and different technical capabilities.
Fault tolerance	Service replication across different providers in case one provider faces an outage the service placed on other providers can be activated as a failsafe.
Improved QoS	Minimizing the latency and delays by serving the request from a more geographically nearest provider or reducing the response time by serving the request from a more capable provider.
Cost efficiency	Can shuffle between providers for a cheaper provider. For example only using spot instance from different providers.
Reducing Service Level Agreement (SLA) Violation	In the case of resource scaling out, cloud service provider (CSP) can reduce it is penalization by renting resources from other federation members.
Provider independence	The consumer would not be dependent upon a single provider.
Contract ending	If a contract with one provider is on the verge of ending, no worry of service blockage.

9.3   Architectural-Based Cloud Security Implementation

There are two kinds of architectural levels in cloud security:

1. Simple Storage Service or Simple Storage Servers

2. Operational server also known as servers for computational purpose

The limit server gives the limit and change. Figure 9.1 demonstrates the working of the general furthest reaches of MQMCE.

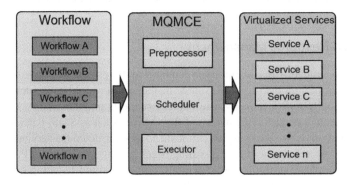

Figure 9.1   Overview of MQMCE.

The number of communication from client to server shown in Figure 9.2.

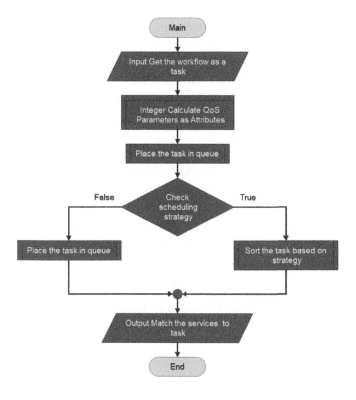

Figure 9.2   MQMCE scheduler process.

Finally the tasks were differentiased into three types namely:

1. Task Assignment.

2. Task scheduling.

3. Task Execution.

Figure 9.2 shows the scheduling stategy.these are the three things necessary for QoS. Pre-processing is a thing which can be perfomed before the task comes into the pictue. Qos is needed for saying the underneath the quality. Task execution explains the step by step procedure for perfoming the task on the framework. Work process $W(i)$ addressed by 5 types of tuples.

$$W(i)[T(ij), (TQ)i, (CQI), RLQi, A(vK)] \tag{9.1}$$

where,

- $T(ij)$ is number of restricted endeavors.

- $TQ(i)$ is the timeshare for work process.

- (CQI) is incurred significant damage sum for work process.

- $A(vK)$ is the general availability of benefits for customer essentials.

- $RLQ(i)$ is the relentless quality amount of application.

Let us consider T as a cluster of undertaking, S be the set of open organizations, MQMCE design the plan of the execution by comparing errand with the sensible organization by succeeding of for diminishing the turn-around time, diminish the holding up time, increment reaction time, increment asset usage and lessen a cost as a solitary target way.

$$TQ(t_i) = Min(T(t_i, R)) + VT(t_i, R) \times \frac{QoS(time) - MinT(w)}{\Sigma VT(t, R)} \qquad (9.2)$$

$$RLQ(t_i) = m_S(t_i) \qquad (9.3)$$

a) The measure of associations in the cloud is limited. What's more, as a rule, the measure of errands holding up which needs to execute, is higher than the association check.

b) The assignments which have a place in the working technique with least time surplus and cost surplus steady quality surplus ought to be masterminded first. The reason takes after the above.

c) The assignment with the smallest covariance ought to be held first.

d) The errand with enduring quality executed by the sorting out figuring. MQMCE algorithm There is two estimations are utilized for mapping associations to client necessities: sorting the task, scheduling system, assume the work strategy as attempts T and assets as an association's S.

e) Extract the data of every undertakings and if any assignment is prepared errand in the all errands and expects that the prepared errand as t.

f) The system is executed to the point that the minute that all the game-plan of masterminded tries is in arranging. Sort `Task(S)`,

9.4 Expected Results of the Process

In our investigations, we restricted the number of assets to 12, as we found that, for these sorts of work process applications, a few assets are not utilized by any stretch of the imagination. Figure 9.3 demonstrates the asset loads when booking the manufactured work process on 12 assets.

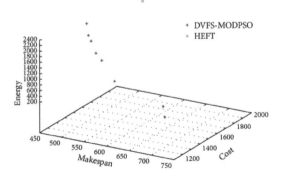

Figure 9.3 Obtained non-dominated solutions for the parallel workflow.

Besides, despite the fact that the number of assets expanded, the aggregate cost and aggregate vitality utilization generally wasn't diminished, as shown in Figure 9.4.

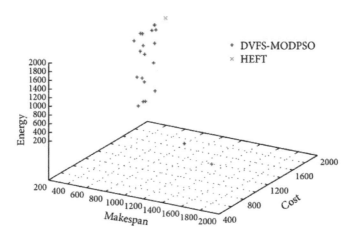

Figure 9.4   Obtained non-dominated solutions for the hybrid workflow.

From this figure, we can see that the QoS measurements diminish right off the bat, as the quantity of assets increases until reaching the number 6. This can be explained by the fact that while expanding the number of assets; there are fewer errands executed in an asset, along these lines, assignments can increase their execution times and the assets have a greater opportunity to downsize their voltages and frequencies which can be extremely viable in diminishing aggregate vitality utilization. In the wake of accomplishing 6 assets, the QoS measurements start to rise; the reason for this is that time executions are commanded by interprocessor interchanges, subsequently diminishing the open doors for downsizing voltages and frequencies of assets. Therefore, the edge quantities of assets that limited the QoS measurements could be acquired.

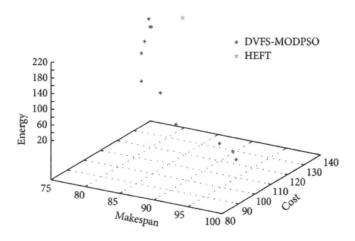

Figure 9.5   Obtained non-dominated solutions for the synthetic workflow.

9.5   Conclusion

Cloud technology has increased the likelihood of providing anything as an association over the Internet. In the interim, different clients benefit from various quality of service necessities. The booking system ought to be made for different types of work with various quality of service prerequisites. The Multi-workflow QoS-Constrained Scheduling strategy accomplishes the client's different QoS targets; for example, execution time, execution cost and, moreover, ceaselessly planing the types of work. In existing tallies, they focus just on cost or time or both, yet not on unchanged quality and accessibility. In this proposed figuring fulfill the various Quality of Service like time, cost and furthermore consistency and transparency. This leads to planning done to a client's paticular QoS prerequisites in a solitary target way. In future work, a combination of MQMCE with MOGA will be used to upgrade the above QoS in light of more client necessities.

References

1. Yu, J., Buyya, R., & Tham, C. K. (2005, July). Cost-based scheduling of scientific workflow applications on utility grids. In e-Science and Grid Computing, 2005. First International Conference on (pp. 8-pp). Ieee.

2. Salehi, M. A., Javadi, B., & Buyya, R. (2012). QoS and preemption aware scheduling in federated and virtualized Grid computing environments. Journal of Parallel and Distributed Computing, 72(2), 231-245.

3. Lin, C., & Lu, S. (2011, July). Scheduling scientific workflows elastically for cloud computing. In Cloud Computing (CLOUD), 2011 IEEE International Conference on (pp. 746-747). IEEE.

4. Liu, K., Jin, H., Chen, J., Liu, X., Yuan, D., & Yang, Y. (2010). A compromised-time-cost scheduling algorithm in swindew-c for instance-intensive cost-constrained workflows on a cloud computing platform. The International Journal of High Performance Computing Applications, 24(4), 445-456.

5. Selvarani, S., & Sadhasivam, G. S. (2010, December). Improved cost-based algorithm for task scheduling in cloud computing. In Computational intelligence and computing research (iccic), 2010 ieee international conference on (pp. 1-5). IEEE.

6. Xu, M., Cui, L., Wang, H., & Bi, Y. (2009, August). A multiple QoS constrained scheduling strategy of multiple workflows for cloud computing. In Parallel and Distributed Processing with Applications, 2009 IEEE International Symposium on (pp. 629-634). IEEE.

7. Parsa, S., & Entezari-Maleki, R. (2009). RASA: A new task scheduling algorithm in grid environment. World Applied sciences journal, 7(Special issue of Computer & IT), 152-160.

8. Salehi, M. A., Javadi, B., & Buyya, R. (2012). QoS and preemption aware scheduling in federated and virtualized Grid computing environments. Journal of Parallel and Distributed Computing, 72(2), 231-245.

9. RajkumarBuyya, CheeShinYeo, Srikumar Venugopal, JamesBroberg, and IvonaBrandic.Cloud Computing forms: Vision, Hype, and Reality for Delivering Computing as the 5th Utility", Future Generation Computer Systems, Elsevier Science, Amsterdam, June 2009, Volume 25, Number 6, pp.599-616.

10. Zhao, H., & Sakellariou, R. (2006, April). Scheduling multiple DAGs onto heterogeneous systems. In Parallel and Distributed Processing Symposium, 2006. IPDPS 2006. 20th International (pp. 14-pp). IEEE.

11. Yu, J., & Buyya, R. (2006, June). A budget constrained scheduling of workflow applications on utility grids using genetic algorithms. In Workflows in Support of Large-Scale Science, 2006. WORKS'06. Workshop on (pp. 1-10). IEEE.

12. Blythe, J., Jain, S., Deelman, E., Gil, Y., Vahi, K., Mandal, A., & Kennedy, K. (2005, May). Task scheduling strategies for workflow-based applications in grids. In Cluster Computing and the Grid, 2005. CCGrid 2005. IEEE International Symposium on (Vol. 2, pp. 759-767). IEEE.

13. Liu, K., Jin, H., Chen, J., Liu, X., Yuan, D., & Yang, Y. (2010). A compromised-time-cost scheduling algorithm in swindew-c for instance-intensive cost-constrained workflows on a cloud computing platform. The International Journal of High Performance Computing Applications, 24(4), 445-456.

14. Salehi, M. A., Javadi, B., & Buyya, R. (2012). QoS and preemption aware scheduling in federated and virtualized Grid computing environments. Journal of Parallel and Distributed Computing, 72(2), 231-245.

15. Lin, C., & Lu, S. (2011, July). Scheduling scientific workflows elastically for cloud computing. In Cloud Computing (CLOUD), 2011 IEEE International Conference on (pp. 746-747). IEEE.

16. Liu, K., Jin, H., Chen, J., Liu, X., Yuan, D., & Yang, Y. (2010). A compromised-time-cost scheduling algorithm in swindew-c for instance-intensive cost-constrained workflows on a cloud computing platform. The International Journal of High Performance Computing Applications, 24(4), 445-456.

17. Selvarani, S., & Sadhasivam, G. S. (2010, December). Improved cost-based algorithm for task scheduling in cloud computing. In Computational intelligence and computing research (iccic), 2010 ieee international conference on (pp. 1-5). IEEE.

18. Xu, M., Cui, L., Wang, H., & Bi, Y. (2009, August). A multiple QoS constrained scheduling strategy of multiple workflows for cloud computing. In Parallel and Distributed Processing with Applications, 2009 IEEE International Symposium on (pp. 629-634). IEEE.

19. Mandal, A., Kennedy, K., Koelbel, C., Marin, G., Mellor-Crummey, J., Liu, B., & Johnsson, L. (2005, July). Scheduling strategies for mapping application workflows onto the grid. In hpdc (pp. 125-134). IEEE.

20. Yu, J., Buyya, R., & Tham, C. K. (2005, July). Cost-based scheduling of scientific workflow applications on utility grids. In e-Science and Grid Computing, 2005. First International Conference on (pp. 8-pp). Ieee.

CHAPTER 10

AN ON-DEMAND AND USER-FRIENDLY FRAMEWORK FOR CLOUD DATA CENTRE NETWORKS WITH PERFORMANCE GUARANTEE

P. Srinivas Kumar[1], Abhishek Kumar[2], Pramod Singh Rathore[2], Jyotir Moy Chatterjee[3]

[1] Department of Computer Science & Engineering, Sri Satyasai University of Technology and Medical Sciences, Sehore, Madhya Pradesh, India

[2] Computer Science Department, Aryabhatta College of Engineering & Research Center (ACERC Ajmer), Rajasthan, India

[3] Asia Pacific University of Technology & Innovation, Kathmandu, Nepal.

Abstract

Distributed computing, a sort of web benefit provisioning model, gives enormous advantages over conventional IT benefit conditions with the assistance of virtualization innovation. As distributed computing isn't a completely developed worldview, it poses numerous open issues to be tended to. Because of its unpredictable and dispersed design, the key research issue in distributed computing is effective asset provisioning. Diagram-based portrayals of complex systems provide less difficult perspectives and chart hypothetical procedures provide easier answers to a great many issues characteristic of systems. Subsequently, this chapter starts with an investigation of chart hypothesis applications in PC systems with a particular spotlight on diagram hypothesis applications in distributed computing. This work focuses on fundamental asset provisioning issues that emerge in distributed computing situations and presents some applied diagram hypothetical recommendations to address these issues.

Keywords: Computer network, cloud computing, graph theory, resource provisioning

Dac-Nhuong Le et al. (eds.), Cyber Security in Parallel and Distributed Computing, (149–262)
© 2019 Scrivener Publishing LLC

10.1   Introduction

This chapter discusses the development of distributed computing. It uses existing appropriated figuring models, such as framework processing and utility registering. Extensive scale preparation and capacity of information are particularly rearranged with the approach of savvy distributed computing arrangements. The Cloud Data Center (CDC) is extremely mind-boggling, with assets circulated all around, prompting a few issues. The creators of Cloud have seen to a few keys and essential distributed computing issues like asset provisioning, security, protection, vitality, and interoperability; however, this rundown isn't restricted. From the point of view of the cloud specialist co-op and cloud benefit customer, these issues paint a diverse picture. While distributed computing provides a chance to relocate the IT business administration on the web, these key issues should be settled before it is acknowledged as an effective business model [1]. This article distinguishes the chances of chart theory-based answers [2] for the asset provisioning issues characteristic in distributed computing. To begin with, it begins with chart hypothesis applications in different areas of PC systems and afterwards investigates its acceptability to address the asset provisioning issues of the cloud. Chart hypothesis is a piece of a discrete arithmetic and valuable structure to show the connection between objects. Diagram hypothesis principally discovers its applications in science, and electrical system.

Computational calculations and booking. Diagram hypothetical systems are increasingly utilized by software engineering applications, particularly in demonstrating and steering systems. Addressing an issue in diagram form can give an alternate perspective and makes an issue substantially easier to understand. It provides apparatuses to take care of an issue and a set of systems for investigating diagrams.

This chapter is divided into two basic parts. The first part gives a review of diagram hypothesis applications in PC systems. As cloud server farm has an arrangement of interconnected frameworks, chart hypothetical arrangements on PC systems can be well-connected on a cloud with reasonable changes to address its issues. The second part gives a review of chart hypothesis applications. The fundamental thought behind this work is to discover the degree of immateriality of chart hypothesis to address asset provisioning issues in the cloud.

10.1.1   Key Research Problems in This Area

A lot of information from individuals about an association is built-in from the beginning to know precisely how secure a system is [2]. The problems associated with disseminated processing are [3]:

A. Cloud securely utilizes data by sending it to the server and storing and retrieving it for the client without any data loss or other problems.

B. Relentless quality in cloud servers experience server downtimes and stoppages.

C. Legitimate concerns remain about the cost of security of single complete with administrative areas.

D. Consistency of numerous headings for identifying and eliminating user requirements.

E. Convinient server management do not authorize users.

A invalid service provider loses everything without proper connection.

10.1.2 Problems with Interoperability

1) Intermediary Layer acts as the virtual gateway for performing the user tasks without installing on the user device (e.g., VM).

2) Open Standard Standardization has a better average response for solving the interpoperability problem.In that case case CSP just remove as the interoperability problem doenn't have in industrial cloud vendors.

3) open API SUn have started late forcing SUN open cloud platform under creattive cloud platform.

4) SaaS and PaaS interoperability while the earlier 1 handles the iaas interoperability.

A meeting of authorities in the field of data mining raised the issue of working up a data mining standard on the cloud, with a particular spotlight on *"the handy utilization of factual calculations, solid creation organization of models and the reconciliation of prescient investigation"* of the different kinds of services such as SaaS, PaaS, and IaaS.

10.2 Difficulties from a Cloud Adoption Perspective

Well-documented security issues, such as data mishaps, phishing, and Black Hat, are veritable risks to an affiliation's data and programming.

- *Multi-Tenancy and Resource Pooling*: These pose new security challenges to disseminated processing.

- *Costing Model*: Cloud clients must consider the tradeoffs among count, correspondence, and joining.

- *Charging Model*: From a cloud provider's perspective, the adaptable resource pool [5] has made the cost examination fundamentally more complicated than in a standard server.

- *Organization Level Agreement*: It is key for buyers to get guarantees from providers on advantageous terms.

10.3 Security and Privacy

Conveyed processing can give unending computing resources on demand in light of its highly flexible nature, which eliminates the necessity for cloud authority associations to prepare on hardware provisioning. Various associations, for instance, Amazon, Google, Microsoft and so on, have stepped up the pace of making disseminated processing structures and enhancing its organizations, providing for a greater number of customers. Zhag et al. investigated the security and assurance stresses of energy dispersed processing structures provided by a number of associations [6]:

1. *Availability*: The goal of openness for disseminated processing systems (*tallying applications and its establishments*) is to ensure its customers can use them at whatever point, at wherever.

2. *Confidentiality*: It infers keeping customers' data secret in the cloud systems.

3. *Data Integrity*: In the cloud structure means to ensure information dependability (*i.e., not lost or balanced by unapproved customers*).

4. *Control*: In the cloud structure means to deal with the use of the system, including the applications, its establishment and the data.

5. *Audit*: Oversees what's happening in the cloud system. Audit-ability could be incorporated as an additional layer in the virtualized movement of system

10.3.1   Resource Provisioning

The authors prescribed that not all standard resource provisioning where resources are provisioned as it is by all accounts, cloud demands capable resource provisioning computations to course of action virtualized advantages for meet SLA necessities. Virtualized server ranches are envisioned to give better organization flexibility, cut down cost, adaptability, better resources utilize and imperativeness capability, yet virtualization is certainly not a straightforward task to do. [7-9] discussed that customers and corporate information harp on pariah structures, it's not possible for anyone to guarantee how anchor the data are. It is slanted to spillage of information and strike. Its a fundamental issue that should for anticipation of by all the cloud master coops to hold their business in the market. They should figure out how to guarantee data and its security. Five most illustrative security and insurance qualities mystery, reliability, openness, obligation, and assurance preservability. [10-13] suggested that the overall public cloud offers pay per use, which can give insignificant exertion options to at this very moment ventures. All things considered, for whole deal use, adventure IT affiliations may be in a perfect circumstance making a capital theory to purchase additional gear and programming. Tries need to coordinate a gain back the first speculation examination to choose if open or private cloud would be cleverer for them. From the perspective of the provider, they are enthused about purchaser faithfulness and making pay out of their organizations. From the perspective of a buyer, they are possessed with monetarily smart game plans. To change these two centers, functional cloud courses of action ought to be made.

10.3.1.1 Unwavering Quality

The authors in [14-18] conveyed that in light of high framework uncommonness and streamed structure, even completely massed data centers are liable to boundless. Denounce tolerant structures ought to be endeavored to address courageous quality concerns. As a result of the reflection thought of cloud condition, there builds up a need to wind up new or extend standard charge tolerant procedures. VM development and server establishment is the major undermining factor for change in accordance with non-essential frustration as they get advantage downtime.

10.3.1.2 Interoperability

The authors in [19-22] suggested that interoperability of heterogeneous cloud is troublesome in perspective of this undeniable hypervisor and VM progresses. The stages in like manner use diverse safety efforts and organization interfaces. Various dealers with different thing estimates pose difficulties for interoperability. Cloud determination will be stopped if there is anything but a better than average technique for planning data and applications transversely over fogs; hereafter a bound together cloud interface and open rules ought to be created Energy.

The authors in [23-26] suggested that growing enthusiasm for computational power prompts setting up tremendous scale server ranches. On the contrary side, the power use of these huge scale server ranches is gigantic. Along these lines, the framework of essentialness capable gear and sharp resource organization frameworks are required. As a result of huge power use, carbon dioxide surge is in like manner [8] all the all the more adding to the nursery affect. From now on the amount of practices ought to be associated with achieve imperativeness efficiencies, for instance, change of use's figurings, essentialness viable gear, and essentialness capable resource organization systems on a virtualized data focus. Out of all these recently made reference to scratch issues, this work gives watchful thought to resource provisioning issue and utilization of graph theory on it. Assets giving in cloud. The term cloud organizations are a general class that encompasses the bundle IT resources gave over the web. The enunciation may in like manner be used to depict capable organizations that assistance the assurance, course of action and advancing organization of various cloud-based resources.

10.3.2   How Do We Define Cloud?

The concept of cloud administrations covers an extensive variety of assets that a specialist organization conveys to clients through the web, which, in this unique circumstance, has comprehensively turned out to be known as the cloud. Qualities of cloud administrations incorporate self-provisioning and versatility; that is, clients can arrange benefits on an on-request basis and close them down when no longer essential. Furthermore, clients normally buy into cloud administrations, paid for in a month to month plan, i.e., instead of paying for programming licenses and supporting server and system framework forthright. In numerous exchanges, this approach makes a cloud-based innovation an operational cost, instead of a capital cost [9]. From an administration stance, cloud-based innovation gives associations a chance to access programming, stockpiling, registering and other IT foundation components without the hassle of keeping up and redesigning them.

10.3.3   Public vs Private Cloud-Based Services

Cloud benefits that a specialist co-op offers to various clients through the web are referred to as open cloud administrations. The SaaS, PaaS and IaaS suppliers may all be said to give open cloud-based administrations.

Private cloud administrations, interestingly, are largely not accessible to an individual or corporate clients or endorsers. Private cloud-based administrations utilize advances and methodologies related to open mists, for example [10], virtualization and self-benefit. Be that as it may, private cloud administrations keep running without someone else's framework and are devoted to inside clients, as opposed to various outside clients.

10.3.3.1 Cloud Services

Cloud administrations includes proficient administrations that empower clients to convey the different kinds of cloud administrations. Counseling firms, framework integrators, and other channel accomplices may offer such administrations to enable their customers to embrace the cloud-based innovation.

In this unique situation, cloud administrations may incorporate any or the majority of the accompanying offerings: cloud-availability appraisal, application legitimization, relocation, organization, customization, private and open cloud combination- half breed mists- and progressing administration. Organizations having considerable authority in cloud administrations have turned into an appealing security highlight for vast IT administrations suppliers- Accenture, IBM, and Wipro, for example- that look for mastery in cloud counseling and arrangement [11].

10.3.3.2   Cloud Services vs Web Services

Cloud administrations are infrequently considered synonymous with web administrations. The two fields, albeit related, are not indistinguishable. A web benefit gives an approach to applications or PCs to speak with each other over the World Wide Web.

10.3.3.3   Efficient Monitoring for Provisioning CDC Resources

In errand, stack adjusting is confounded distributed computing condition because of its unique heterogeneous design, dynamic conduct and asset heterogeneity. Observing assets is required before performing booking and load adjusting.

10.3.3.4   Optimal VM Placement and Migration in CDC for Energy-Efficient Resource Provisioning

Keeping a considerable measure of PMs and VMs running in the server farm devours more vitality, prompting higher working expenses. Thus, recognizing physical machines with slightest load and moving its heap to some other physical machines, and after that, closing them down, spares vitality. Preservation of vitality might be better accomplished through ideal arrangement of VMs on the PMs and performing VM movements, with the goal that vitality utilization might be kept up at an attractive level [12].

10.3.3.5   Appropriate Locating of CDCs and Allocation of CDCs to the Source of Requests

The solicitations for the CDC administrations can originate from various parts of the world. The term wellspring of demands/customers indicates the clients who make solicitations to different cloud server farm administrations. The separation between the cloud server farm and the wellspring of solicitations is a main consideration affecting the nature of administration as far as reaction time and idleness. Cloud server farm designation is one of the significant issues in distributed computing [13]. A proficient designation of cloud server farm to the wellspring of solicitations may enhance the nature of administrations.

10.3.3.6   Clustering Distributed CDCs for Faster Server Provisioning

Cloud server farms are regularly conveyed over the world to expand the accessibility of administrations by remote replication, which is a sort of excess system. It is conveyed basically for fiasco recuperation [14]. Locale astute grouping sent cloud data centers will give fast reactions.

10.3.3.7   Uniform Task of Customers to CDC Servers

In a conveyed cloud server farm condition, stack adjusting systems guide the solicitations to the nearest source or to the source which is most able to serve the demand. Assortment of calculations is utilized to perform stack adjusting. Be that as it may, a trade-off dependably exists between picking the nearest cloud server farm and adjusting the heap of cloud server farm. Now and again a cloud server farm nearer to the client area might be piles of data of the this situation, the solicitations will be directed to a far off cloud server farm which is equipped for taking care of the solicitations. Subsequently, there emerges a need to manage this trade-off while considering both closeness and load in the meantime.

10.3.4   Traffic-Aware VM Migration to Load Balance Cloud Servers

After getting the heap data, the cloud merchant must call upon stack adjusting methodology to disseminate the heap consistently over the hosts in the CDC. It should be possible by relocating a portion of the VMs [15] from overburdened to underloaded hosts to consider just server-side imperatives. System side requirements additionally should be considered to upgrade the execution of CDCs.

10.3.4.1 Graph Theory Applications in Computer Networks

This segment gives a rundown of works connected to diagram hypothesis in different kinds of PC networks. Table 10.1 records a portion of the conceivable chart hypothesis applications in different sorts of systems. Since the cloud is somewhat arranged, this conventional chart of hypothetical procedures can be broken down according to their appropriateness to address asset provisioning issues in cloud and also introduces some calculated recommendations for it.

Table 10.1   Graph theory in computer networks.

Author	Graph theory technique	Issue addressed	Type of network
Wang et al. (2006; Tamura and Nakano, 2011; Tamura et al., 2008)	Graph coloring	Interference reduction, Interference Aware TDMA Link scheduling, Job Scheduling/ Assignment problems, Resource allocation	Wireless networks-Mobile Adhoc Networks and Sensor networks
Alzoubi et al. (2002; Scheideler et al., 2008; Wu and Li, 1999; Erciyes et al., 2007; Liu et al., 2007; Dai and Wu 2004; Muhammad 2007)	Dominating set and Connected dominating set	Routing, fault tolerance, energy- efficiency, delivery delay reduction, connectedness, Virtual backbone construction for efficient routing, overlay network construction, Search space reduction, Clustering nodes	
Kawahigashi et al. (2005)	Random graphs	Connectivity, scalability, Routing, Congestion handling, Modeling the network	
Meghanathan (2012)	Shortest path algorithms	Route computation for communication	
Wang and Li (2006)	Spanner	Minimum power assignment	
Dong et al. (2010)	Topological graph	Network Coverage problem	
Newsome and Song (2003)	Graph embedding	Routing	
Prasanna et al. (2014)	Graph labeling	Fast communication via radio labeling	
Bose et al. (2001)	Gabriel graph, unit graph	Routing with guaranteed delivery	
Xie et al. (2010)	DAG	Workflow modeling, Loop-free routing	
Xie et al. (2014)	DAG	Task Scheudling	Network embedded systems
Nakayama and Koide (2013)	Network flow	Flow optimization	Mesh network
Fatmi and Pan (2014)	Tree	Data center/ network modeling	Datacenter
Bunke et al. (2006)	Graph matching	Abnormal event detection in network by graph comparison	General network
Jana and Naik (2009)	Spanning and minimum spanning tree algorithms	Loop-free connectedness, clustering	
Wang et al. (2012)	Graph traversal	Searching an object	General network query optimization
Maldeniya et al. (2013; Tang et al., 2008)	Graph partitioning	Clustering, faster communication	Real road networks, World Wide Web
Dai et al. (2007; 2009)	Virtualized graph model	Grid service reliability evaluation	Grid
Venugopal and Buyya (2006)	Set covering problem	Mapping applications with data sets	
Xiao and Parhami (2003)	Cayley digraphs	Design of scalable Interconnection networks	
Bentley (1979)	KD-Tree	Multi-dimensional search	Database
Potluri and Singh (2012)	Capacitated dominating set	Minimum capacitated dominating set construction	Wireless networks
Bar-Ilan et al. (1992)	Facility location problem	Locating centers	General facility

10.3.4.2 Graph Theory Applications in Cloud Computing

This segment gives a rundown of works connected to diagram hypothesis in the cloud. Jansen [14] proposed a heuristic in light of hypergraph and its apportioning for advancing logical work process execution. Rodrigues et al. [15] showed the dependability of the cloud administrations. Ballani et al. showed organization, flood, timeout, missing asset, equipment, programming and database disappointments utilizing Markov models [16]., queuing theory, and graph theory. Xie et al. [17] investigated how to ideally convey programming applications on the offered framework in the cloud while limiting the system use. Particularly with regards to portable registering. They outlined and assessed diagram apportioning calculations that allot programming segments to machines in the cloud while limiting the required transfer speed. Popa *et al.* [18] proposed CAM, a cloud stage that gives an imaginative asset scheduler especially intended for facilitating MapReduce applications in the cloud [17].

CAM utilizes a stream organize-based calculation that can enhance MapReduce execution under the determined limitations. Ballani *et al.* [16] proposed enterprise topology graphs (ETG) as the formal model to depict a venture topology. Authors spoke to the physical system of the cloud as a diagram which considers the goal of limiting the blockage. Popa *et al.* [18] showed a registering cloud as a type of processing chart, for example, administrations or licensed is permission on the hub diagram as an edge of the graph. In a like manner, Ballani *et al.* proposed cloud estimation as a course of action of routes in a subchart of cloud [19] to such a degree that each edge contains a predicate that is surveyed to be valid. Finally, they present a course of action to calculate cloud estimations and model-based testing criteria for test cloud applications. Peng *et al.* [5] constructed a strategy for groups of VM [20] by vitality minimization in view of chart hypothesis.

At that point, Joe Wenjie Jiang *et al.* [21] studied a joint tenant (e.g., server or virtual machine) placement and routing problem to minimize traffic costs. Divakaran *et al.* showed formal security for hypervisor-based virtual machine frameworks in view of the chart theory [22]. From Table 10.2 summarizes the basis of graph theory techniques proposed in cloud and indicate the limitations of each approach. In this way, it opens a lot of chances to apply diagrammed hypothetical procedures to address asset provisioning issues in the cloud.

Table 10.2 Grap theory in cloud

Author	Graph theory technique	Issue addressed	Limitation
Çatalyürek *et al.* (2011)	Hypergraph	Modeling cloud network	Scheduling is done in two-phases which increases makespan. If done in single phase, it may minimize the makespan of the workflow. This work didn't consider dynamic workflows whose execution pattern changes over time as well.
Dai *et al.* (2009)	Spanning tree	Cloud service reliability	Cloud service reliability model and evaluation algorithm have not been validated by simulation and real-life data. They have proposed only theoretical model.
Verbelen *et al.* (2013)	Graph partitioning	Software deployment in mobile cloud	This work considered only minimizing the bandwidth between software components. It didn't minimize the execution time of tasks. This work provide scope for integrating their algorithms to address energy consumption objective.
Li *et al.* (2012)	Flow network algorithms -Ford-Fulkerson	Optimizing MapReduce performance in cloud	Validation of min-cost flow model for data and VM placement is to be done in larger real VM clusters.
Binz *et al.* (2012)	Topological graph theory	Topology management in cloud	Enterprise Topology Graph (ETG) is to be built as reusable building blocks to address specific problem domains with broad set of basic operations.
Bansal *et al.* (2011)	Graph mapping	Congestion minimization in cloud network	Only mapping of two classes of workloads, namely depth-d trees and complete graph are considered.
Chan *et al.* (2009)	Predicate-based graph	Modeling and Testing cloud	This model supports only stateless atomic operations expressed in context free grammar. Some other attributes such as scalability, exception handling, dynamic binding, service interactions can also be considered to make the model valuable.
Peng *et al.* (2015)	Graph cut theory	Virtual Machine (VM) clustering in cloud	Time taken for VM clustering is a valuable parameter, which is not mentioned. Not mentioned the applicability of
Zegzhda and Nikolsky (2014)	Graph model	Security model for VM hypervisor in cloud	hypervisor security model on the specific type of hypervisor architectures, namely hosted or bare-metal.

Following are some proposals for applying diagram hypothesis for asset provisioning issues in distributed computing. CAM uses a stream-based estimation that can upgrade MapReduce execution under the decided upon restrictions. Ballani *et al.* [19] proposed enterprise topology graphs (ETG) as the formal model to delineate a wander topology. Guo *et al.* [20] addressed the physical arrangement of the cloud as an outline considering the objective of constraining blockage. Jiang et al. [21] enlisted the cloud as a kind of outline; a handling resource [23], for instance, in which organizations or authorized developers get rights based on a chart focal point and use the preferred standpoint as a predicate associated with each edge in the outline. Similarly, they propose exhibiting cloud estimation as a strategy of courses in a subgraph of the cloud to such an extent that the point of each edge contains a predicate that is assessed to be valid. Finally, they describe an approach of tallies with cloud calculations and model-based testing criteria for test cloud applications. Chen and Shen [24] constructed a VM bundle technique by imperative minimization taking into account the diagram theory. After that they modified the sending of VM parties into most advanced VM parties. Lewis [25] described a formal approach to security for virtual machine hypervisors combined structures from the perspective of the graph theory. From Table 10.2, it is seen that it is not that much important work on applications to aggregate and most of this has not regarded its[26] application resource provisioning. Thusly, it opens a huge amount of opportunities to apply chart theoretical methods to address resource provisioning issues in the cloud.

The going with region shows some connected [27] recommendations for applying graph theory for resource provisioning issues in conveyed registering.

10.4 Conclusion and Future Work

In this analysis, an investigation was done on the utilization of diagram hypothesis ideas in PC systems and its acceptability to address asset provisioning issues in the cloud. In the future, we might want to extend the research to include other areas of distributed computing.

References

1. Dillon, T., Wu, C., & Chang, E. (2010). Cloud computing: issues and challenges. In Advanced Information Networking and Applications (AINA), 2010 24th IEEE International Conference on (pp. 27-33). IEEE.

2. Shankarwar, M. U., & Pawar, A. V. (2015). Security and privacy in cloud computing: A survey. In Proceedings of the 3rd International Conference on Frontiers of Intelligent Computing: Theory and Applications (FICTA) 2014 (pp. 1-11). Springer, Cham.

3. Yang, J., & Chen, Z. (2010). Cloud computing research and security issues. In Computational intelligence and software engineering (CiSE), 2010 international conference on (pp. 1-3). IEEE.

4. Zhang, S., Zhang, S., Chen, X., & Huo, X. (2010). Cloud computing research and development trend. In Future Networks, 2010. ICFN'10. Second International Conference on (pp. 93-97). IEEE.

5. Peng, J., Zhang, X., Lei, Z., Zhang, B., Zhang, W., & Li, Q. (2009). Comparison of several cloud computing platforms. In Information Science and Engineering (ISISE), 2009 Second International Symposium on (pp. 23-27). IEEE.

6. Zhang, S., Chen, X., Zhang, S., & Huo, X. (2010). The comparison between cloud computing and grid computing. In Computer Application and System Modeling (ICCASM), 2010 International Conference on (Vol. 11, pp. V11-72). IEEE.

7. Alabbadi, M. M. (2011). Cloud computing for education and learning: Education and learning as a service (ELaaS). In Interactive Collaborative Learning (ICL), 2011 14th International Conference on (pp. 589-594). IEEE.

8. Kalagiakos, P., & Karampelas, P. (2011). Cloud computing learning. In Application of Information and Communication Technologies (AICT), 2011 5th International Conference on (pp. 1-4). IEEE.

9. Mell, P., & Grance, T. (2011). The NIST definition of cloud computing.

10. Sun Microsystems Unveils Open Cloud Platform, [Online]. Available: http://www.sun.com/aboutsun/pr/2009-03/sunflash.20090318.2.xml,2 009.

11. Dawoud, W., Takouna, I., & Meinel, C. (2010). Infrastructure as a service security: Challenges and solutions. In Informatics and Systems (INFOS), 2010 the 7th International Conference on (pp. 1-8). IEEE.

12. Itani, W., Kayssi, A., & Chehab, A. (2009). Privacy as a service: Privacy-aware data storage and processing in cloud computing architectures. In Dependable, Autonomic and Secure Computing, 2009. DASC'09. Eighth IEEE International Conference on (pp. 711-716). IEEE.

13. Grobauer, B., Walloschek, T., & Stocker, E. (2011). Understanding cloud computing vulnerabilities. IEEE Security & Privacy, 9(2), 50-57.

14. Jansen, W. A. (2011). Cloud hooks: Security and privacy issues in cloud computing. In System Sciences (HICSS), 2011 44th Hawaii International Conference on (pp. 1-10). IEEE.

15. Rodrigues, H., Santos, J. R., Turner, Y., Soares, P., & Guedes, D. O. (2011). Gatekeeper: Supporting Bandwidth Guarantees for Multi-tenant Datacenter Networks. In WIOV.

16. Ballani, H., Costa, P., Karagiannis, T., & Rowstron, A. (2011). Towards predictable datacenter networks. In ACM SIGCOMM Computer Communication Review (Vol. 41, No. 4, pp. 242-253). ACM.

17. Xie, D., Ding, N., Hu, Y. C., & Kompella, R. (2012). The only constant is change: incorporating time-varying network reservations in data centers. ACM SIGCOMM Computer Communication Review, 42(4), 199-210.

18. Popa, L., Yalagandula, P., Banerjee, S., Mogul, J. C., Turner, Y., & Santos, J. R. (2013). Elasticswitch: Practical work-conserving bandwidth guarantees for cloud computing. In ACM SIGCOMM Computer Communication Review (Vol. 43, No. 4, pp. 351-362). ACM.

19. Ballani, H., Jang, K., Karagiannis, T., Kim, C., Gunawardena, D., & O'Shea, G. (2013). Chatty Tenants and the Cloud Network Sharing Problem. In Nsdi (Vol. 13, pp. 171-184).

20. Guo, C., Lu, G., Wang, H. J., Yang, S., Kong, C., Sun, P., ... & Zhang, Y. (2010). Secondnet: a data center network virtualization architecture with bandwidth guarantees. In Proceedings of the 6th International COnference (p. 15). ACM.

21. Jiang, J. W., Lan, T., Ha, S., Chen, M., & Chiang, M. (2012). Joint VM placement and routing for data center traffic engineering. In INFOCOM, 2012 Proceedings IEEE (pp. 2876-2880). IEEE.

22. Divakaran, D. M., Le, T. N., & Gurusamy, M. (2014). An online integrated resource allocator for guaranteed performance in data centers. IEEE Transactions on Parallel and Distributed Systems, 25(6), 1382-1392.

23. Wang, M., Meng, X., & Zhang, L. (2011). Consolidating virtual machines with dynamic bandwidth demand in data centers. In INFOCOM, 2011 Proceedings IEEE (pp. 71-75). IEEE.

24. Chen, L., & Shen, H. (2014). Consolidating complementary VMs with spatial/temporal-awareness in cloud datacenters. In INFOCOM, 2014 Proceedings IEEE (pp. 1033-1041). IEEE.

25. Lewis, H. R. (1983). Computers and Intractability. A Guide to the Theory of NP-Completeness.

26. Hoffman, K. L., & Ralphs, T. K. (2013). Integer and combinatorial optimization. In Encyclopedia of Operations Research and Management Science (pp. 771-783). Springer US.

27. Hopcroft, J. E., & Karp, R. M. (1973). An $n^{5/2}$ algorithm for maximum matchings in bipartite graphs. SIAM Journal on computing, 2(4), 225-231.

28. Kumar, P. S. An Approach towards economical hierarchic Search over Encrypted Cloud. DOI: http://dx.doi.org/10.15439/2017KM38 ACSIS, Vol. 14, pages 125129 (2017)

29. Le, D. N., Kumar, R., Nguyen, G. N., & Chatterjee, J. M. (2018). Cloud Computing and Virtualization. John Wiley & Sons.

30. Venkatesh, A., & Eastaff, M. S. (2018). A Study of Data Storage Security Issues in Cloud Computing.

PART III

Cybersecurity Applications and Case Studies

CHAPTER 11

CYBERSECURITY AT ORGANIZATIONS: A DELPHI PILOT STUDY OF EXPERT OPINIONS ABOUT POLICY AND PROTECTION

Holly Reitmeier[1], Jolanda Tromp[2], John Bottoms[3]

[1] State University of New York at Oswego, Oswego, New York, USA

[2] Duy Tan University, Danang, Vietnam

[3] FirstStar Systems, USA

Emails: holly.reitmeier@oswego.edu, jolanda.tromp@duytan.edu.vn, john@firststarsystems.com

Abstract

Cybercrime is becoming more and more prevalent in today's society and attackers are continuously discovering new methods to hack systems. Monitoring and maintaining computer network security is a complex process that presents unique challenges. If security is not constantly strengthened, cyber threats have the potential to affect millions of systems, all of which share similar vulnerabilities.

The issues surrounding cybercrimes are exponentially different than other types of crimes carried out in society. Therefore, federal law enforcement agencies are faced with the difficult task of generating new approaches to combat them. This chapter explores the concepts of cybercrime and cybersecurity, presents the statistical impact it is having on organizations, and demonstrates the importance of an effective cybersecurity policy manual. It also describes the methodology used for this research, analyzes the data provided by expert testimonials, and introduces the development of a new innovative technological method (Blockchain) to minimize the risk of the cyber world. The analyses cover the extent to which Blockchain applications could help strengthen cybersecurity and protect organizations against cyberattacks, and what kind of research directions are essential for the future.

Keywords: Cybercrime, cybersecurity, cyber world, Blockchain, Delphi

Dac-Nhuong Le et al. (eds.), Cyber Security in Parallel and Distributed Computing, (163–262) © 2019 Scrivener Publishing LLC

11.1   Introduction

This chapter is focused on cybersecurity policies and prevention. Cybercrimes are becoming more prevalent in cyberspace, and organizations must take proactive measures to minimize the risk of a breach of sensitive information. In order to elicit the perceptions of cyber-security experts and gain an understanding of the industry, we collected their expert opinion about Blockchain technology and the extent to which may be a viable cybersecurity method of protection. The data was collected using the Delphi Method, which is a systematic interactive way of gaining opinions/forecasts from a panel of independent experts. The anonymous gathering of information through surveys across a diverse population provided a more accurate and meaningful response. The Delphi method was especially useful in reducing ambiguity through the use of experts and analyzing relevant and timely issues facing the cybersecurity industry. In essence, the Delphi method has potential to provide both rigor and relevance to. The methods of analysis will be explained in-depth in the context of the report and detailed descriptions of the research tools can be found in [16]. The potential contribution of this work is that it is a pilot study, with guidelines to perform a similar study on a much larger scale.

11.1.1   What is Cybercrime?

Computers and Information Technology (IT) first emerged into the business world in the 1960s. Since then, cybercrime has steadily been on the rise. The cyber-security community and major news media have largely concurred on the prediction that, "Cybercrime damages will cost the world $6 trillion annually by 2021. This is up from $3 trillion just a year ago [12]." The rapidly evolving phenomenon, the Internet of Things (IoT) has dramatically changed the way business is conducted. Organizations must acknowledge that the use of these new digital assets and devices for accessing them present ongoing threats to the security of critical business information. "Internet of Things refers to things having identities and virtual personalities operating in smart spaces using intelligent interfaces to connect and communicate within social, environmental, and user contexts [15]." The IoT is widening the sphere of physical security of cybersecurity, as smart devices connected to business systems via the Internet may be located outside of established secure perimeters. As a result, this is a leading factor as to why corporate data is becoming increasingly harder to protect. IoT devices may be hacked remotely or through hardware changes if the device can be accessed, such as is the case for large exterior complexes such as chemical plants. Both the operating system and application vulnerabilities leave organizations open to attack.

Organizations today are able to spread information quicker than ever before. However, the tools and platforms that allow companies to instantaneously connect internally and externally with customers, suppliers and partners are subject to the serious risk of exposure. Not only does cybercrime significantly hinder business functions, but it can also result in serious reputational damage when not handled properly. According to a report by Forbes Insight and IBM, 46 percent of companies have suffered reputational damage due to a data breach [10]. The stakes are clearly high when it comes to data breaches.

Therefore, it is vital to the success of an organization that it takes a proactive stance when it comes to preventing and combating cybercrime.

11.1.2   What is Cybersecurity?

In recent years, researchers and cybersecurity experts have really begun to warn organizations that the rise in cybercrime will fundamentally change businesses policies. Ginni Rometty, IBM's chairman, president and CEO, stated that: *"Cybercrime is the greatest threat to every company in the world."* What will it take for organizations to maximize the benefits of the various technologies available to them, while deriving methods to mitigate cybercrime risks?

Cybersecurity refers to the ability to control access to networked systems and the information they contain [2]. When controls are effective, networks are considered to be reliable and credible digital infrastructures. However, when cybersecurity controls are nonexistent, incomplete, or flawed, hackers have the ability to illegally gain access to sensitive information. There are four different perimeters around a secure data asset [16]

1. Physical security: area in which all critical cyber assets reside.

2. System perimeter: necessary safeguards at the entrance of a privately owned network to secure it from hackers.

3. Access perimeter: all of the points of physical ingress or egress through the nearest physically secured *"four-wall"* boundary.

4. Electromagnetic spectrum: protected global connectivity and movement within cyberspace.

Data is the heart and soul of an organization. Protecting and securing sensitive information is incredibly challenging, and when it comes to doing so, hackers have the advantage. It only takes one successful hacker to create huge damage, while it takes an organization a substantial amount of resources to prevent being hacked.

11.1.3   Purpose of This Cybersecurity Pilot Study

The aim of this Cybersecurity Pilot Study is to understand cybersecurity professional's perceptions, opinions, beliefs and attitudes regarding the effectiveness of cybersecurity initiatives. Particular focus is on control of information and the prevention of unauthorized access at organizations. The purpose of the literature review portion is to present the statistical impact cybercrime is having on organizations, and demonstrate the importance of an effective cybersecurity policy manual. Economic crime has gone digital, and when incidents occur, they attract major media attention. For example, the recent Google Docs phishing attack exposed how hackers could use Google Docs to obtain customer's personal information. The research conducted in this case study is performed using the Delphi method, which will be explained later in the report, to determine the extent in which Blockchain applications would help to strengthen cybersecurity and protect organizations against these types of cyberattacks.

11.1.4   Methods of Cybersecurity Professionals

It is simply not possible for organizations to prevent all forms of attacks posed by hackers because of the complexity of security challenges. However, it is the responsibility of security professionals to take adequate measures to plan and prepare for cyberattack crises.

The literature on the subject points out that too few individuals are employed at organizations to prevent and handle breaches [12]. What separates a secure organization from the rest is one that has developed methods to detect attacks as soon as they happen, and one that has the ability to respond immediately to any incidents that occur. Cybersecurity is explained in terms of three triads that describe the objectives of security professionals and their methods [2]. They are:

1. Prevent, Detect and Respond

2. People, Processes, Technology

3. Confidentiality, Integrity, Availability

These nine terms represent the common goals and methods common to both technology management and to cybersecurity management as a specialized field.

IT is continuously changing and hackers are constantly discovering new ways to breach defenses and exploit system weaknesses. Therefore, organizations need to understand that they have to allocate personnel to stay informed of each new potential weakness. Federal governments and business entities are having an incredibly difficult time combating economic crime. Therefore, regulations and standards need to be created and modified to assist with this. It is virtually impossible for an organization to completely eliminate the vulnerabilities contained in its computer system. Therefore, they need to have an effective cybersecurity policy manual and incident response plan in place. However, it has been found that many are substantially underprepared to handle cyber threats. Additionally, studies show that many CEOs are not even fully aware of the International Organization for Standardization (ISO) policies and standards that pertain to their organizations and are crucial for effective IT governance [11].

11.2   Shocking Statistics of Cybercrime

Business organizations are being exposed to more threats than ever and the data shows that cybercrimes are continuing to intensify. The 2016 Internet Crime Report [8] produced by the United States Federal Bureau of Investigation presents valuable information for organizations and cybersecurity professionals. Additionally, the 2016 Global Economic Crime Survey prepared by PricewaterhouseCoopers [3] highlights the fundamentally flawed incident response plans the majority of business organizations currently have in place.

11.2.1   Role of the Internet Crime Complaint Center

Internet crime is unlike any other type of crime and presents unique challenges that are difficult to detect and deter. Therefore, the Internet Crime Complaint Center (IC3), a multi-agency task force, was developed. It includes members from the Federal Bureau of Investigation (FBI), the National White Collar Crime Center (NW3C), and the Bureau of Justice Assistance (BJA). The IC3's role in helping to prevent Internet crime is best described as an intricate puzzle. Each piece is intended to fit together to effectively address the serious risk cybercrime poses to global organizations [8]. The nine pieces of the puzzle are:

1. Detection: evidence of fraud, presence of fraud, attempt of fraud.

2. Complaint: statement of distress filed by either actual victim or third party.

3. Mitigation: effort to stop fraud, reduce losses, and attempt recovery.

4. Liaison: collaboration with all levels of Law Enforcement.

5. Analysis: data that has been assessed or is available for assessment.

6. Deterrence: action or events to prevent fraud through instilling fear of consequences.

7. Investigation: gathering of information and conducting interviews to obtain evidence.

8. Prosecution: legal action brought against the perpetrator.

9. Prevention: measures to stop fraud from occurring.

In 2016, there were nearly 300,000 complaints received that included over $1.33 billion in losses [8]. Comparing these figures to those from the 2015 report [8], these figures have increased by approximately five-percent from just the previous year. Additionally, the IC3's Public Value Graph (see Figure 11.1) illustrates that losses in monetary amounts were under $1 billion just seven years ago in 2010, and now have surpassed that mark. The bar graph shows the total number of complaints and overall victim losses for the years 2010 to 2016.

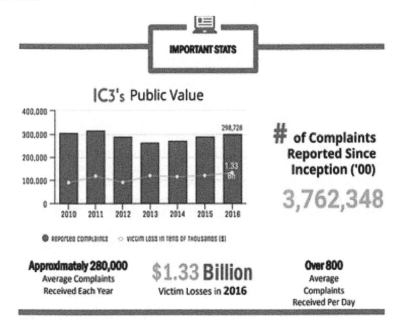

Figure 11.1   Internet Crime Complaint Center(IC3) public value of overall statistics 2016.

Subsequent sections of the IC3 report more specifically pertain to the purpose of this study, as they present the figures in terms of the various cybercrime types. In 2016, there were nearly 3,500 reports of a corporate data breach, almost 20,000 phishing scheme reports, and approximately 2,000 issues regarding currency exchange [8]. In comparison, there were almost 1,000 more corporate data breach reports in 2016 than in 2015 [8]. These numbers corroborate the findings that cybercrime is continuing to escalate.

11.2.2   2016 Global Economic Crime Survey Report

The 2016 Global Economic Crime Survey, conducted by PricewaterhouseCoopers (PwC) [3], interviewed over 6,000 organizations in 115 countries. Despite the marginal decline in economic crime reported overall, it found that Internet crime and the financial cost associated with each fraud is on the rise. With 14 percent of respondents experiencing losses of more than $1 million in the last two years, chief financial officers (CFOs) need to be key players in addressing the problem [3]. The survey points out that too many business organizations are not adequately bridging the gap between IT teams and senior management in terms of effective information exchange. This significantly interferes with planning for and handling of corporate data breaches. A strong relationship between the cybersecurity team at a company and the CFO and other key players is crucial when serious issues such as potential security breaches are on the table. One of the problems is that these two departments speak very different "languages" and have different skill sets, which creates disconnect. It is one thing to listen to the advice from the cybersecurity experts, but that advice is only useful to the extent it is acted upon. Financial information has shifted to digital channels such as Excel spreadsheets, the Cloud, servers that allow people to share docs, non-encrypted email exchange and mobile transactions. Therefore, the two departments are now highly interdependent on one another. The devastating figures presented by the IC3 and PwC clearly indicate that measures need to be taken to correct this issue. The question is, why do so many organizations have disconnects between the responsible parties and how can that be resolved?

11.2.3   Inadequate Preparation at Organizations

Hackers are constantly developing new ways to initiate data leaks. Furthermore, they are able to remain on a company's network for an extended duration without it ever being detected. Given the increase in the complexity of cybercrime, leaks are no longer solely an IT problem. Addressing the importance of cybersecurity starts with upper-level management at an organization and flows downward. However, the figures presented above show that more must be done to harness the intelligence of network and information security. Stakeholders must be assured of strong relationships between departments, in which information can be exchanged for investigative and intelligence purposes. Many organizations are not taking appropriate proactive measure against cyber threats. The PwC Global Economic Crime Survey found that less than 50 percent of executives even request information about their organization's level of readiness to combat cybercrime [3]. It is very despairing for stakeholders of companies to be presented with this type of information when huge corporate security breaches are frequently occurring and the literature seems to indicate that not enough is being done to prevent future ones in response. It is a serious problem when only 37 percent of the organizations that responded to the PwC Global Economic Crime Survey reported to having a cybersecurity policy in place [3]. If 63 percent of organizations report that they do not have a cybersecurity policy in place, this raises some serious question as to their level of awareness and ability to respond to the cyber risks at stake.

11.2.4   Organizations: Be Aware, Be Secure

There has to be a fundamental understanding that while using the Internet to conduct business activities has an abundance of advantages, there are serious cyber risks associated with it. It is critical that organizations consider incident handling as a core component of cyber defense, and ensure that all the necessary parties involved in protecting critical online assets are working together effectively. The reason why society knows about the cybercrime figures referenced in Sections 11.2.2 and 11.2.3 is that they were detected and investigated. Prevention measures taken by the IC3 will only help organizations strengthen their defenses if executives are willing to learn from previous experience. Ultimately, the aim of Internet Crime reports and surveys like the ones mentioned above is to improve the overall security of organizations and avoid costly and damaging incidents in the future. There is no universal solution to combating cybersecurity. However, policies and recommendation guidelines have been established to help reduce criminal activity in cyberspace. For an organization, the extent in which cybersecurity policies are effective revolves entirely around its Cybersecurity policy manual. The question is what policies have been set forth and what information should be included in the policy manual? The following section contains this vital information.

11.3   Cybersecurity Policies for Organizations

The statistics that have been reviewed regarding cybercrime referenced in the previous section show that cybersecurity policy initiatives are pertinent to protect sensitive data at an organization. The word "Policy" is applied to a variety of situations that concern cybersecurity. It has been used to refer to laws and regulations concerning information distribution but is generally associated with maintaining cybersecurity in today's business world [2].

The standards and guidelines set forth by the International Organization for Standardization (ISO) in ISO 27001, strongly recommend that all private and public sector organizations develop, implement, and maintain an appropriate cybersecurity defense policy. The purpose of the ISO is to create documents that provide requirements, specifications, guidelines or characteristics that can be used consistently to ensure that materials, products, processes and services are fit for their purpose [11]. ISO 27001 provides best practice recommendations on information security management for use by those responsible for initiating, implementing or maintaining information security management systems [11]. For an organization, its cybersecurity strategy entirely revolves around a policy manual. The purpose of a written security policy is to ensure that information is accessible only to those authorized to have access. Determining what information needs to be included in the policy manual and how it is validated should be a top priority of every organization. By creating a multi-layered plan to prevent cyberattacks, an organization can substantially reduce its risk exposure.

The Cybersecurity Policy Handbook [6], developed by Accellis Technology Group, suggests a four-layer framework for an organization's policy manual. The Accellis security team has ten years of expertise with developing these types of written policies, and has created plans for the U.S. government, law firms and region-specific companies.

Their four-feature approach is in the areas of:

1. Application Security: controls within line-of-business applications such as practice management, time and billing, and accounting.

2. IT Infrastructure Security: actual devices and activities that protect against all points of ingress into the business environment.

3. Education & Policy Enforcement: the creation of policies and plans that constitute the cybersecurity framework, such as written security policies, incident response plan, and disaster recovery plan.

4. Continual Assessment & Improvement: ongoing process for the testing. of new attack vectors, the effectiveness of the CS framework, and testing for weaknesses in the approach.

Creating and carrying out policies at an organization is highly complex. Therefore, there are people and companies that solely focus on selling handbooks that contain policy manual templates and consulting services to assist with this. At the basic level, these handbooks recommend defining the goals of the organization, defining roles and responsibilities, establishing an incident response plan, and developing and conducting continual education to reinforce the policies and controls in place [6]. See [16] to review a sample Applications Security and Operations Cybersecurity policy manual table of contents template.

There are various elements that must be adequately addressed for an organization to effectively prevent and protect itself from cyber threats. These include components such as:

- Creating a systems access policy.

- Vendor compliance policy.

- System management policy.

- Email policy.

- Encryption policy.

- Password management policy.

- Backup and recovery policy.

In today's business world that has been radically transformed by the IoT, it is vital to an organization's security over cyberspace to develop an effective policy manual. Organizations should consider hiring cybersecurity experts to offer their recommendations on how to create or improve their policy manuals. Whether the policy manual is written internally or with the help of a third party security company it should be written with several goals. These include:

- It should define how information (*and knowledge*) security is accomplished within a company or enterprise, including who is responsible for what.

- It should inform the users that they are a part of that secure system, and that involves responsibilities on their part.

- The policy manual should clearly describe what is expected of them, and the consequences of allowing breaches to the system.

It is also important to stress that while the goals include halting the leak of information it also includes the forensic of incidents. This means that when a security leak occurs one of the products of the investigation is a set of "Principled documents" that form the basis for litigation. All forms of personal information and Internet correspondence, both internally and externally, have value. These need to be protected, just like every other asset at the organization [11]. In the survey conducted by PwC, it was found that 40 percent of CEOs are not worried about cybersecurity, and do not even consider security standards in these areas [3]. When it comes to the cybersecurity of an organization, there is no such thing as being over-prepared.

11.3.1   Classification of Cybersecurity at an Organization

It is helpful to consider the three-levels of security classification regarding the evaluation and monitoring of a system. There are levels A, B and C, of security evaluations. These levels are identified by their security as follows:

- A: System that is mathematically proven to be secure.

- B: System that has been evaluated for secure policies against best practices.

- C: System that has not been evaluated.

It is inexcusable for any company or organization in today's society to fall under a C classification with all the information available regarding the seriousness of cybercrime [5].

11.3.2   Pyramid of Cybersecurity

Cybersecurity can be represented as a pyramid illustrating the persistent problems with IT security, data protection and the complexity of the industry. See Figure 11.2 showing the IT and non-IT environment. At the base of pyramid are the Three Laws of Information and Communication Technology (ICT) Security, the middle sections are Testing source code and creating a Reliable login, and at the top is Critical Data.

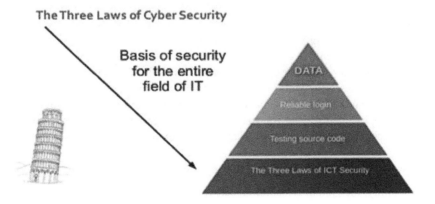

Figure 11.2   Pyramid of cybersecurity 2017.

The Three Laws of Cybersecurity set rules to prevent editing files by a virus or hackers. The Three Laws of Cybersecurity, are [13]:

1. The checksum of the file on the user's device must always be the same as the checksum of the same file by the author SW,

2. The network shall enable checksum verification,

3. The operating system has to verify the checksum before starting an application and before using unverified system files,

It is important to note that these are not exact laws in which the functions and procedures can be described accurately. The three laws are general rules which help to achieve cybersecurity and secure financial transactions over the Internet. To properly place secure perimeters around an operating system, all subordinates within an organization are expected to modify their behavior in compliance with the policies. Analysis of the source code and strategically setting policies for user login will help protect individuals from hacking into the system. Given that this information is out there and there are tools available to assist with this, it is concerning that 63 percent of organizations still do not have cybersecurity policies. Organizations must take advantage of the technologies and tools available to them to achieve secure networks, such as blockchain technology explained in the next section.

11.4 Blockchain Technology

Blockchain technology is not yet mainstream, but is a distributed database that is used to maintain a continuously growing list of records. These individual records are referred to as blocks, since as more records are produced it starts to form a chain. It is anticipated to be a feasible tech solution that has the ability to transform the business ecosystem. In 2009, Bitcoin, the most prolific worldwide cryptocurrency system was introduced. It allows users to exchange currency through a decentralized system in which the integrity of the information is protected and there is complete transparency, operating independently of a central bank [18]. The emergence of Blockchain is considered to be the most applicable component to come out of the introduction of bitcoin.

The underlying concept of Blockchain is that a digital, distributed transaction ledger that continuously updates its extensive list of data records, will improve the cybersecurity at organizations. Blockchain is managed by a peer-to-peer network collectively adhering to a protocol for validating newblocks. All the data for each bitcoin transaction is grouped into a block that is then placed on the blockchain ledger. Each block is time stamped, encrypted, validated anonymously, recorded by multiple computers and permanent [1]. It can be used to trace the entire path of a particular bitcoin since it was created. Once information is entered into a blockchain, that information can never be altered or erased, which ensures its integrity and transparency. Every computer in the system has a copy of the blockchain so that users can quickly detect any discrepancy, or signs of hacking attempts.

The key characteristics of Blockchain are:

- Reliability: the system can continuously run without the fear of shutdown or interruption.

- Transparency: all transactions are visible to every member of the blockchain.

- Immutability: it is incredibly difficult to make changes to the blockchain without detection.

- Irrevocability: nature of the blockchain makes it possible for all transactions to be binding and final.

In the past few years, interest in Blockchain technology has substantially increased among researchers, investors and the cybersecurity community. According to Gartner's technology hype cycle graph, Blockchain technology is at the peak of inflated expectations [1].

With all the hype surrounding Blockchain, millions of dollars are being spent by organizations around the globe in order to experiment and test this new technology. Capital investments into organizations providing Blockchain services have soared from only $3 million in 2011 to nearly $500 million today [18]. The ever growing excitement of Blockchain applications is a direct result of the various benefits associated with it. Some of these include decentralized trust (*governing principle of the network*), transparency (*distributed network architecture*) and efficiency (*transactions can be completed without an intermediary*). Its flexible design gives it the ability to not only impact financial services, but other industries as well. A few of the primary potential industries include Smart Contracts, Automated Auditing, and the one featured in this pilot study, Cybersecurity. Cybersecurity has the ability to be vastly strengthened because the nature of the Blockchain enables the immediate detection of data manipulation and verifies the integrity of IT systems [18]. However, the literature indicated that there is currently still a lot of uncertainty associated with the technology. Challenges such as regulation and scalability are currently holding up mainstream adoption. Cybersecurity experts are currently in the process of performing the necessary research and testing protocols so that Blockchain is ready for adoption in the near future. Just imagine the endless possibilities that could result from this technology if organizations choose to incorporate it into the cybersecurity policy manuals.

11.5   Research Methodology

This section describes the pilot study proposition, research perspective, study design, and procedures followed. The focus of this research is to interpret and analytically disclose the opinions of the human subjects regarding the cybersecurity industry.

The focus is on expert opinions regarding cybersecurity and the future of Blockchain applications. The primary goal is to develop a survey instrument that captures the testimonials of expert insight on cybersecurity policies and initiatives. Based on the literature review portion of this Cybersecurity Pilot Study, it was identified that Blockchain technology has the potential to be a viable solution for improving the security of the Internet. But do the experts agree with this proposition? The respondents to the survey were recruited from various backgrounds, with highly regarded credentials. The researcher sought to discover the extent to which experts believed Blockchain applications could revolutionize the business world.

11.5.1   Quantitative and Qualitative Data Collection

The research conducted for the study reported here, applies a Delphi style survey. A combination of quantitative scales and qualitative open-ended responses are utilized to collect the information. The primary information is obtained through the survey that is distributed to elicit the anonymous opinions of the experts, after requesting permission to do so (see [16] for details of the survey). The secondary information is compiled from a variety of sources including literature, journals and articles. The Delphi Method originated in the American business community, and has since been widely accepted globally in many industry sectors, including health care, defense, business, education, and information technology [17].

One of the unique values of the Delphi method is that it facilitates a dialog that shares knowledge and considerations among participants as they work toward a collaborative response to the questions. The net result of this is that that in the majority of uses of the Delphi method, the group's results are better than that of most participants. Therefore, it is believed that as knowledge engineering systems evolve which are used in global collaborative projects, the Delphi style survey will play an important part of working towards consensus. It is used in this Cybersecurity Pilot Study to collect and analyze the opinions of cybersecurity experts using a survey interspersed with feedback.

11.5.2 Design of the Study

The design of this study is based on deductive reasoning. A deductive approach is applied, which means that a hypothesis was developed from an existing proposition and then a research strategy was designed to test the hypothesis. Information is collected from cybersecurity experts regarding the following hypothesis:

H1: *Use of Blockchain applications will help to strengthen cybersecurity and protect organizations against cyberattacks.*

The target population of this research is comprised of cybersecurity experts, which is defined as individuals who work(ed) in cybersecurity or a related IT field for a minimum of three years. This information was part of the Screening Questions, as listed in Expert Respondent Sufficiency & Qualifications [16]. The sample consists of professionals that work in the industry with jobs relating to cybersecurity policy initiatives, and developing technologies available to protect organizations from cyber threats. Ten potential respondents recruited from networking events, university connections and LinkedIn were approached via a carefully crafted email (see [16] for the survey invitation). At the end of the invitation, participants who wished to have the results of the pilot study shared with them had the option to provide an email address. Prior to participating in the Online Cybersecurity Survey, the eight respondents were ensured of their complete anonymity.

11.5.3 Selection of the Delphi Method

The original Delphi method was developed by Norman Dalkey of the RAND Corporation in the 1950s for a U.S. sponsored military project. The method entails a group of experts who anonymously reply to surveys and subsequently receive feedback in the form of a statistical representation of the "group response," after which the process repeats itself [17]. The goal for this pilot study is to reduce the range of responses and arrive at something closer to expert consensus. It was chosen as an effective methodology for this query of experts and stakeholders because of the following reasons:

1. The complexity of the cybersecurity industry requires knowledge from individuals who understand the different economic, social and political implications.

2. It does not require the experts to be present physically, which would have been impractical for this study.

3. The Delphi method size requirements are modest. The method can be utilized with as few as two respondents [14].

The sample size of this study contained eight expert respondents. Within the scope and time limitations of this pilot study, this sample size was considered commendable. It is important to bear in mind that this is a pilot study; the aim is to test the format and provide the feasibility for a much larger version.

11.5.4   Procedure of Utilization of the Delphi Method

The procedure undertaken by the researcher involves three general steps:

1. Brainstorming of related questions.

2. Distributing a series of quantitative and qualitative questions to qualified experts.

3. Narrowing in on the scope and quality of the responses by means of second round open-ended questions.

The Delphi survey was created using the Google Forms online survey application that is directly accessible via a one-click link shared by email. This has the added benefit that the data is directly collected and stored in digital format, thus saving the researcher time and resources. Furthermore, it reduces the chance of transcription errors that are common to collecting data with the traditional pen and paper format. Another added benefit of this delivery method is that the respondents were free to use whichever response platform was most convenient, such as laptop, IPad/tablet or smartphone, thus reducing obstacles in answering the survey. And finally, another advantage of this is that it speeds up the turnaround time between iterations of the Delphi Method. This is an important success factor in terms of scalability of this study, i.e., so that the study can be performed with a larger number of respondents in the future.

In terms of this pilot study, the purpose of the first round is to gain a basic understanding of the respondents' perceptions of cybersecurity practices at organizations through multiple quantitative and qualitative survey questions. In the second round, each Delphi participant receives another series of open-ended questions to respond to and is asked to review the key findings summarized by the researcher based on the information provided in the first round. After this is completed, a general inductive approach is taken by the researcher. The objectives are to establish a link between the research proposition and the findings provided by the respondents, and to condense the qualitative data into a brief summary format. In response to this challenge, the researcher categorizes and codes the qualitative data to hopefully achieve the desired level of consensus. It is important to note that theoretically the Delphi process can be continuously iterated when it is determined that additional iterations beyond three are needed or valuable, given more time and resources. For this study, three rounds was considered sufficient for a pilot, as proof-of concept, given the time limitations. The specific information pertaining to each round is provided below.

11.5.5   Delphi Activities (Iteration Rounds) of This Pilot Study

1. **Round #1: Initial collection**. The first survey is distributed on the same day that the expert agrees to serve as a respondent to the survey. The survey contains a series of varying complexity level questions, each corresponding to the research proposition. The researcher requests permission to collect richer data by means of second round open-ended follow-up questions. After gaining approval, this leads to the second round of the Delphi Method.

2. **Round #2: Richer data collection.** The Delphi study is flexible in its design, which allows for the second round of follow-up questions in this study. The goal is to understand the importance and narrow in on the scope of the responses based on the

differing perspectives. The respondents are asked to review the key findings compiled by the researcher based upon the responses provided in Round #1. As a result, this provides more concise and richer data because of an additional iteration and participant response revision due to feedback.

3. **Final analysis**. The goal of the final phase of the study is to reach a consensus and analyze the major themes to see as to whether or not the research proposition in this pilot study is validated. The researcher uses information provided in both the first and second round to categorize, code, and identify themes among the responses.

This Cybersecurity Pilot Study [16], is exploratory in nature. It aims to explore a topic in which the research proposition being evaluated has no clear, single set of outcomes. It involves incrementally developing deep understanding through the collection of multiple types of data about the complex issues organizations in today's business world face with regards to cybercrime.

The aim of the research is the inquiry into cybersecurity experts' perceptions, opinions, beliefs and attitudes towards organizations implementing Blockchain technology to prevent against cyberattacks. There is a combination of questions, some using the Likert Scale. The rating scale (1-5) ranged from 1- Strongly Disagree to 5- Strongly Agree. The remaining questions solicit a series of short responses (Refer to [16]). Through the series of open-ended questions, the experts focused on several different topics: Cybersecurity Governing Policies, Cybersecurity at Organizations, Cybercrime Prevention, and Blockchain Technology.

11.6   Results of the Cybersecurity Delphi Study

The results were collected over a period of four weeks, and vary in type with each round. The first round was primarily focused on individual brainstorming function as the experts responded to a series of questions regarding cybersecurity policy and protection. After gaining a fundamental understanding of the expert opinions, the researcher carefully organized the data to look for patterns in the responses. In the second round, findings from the first round were presented to the respondents and they were asked to open-endedly respond to four key insights. The final round required the researcher to code and categorize the textual responses to the open-ended questions, ultimately looking for common themes.

11.6.1   Results from Round One

In the first round, eight experts responded to a series of quantitative and qualitative questions relating to cybersecurity and Blockchain technology. Four distinct findings emerged from the experts in round one. These are described below.

11.6.1.1   *Expert Level Awareness of Cybersecurity*
Of those responding, 62.5% were "Very aware" of cybersecurity and the remaining 37.5% are *Moderately aware* (see Figure 11.3). Therefore, the researcher sought to investigate what each expert would recommend in regards to creating a cybersecurity policy.

11.6.1.2   *Cyber Incident Response Plan*
As shown in Figure 11.4, 75% of 8 respondents either "Strongly Disagree" or "Disagree" that the majority of organizations have an effective cyber incident response plan.

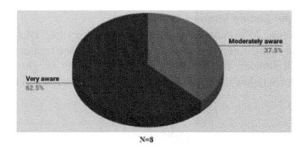

Figure 11.3   Expert-level-awareness of cybersecurity.

Therefore, the researcher sought to determine what each expert believes should be done to correct this.

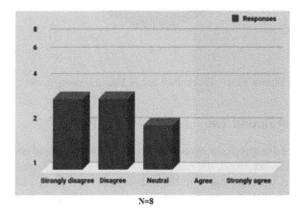

Figure 11.4   Effective incident response plans.

11.6.1.3 Federal Government Cybersecurity Initiatives

As shown in Figure 11.5, 62.5% of respondents believe that federal governments need to improve cybersecurity initiatives. Therefore, the researcher sought to examine what measures governments should take in this regard.

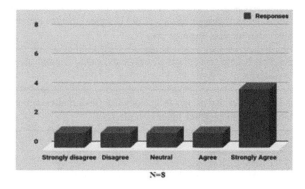

Figure 11.5   Federal Government cybersecurity initiatives.

11.6.1.4 *Blockchain Secure Internet Transactions*

Of those responding, 75% believe that using a technology like Blockchain is a more secure method than using intermediaries to complete Internet transactions (See Figure 11.6 below and in Reitmeier, 2017). Therefore, the researcher sought to determine why Blockchain would or wouldn't help to strengthen an organization's cybersecurity policy manual.

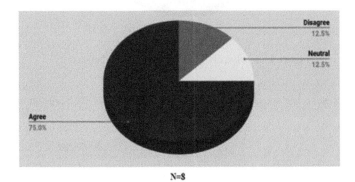

N=8

Figure 11.6   Blockchain secure Internet transactions.

11.6.2   Results of Round Two

Six of the initial round respondents agreed to participate in the second round of open-ended questions. For the second round, the major findings from Round 1 were summarized and the four key insights were presented to the respondents (see Table 11.6.2). The findings were revealed via email to the six respondents who agreed to review the updated survey statements.

Table 11.1   The major findings from Round 1 and the 4 key insights presented to the respondents.

Key Findings from Round 1
• 62.5% of respondents are "Very aware" of cyber-security and the remaining 37.5% are "Moderately aware."
• 75% of respondents either "Strongly Disagree" or "Disagree" that the majority of organizations have an effective cyber incident response plan.
• 62.5% of respondents believe that federal governments need to improve their cyber-security initiatives.
• 75% of respondents believe that using a technology like Blockchain is a more secure method than using intermediaries to complete Internet transactions.

The top four findings were structured into open-ended questions for the experts to respond to (see Reitmeier, 2017, for more detail) and these were sent to them via email. The experts were asked to be as specific as possible answering the following questions:

1. If you were (or are) in charge of setting the cybersecurity policy at the organization you work for, what would you do, specifically, to reduce the vulnerability of online data and protect data integrity?

2. What should be done to encourage and/or mandate organizations to create and implement an effective cyber incident response plan?

3. What measures should be taken by federal governments to improve cybersecurity standards?

4. Please provide justification as to why you believe or do not believe the use of Blockchain applications would help to strengthen the cybersecurity policy manual at an organization.

The feedback from the open-ended questions are noted in Tables 11.2 to 11.5. Responses were categorized and coded so that the major themes could be identified and categorized by the researcher. The full expert responses used for the inductive analysis are provided in the appendices of [16].

Table 11.2   Cybersecurity policy within an organization.

Categories	*Question 1:* If you were (or are) in charge of setting the cyber-security policy at the organization you work for, what would you do, specifically, to reduce the vulnerability of online data and protect data integrity?			
	Policy Manual	*Stricter Enforcement*	*Training*	*Continuous Monitoring*
Codes	Determine requirements Survey commercial vendors Implement and revise	Validate existing policies Require employees to modify behavior to conform Hire the right people	Practice & Test Educate all employees	System management Emergency response plan

Table 11.3   Effective cyber incident response plan mandates.

Categories	*Question 2:* What should be done to encourage and/or mandate organizations to create and implement an effective cyber incident response plan?			
	Increase awareness	*Legislation*	*Professional Associations*	*Demonstrate Benefits*
Codes	Global wide effort Relevant literature and figures	New assessment model Collaborative effort CSIRT @ every company	Key external stakeholders Law enforcement	Reduced costs Aggregate risk analysis

Table 11.4 Federal Government cybersecurity initiatives.

Categories	*Question 3:* **What measures should be taken by federal governments to improve cyber-security standards?**			
	New communication protocols	*Enhancement of Software Platforms*	*Collaboration*	*Modification*
Codes	Cryptographic technology Encryption technology	Modify and adapt SPIRNet for use within the U.S Blockchain	Department of Homeland Security	Internet commerce Future systems (VR)

Table 11.5 Blockchain technology for secure Internet transactions.

Categories	*Question 4:* **Please provide justification as to why you believe or do not believe the use of Blockchain applications would help to strengthen the cyber-security policy manual at an organization.**			
	Efficiency	*Adaptability*	*Challenges*	*Uncertainty*
Codes	No single point of failure Quick detection of hack attempts Transparency	Has potential to improve every industry	High implementation Costs Internet is currently not compatible	No standard of crypto currency More research & testing

After the findings were categorized and coded, it allowed for the themes to be identified. The following section highlights the key themes that emerged from the research.

Question #1: *If you were in charge of setting the cybersecurity policy for an organization, what would you do, specifically, to reduce the vulnerability of online data and protect data integrity?*

Five different themes developed from this question, and are presented below:

1. Determine specific cybersecurity requirements pertaining to that organization. Then survey commercial policy handbook vendors to implement policy.

2. Strong authentication and verification of all executives, employees, and stakeholders is critical. This includes a multifactor and multilayer authentication.

3. It is important that continuous monitoring occurs on a daily basis. This includes system management (ensuring firewall protection) and hardware and software be up-to-date and reviewed.

4. Allocate the necessary resources for creating and validating a cybersecurity policy manual and hire the right people to enforce it.

5. Training on security fundamentals.

Question #2: *What should be done to encourage and/or mandate organizations to create and implement an effective cyber incident response plan?*

Three themes developed from this question, and are presented below:

1. Maintain relationships with key external stakeholders, such as law enforcement.

2. Enact legislation that establishes a new cybersecurity assessment model.

3. It needs to be a cooperative effort to increase the awareness of the seriousness of cybercrimes and the potential they have to impact organizations.

Survey respondent Z is quoted as saying "Professional associations should be encouraged to develop approaches that are beneficial to all members. This would reduce costs and aggregate risk analysis across the group."

Question #3: *What measures should be taken by federal governments to improve cybersecurity standards?*

Three themes developed in response from the experts in relation to the third question.

1. New communication protocols need to be established and enforced such as encryption of communication devices.

2. The SIPRnet approach needs to be modified and adapted for use within the U.S.

3. Current commerce functions and future systems (such as VR) need to be modified by government authorities.

Two of the experts summarized the scope of the question copiously. The responses mentioned that the Department of Homeland Security has to become more involved and should be encouraged to work with industry to develop robust approaches to corporate security.

Question #4: *Please provide justification as to why you believe or do not believe the use of Blockchain applications would help to strengthen the cybersecurity policy at an organization.*

Five major themes developed from the final question.

1. Blockchain technologies do have many important advantages. These include efficiency, transparency, reliability, and quick detection of attempted hack.

2. More research and testing is necessary.

3. The existing Internet commerce mechanism will need either major modification or replacement to take advantage of Blockchain features.

4. Currently, there are no standards for cryptocurrency.

5. Governments worldwide are in the process of creating regulatory policies for the application.

11.6.3 Discussion and Limitations Based on the Results

Reflecting on these themes, it is evident that measures need to be taken to address the fact that many organizations in today's business world are vastly underprepared when it comes to their cybersecurity policy manual. Cybersecurity policies has been sidelined in the rush to gain market share and a competitive advantage over rival organizations. As noted above, it needs to be a cooperative effort to increase the awareness of the seriousness of cybercrimes and the potential they have to impact organizations.

The most common finding in this pilot study is that the majority of organizations do not have an effective cybersecurity policy manual to refer to. Furthermore, the ones that do, are not properly enforcing it. It is crucial that an organization monitors its network security system on a daily basis, to not only reduce vulnerabilities, but also to minimize the threat of being hacked. Ongoing cybersecurity training is vital to the success of an organization. It allows for all employees to be up-to-date on the current policies in place and their role and responsibility if an incident does occur.

There is a tendency at organizations to suggest solutions that do not consider the complexity of the issue of cybercrime in its entirety. However, technologies are emerging that have a broad potential future and which do not require organizations to build their own system in house, such as Blockchain. Blockchain applications offer interesting tools to facilitate the process of transferring sensitive information. The Blockchain design is cryptographically secure, extremely hard to change without permitted access, and updatable only with consensus among all parties in the chain. Those organizations that have realized they need to take their cybersecurity policies seriously have taken an interest in the technology and are investing in its R&D and testing. Blockchain may possess the ability to radically change and enhance the business world at a fundamental level because every 10 minutes, all transactions conducted are verified, cleared, and stored in a block.

There were some issues raised in this pilot study that were unexpected. Although this pilot study reached its aims, there were some unavoidable limitations and shortcomings. First of all, the research was conducted in a one month period. Four weeks is not enough to do justice to and fully understand cybersecurity experts' perceptions, opinions, beliefs and attitudes towards cybersecurity policies at organizations. The results would have been more conclusive if the method had been applied over a longer timeframe.

Second, the sample size of the respondent group is small. Only eight respondents might not represent the majority of the experts in the cybersecurity industry. Additionally, the first round initial survey, was designed to gain a basic understanding of cybersecurity policies and protection mechanisms at organizations. However, it seemed to not provide enough evidence of the impact cybercrimes are having on organizations. In addition to this, two of the eight respondents dropped out after the first round. This hinders the Delphi Method process, and reduced the sample size of the second round collection of richer data. The intent of the Delphi Method is to properly analyze the experts' statements regarding cybersecurity. Therefore, the results are more reliable if multiple iterations are able to be conducted. Despite these limitations, the pilot study research presented key insights into cybersecurity policies and the future of Blockchain technology. A recommendation for a larger scale study of this type is to offer an incentive for respondents who are willing and able to participate in every iteration round. Doing so, would potentially attract the attention of more experts and increase the likelihood that respondents don't drop out.

Ultimately, there are new technologies becoming available that offer the ability to strengthen the cybersecurity policy at an organization. The experts in this study concurred that, currently, too many organizations do not have an effective or validated cybersecurity policy manual. Data is the critical dependency of organizations worldwide, and protecting the integrity of it needs to be of top priority. There is no advantage to waiting for the government to take action, it is the responsibility of the organization to strengthen its cybersecurity policies. There is an endless stream of practical benefits that flow from Blockchain technologies. However, it is important to be aware of the challenges and risks involved in adopting the technology.

11.7 Conclusion

Cybercrime has become a global phenomenon, and as shown, is immensely disruptive to the world of business. As the Internet of Things, Virtual and Augmented reality, and Artificial Intelligence continue to advance, organizations will be fundamentally revolutionized. They will face serious challenges while trying to adapt and optimize the integration of these new technologies with employees, and the cybersecurity policies at the organization. According to Edward Hess, a top authority on organizational and human high performance at the University of Virginia, organizations are expected to undergo critical transformations [9]. They are in four areas:

- *Technology*: integrating new technologies and data analytics into every part of the organization.

- *Systematic Redesign*: creating a technology-enabled Human Excellence System.

- *Leadership*: developing a new model of how to lead and manage others.

- *Human Resource*: transforming human resources functions into human development functions.

As a result, measures must be taken to overcome the challenges the transformations present and keep the threats they pose to the cybersecurity at the organization to the bare minimum. Hess stated that, "The Smart Machine Age will be more disruptive than the Industrial Revolution because of its scope, scale, and the power and quality of what the technology can do (Hess, 2017)." Consequently, to protect e-commerce transactions and increase economic gains through cyberspace, continuous research is needed to control and prevent the associated cybercrime activities. The literature in the cybersecurity field is aimed at discovering the truth behind cybercrime, exposing the alarming statistics, and pointing out that many organizations have fundamentally flawed cybersecurity policy manuals or do not have one at all.

11.7.1 The Literature in the Field

The fact that the information is becoming mainstream regarding cybersecurity is highly beneficial, as it is intended to alert organizations around the globe that each and every day they face the serious risk of being targeted. It is vital to the success of an organization to fully accept the fact that cybercrime is on the rise, and therefore they must utilize the prevention technologies available to assist with maintaining security and protecting its systems and sensitive information. The extent to which a cybersecurity policy is effective at an organization, is highly dependent on its cybersecurity policy manual. If an organization adopts the policy manual suggestions and protection technologies available to it, it is offered the opportunity to stay a step ahead of an attack.

There is a severe lack of monitoring mechanisms and skilled personnel in cybersecurity in the business world. Additionally, rapidly evolving environment complexity, continuous new threats and exploits, and not properly allocating budgets for security initiatives is addressed in the literature [7]. The skills required for hackers to gain access to sensitive information is diminishing, and the hacking techniques are increasing in sophistication. As a result, everyone, from your next-door neighbor to an individual or organization located across the globe, is a potential threat. It is incredibly difficult to understand the complexity of the cybersecurity industry, as cybercrimes are continuing to escalate and new methods are constantly being developed. Therefore, staying up-to-date on the research and testing pertaining to cyber threats is crucial.

11.7.2   Next Steps for Future Research

There is a high anticipation that Blockchain technology will have the ability to transform the way business is conducted. Arvind Krishna, senior vice president at IBM Research, stated that [4]:

"Over the past two decades, the internet has revolutionized many aspects of business and society. Blockchain could bring to those processes the openness and efficiency we have come to expect in the internet era."

Further investigation of Blockchain is necessary, but there is a growing expectancy that it will be extremely beneficial for organizations. It is predicted to considerably reduce the probability of an organization being hacked, and substantially improve its cybersecurity. Although predictions can be made, there is no way of knowing exactly what the future has in store for the cybersecurity industry. One can only hope that within the next few years, technologies such as Blockchain will undergo the necessary testing phases, and that organizations begin to implement strong encryption technology to secure their data.

Future research is highly recommended to address the question: "How can cybersecurity experts piece together the information and technologies available to make cyberspace more secure than it is currently?" Pilot studies like the one in this account do not have the ability to eliminate cybercrime, nor can they guarantee cybersecurity for all. However, continuous research in the field will inspire innovative and progressive thinking, and create a world where more organizations are conscious of their cybersecurity initiatives. When society as a whole becomes willing and enabled to take adequate action against cyber threats, the Internet will become a better and safer place to conduct business.

References

1. Bashir, I. (2017). Mastering Blockchain. Packt Publishing Ltd.

2. Bayuk, J. L., Healey, J., Rohmeyer, P., Sachs, M. H., Schmidt, J., & Weiss, J. (2012). cybersecurity policy guidebook. John Wiley & Sons.

3. Burg, D., McConkey, K., & Amra, J. (2016). Cybercrime. Price water house Coopers. Document retrieved (15 July 2017), from: http://www.pwc.com/gx/en/services/advisory/forensics/economic-crime-survey/cybercrime.html

4. Bishop, N. (2017). Enterprise Intelligence Brief: Three Experts Discuss Blockchain in Cybersecurity. Security Intelligence. Document retrieved (15 July 2017), from: https://securityintelligence.com/enterprise-intelligence-brief-three-experts-discuss-blockchain-in-cybersecurity/

5. Bottoms, J. (2017). CEO of FirstStar Systems Shares Insights on Cybersecurity. Telephone Interview (22 May 2017), conducted by Holly Reitmeier.

6. Cybersecurity Policy Handbook, Accellis. (2016). Valley View, Ohio: Accellis Technology Group, Inc. Document retrieved (19 July 2017), from: https://accellis.com/wp-content/uploads/Cybersecurity-Policy-Handbook.pdf

7. Effiong, N. (2013). Cyber-Crime Control, Prevention and Investigation (Ph.D.). CranfieldUniversity- College of Management and Technology. Document retrieved (14 July 2017) from: http://www.academia.edu/4259163/Cyber_Crime_Research_Proposal

8. Federal Bureau of Investigation Internet Crime Complaint Center. (2015, 2016). Internet Crime Report. FBI IC3. Document retrieved (24 May 2017), from: https://pdf.ic3.gov/2015_IC3Report.pdf

9. Hess, E. D. (2017). Surving the Digital Age: 4 Corporate Transformations. Darden Ideas to Action.

10. How does a data breach affect your business' reputation?. (2016). [Blog] Cyber Experts Blog at National Cybersecurity Institute (NCI).

11. Moeller, R. R. (2013). Executive's guide to IT governance: improving systems processes with service management, COBIT, and ITIL. John Wiley & Sons.

12. Morgan, S. (2017). Top 5 cybersecurity facts, figures and statistics for 2017.

13. Napravnik, J. (2016). The Three Laws of cybersecurity and SOFTWARE Control Server - Cybersecurity Excellence Awards.

14. Okoli, C., & Pawlowski, S. (2004). The Delphi method as a research tool: an example, design considerations and applications. Information & Management, 42(1), 15-29.

15. Saadeh, M., Sleit, A., Qatawneh, M., & Almobaideen, W. (2016, August). Authentication techniques for the internet of things: A survey. In Cybersecurity and Cyberforensics Conference (CCC), 2016 (pp. 28-34). IEEE.

16. Reitmeier, H. (2017). Cyber-Security at Organizations: a Delphi Pilot Study of Expert Perceptions about Policy & Protection, HCI Project Report, State University of New York, NY, USA.

17. Skulmoski , G. J., Hartman, F. T., & Krahn, J. (2007). The Delphi Method for Graduate Research. Journal of Information Technology Education, 6, 2-12. ¡Document retrieved from: http://www.fepto.com/wp-content/uploads/Delphi-method-for-Graduate-research.pdf¿

18. Wilson Jr, J. D. (2017). Creating Strategic Value Through Financial Technology. John Wiley & Sons.

CHAPTER 12

SMARTPHONE TRIGGERED SECURITY CHALLENGES - ISSUES, CASE STUDIES AND PREVENTION

Saurabh Ranjan Srivastava[1], Sachin Dube[1], Gulshan Shrivastava[2], Kavita Sharma[3]

[1] Malviya National Institute of Technology, Jaipur, India.

[2] National Institute of Technology, Patna, India

[3] National Institute of Technology, Kurukshetra, India

Email: gulshanstv@gmail.com

Abstract

In today's rapidly evolving technological scenario, mobile computing devices are always at an increased risk of being attacked and exploited. Mobile security challenges comprise threats such as physical theft or accidental loss of the device, mobile malware, unauthorized access, mobile-based fraud, espionage and much more. Here, phone calls, SMS, Bluetooth, and web access act as potential security threat channels to a smartphone device. This chapter classifies the various types and details of security threats to a smartphone device. Further case studies about exploits of smartphones by terrorists, user data theft and Smartphone-based fraud are discussed. The chapter concludes with the preventive measures that can be used to improve the security of mobile devices and user data, keeping them from being exploited and attacked.

Keywords: Smartphones, mobile computing, trigger

Dac-Nhuong Le et al. (eds.), *Cyber Security in Parallel and Distributed Computing*, (187–262)
© 2019 Scrivener Publishing LLC

12.1   Introduction

Today mobile phones have almost replaced personal computers and laptops by merging a combination of technologies, to fulfil the basic computational and communication necessities of today's generation. The evolution of mobile devices with constantly growing processing power and larger storage memories, matching the potential of desktop computers can be considered as a true revolution in the world of information technology. This revolutionary growth in complexity and portability has placed mobile devices as extensions of our personality. These extensions store and manage our contacts, messages and emails, track our current location, remember our preferences and appointments and even follow us everywhere.

Due to their portability and versatility of applications, smartphones and tablets are fast becoming the preferred tools for internet browsing, online transactions, auctions and purchases and so on. The ease of interface access for every mobile application has rendered skills and underlying technologies as almost meaningless constraints for the use of these devices. Similar to every technology that created a radical impact in the life of the common masses, and was later exploited for misuse, mobile technology is also under the same spectrum. As the evolution of mobile phones constructed a thriving path for the growth of civil society, it also raised possibilities for cyber criminals to exploit mobile devices as a channel or medium of attack and exploitation.

12.2   Classification of Mobile Security Threats

The wide range of security threats that can attack or exploit mobile computing devices can be categorized into the following categories, which are discussed ahead in this section.

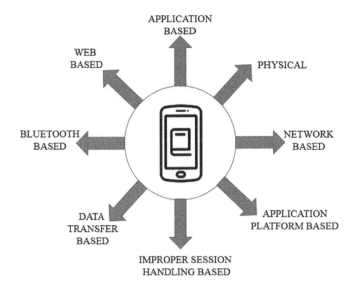

Figure 12.1   Classification of mobile security threats.

12.2.1 Physical Threats

Mobile devices have become common for computing and communication requirements among people because of their portable dimensions and high computing potentials. Due to these features, these gadgets are valuable and demand precautions for their physical security. In addition to the costly hardware that can be resold on the black market of gadgets, the information relevant to a user or organization can also be highly sensitive and worth far more. Due to these factors, stolen and lost mobile devices are one of those most frightening security threats. In terms of threats to physical security, mobile devices such as smartphones, tablets, PDAs, etc., without authentication check mechanisms like passwords, screen locks or fingerprint scans are at high risk [1, 2]. Such undefended devices always remain vulnerable to loss and compromise the stored sensitive information. In the worst case of loss or theft, the hackers or cyber criminals find one mechanism or another to bypass any form of authentication check and gain access to user sensitive information stored on the device.

12.2.2 Web-Based Threats

Modern mobile devices are designed to be persistently connected to WiFi networks or packet data internet to access web services. A major threat to the security of mobile devices arises through these networks. To execute web-based threats on a mobile device, its user must be prompted to visit an unsafe site and naively trigger a malicious process. Web-based threats can be classified into the following classes.

Applications such as email, messaging, Facebook, WhatsApp and Twitter are commonly used to spread links of malicious websites designed to scam the receiving users. Such scams are known as phishing scams [2]. Upon accessing such websites, the user is tricked into feeding his sensitive information like passwords or account numbers, which is captured by criminals for later exploit. The next level of possible threat connected to malicious links is drive-by downloads which automatically download a malicious application on user's mobile device as they access such links. Some of such malicious apps prompt the user to click on or open the download for execution, while other apps can even start automatic execution. Another class of threats is known as browser exploit that utilizes the vulnerabilities present in the web browser installed on the mobile device or applications connected to it such as PDF file reader, flash player, shockwave file player or even image viewer, to damage the normal functionality of the device.

12.2.3 Application-Based Threats

Malicious mobile applications are often connected to websites with acceptable looks and behavior. As discussed in web-based threats, such malicious applications present a wide range of security threats to a mobile device. In continuation to this sequence, even legitimate software applications can also be exploited for deceitful purposes.

Application-based threats fit into one or more of the following classes. The first class of application-based threats is malware. Malware is an intentionally written piece of code to perform malicious actions on a target device [3]. Modern malware applications are capable of adding charges to a user's phone bill, sending unwanted messages to contacts, accessing user's private data or even hand over the control of the mobile device to a remote hacker without the knowledge of the user.

The next class of threatening applications for a mobile device is spyware. Spyware is a malicious application similar to malware, only it does not cause any visible harm to the normal functioning of the mobile device. Instead, a spyware silently collects user's private data without their knowledge or consent. Text messages, phone call history logs, geographical location, browser history, contact list, private photos, contact lists and emails are some of the user data, which are generally targeted by spyware applications. Such data collected by spyware is exploited for financial fraud, blackmailing and even espionage cause a deep risk of privacy threats to the mobile device user. Another type of application-based threat is caused by vulnerable applications that contain faults exploitable for malicious intentions [28]. Such applications are generally legitimate ones with weaknesses due to improper designs or insufficient testing. Vulnerable applications allow access to sensitive user data for a criminal intent, execute fraudulent activities, disrupt the normal functioning of a service or even allow downloads of other similar malicious applications on the user's device.

12.2.4   Network-Based Threats

Modern mobile devices are designed to ensure connectivity to local wireless networks (WiFi, Bluetooth) as well as cellular packet data networks to access web-based services. Threats from such networks are classified under network-based threats. Network exploits utilize flaws present in mobile operating systems or even the platform software on which the wireless or cellular networks function. On connecting to the user's mobile device, these threats can provide the channel to an application or web-based threats [4].

WiFi sniffing is a common class of network threat that captures user data traveling through the network between the device and the network access points. Sending unencrypted data such as usernames, passwords or financial details via websites or applications lacking any security measures puts to privacy and security of user data at potential risk.

The next form of network threat to mobile devices is known as WiFI spoofing, which is executed by hackers by creating bogus WiFi access points for web access generally by using malicious WiFi routers. These WiFi points appear to be freely available public WiFi networks at public places, such as hotels, libraries, airports, railway stations or even coffee shops or hotels, with sufficiently familiar names like "Coffeehouse Freenet" or "Airport Free WiFi" to attract users to connect to them. In worst cases, such malicious services prompt the user to create a user account with a username and password to access the free services. A large number of naive or ignorant users create accounts on such access points by using the same combination of email or username and password, that they use for many other services. This allows hackers to capture the victim's sensitive user information and exploit it for malicious intent. Hence, extreme precaution must be taken while connecting to any new WiFi access point at any public place. In addition to this, users must never use personal details and regular account details to create accounts on such services. Instead, they should always use a unique combination of username and password to create a login on any new service. Compared to random or anonymous WiFi access spots with minimum or no security features, the paid wireless networks controlled by business groups with much more protected and controlled access should be preferred. Analysis of network traffic between router and mobile device of a victim user is known as session hijacking in cybersecurity terms.

In the case of mobile devices, a network attack known as sidejacking is employed to capture data from vulnerable data traffic. For this purpose, hackers use various tools to automate session hijacking via sidejacking attack [24]. A similar tool of this class has been developed by Mozilla as a plugin for Firefox web browser known as "Firesheep." Firesheep

[31] automates sidejacking between vulnerable WiFi networks and victim mobile devices to capture and exploit data traffic using a packet sniffer. Risk of compromise of wireless networks and mobile hotspots can be minimized by disabling automated search and by using secure wireless networks.

12.2.5 Data Transfer-Based Threats

Use of weak encryption algorithms or improper implementation of strong encryption techniques by the application developers can lead to cracked encryption threats. In the first case, many times developers use fragile encryption algorithms with well-known vulnerabilities only to speed up the development process [3, 5]. Such fragility attracts attackers to crack the applications and capture sensitive user data. In the later case, back doors or deficiencies are left open by developers while working with strong encryption techniques, which can also lead to the same impact on the privacy or security of user data. For example, multiple messaging applications provide encryption of user data only at sender and receiver ends. This leaves sufficient space for attackers in intermediate networks to capture the data and exploit it for malicious intent without any requirement of user details and passwords. Satisfactory enforcement of encryption practices through the network only practices encountering data transfer-based threats.

12.2.6 Improper Session Management-Based Threats

Many applications make use of runtime-generated access tokens to enable network access to connected devices. These access tokens also facilitate connectivity between the network and devices without repeated re-authentication for a predefined time limit. Applications with sufficient security features, generate new and confidential access tokens to enable network access for every session. Improper handling of session variables like access tokens, by the application, can naively leak them to malicious actors, risking the entire communication to illegitimate exploits.

12.2.7 Bluetooth-Based Threats

Bluetooth technology allows mobile devices to wirelessly exchange data among devices as well as connect peripherals like mouse and keyboards. But mobile devices with Bluetooth in the activated mode, set to be discoverable for other devices, are exposed to attacks such as blue snarfing, blue jacking and blue jugging discussed below [5]. Theft of private and sensitive user data, such as phone call logs, browsing history, GPS details, contacts, email communications and text messages, can be executed by using malicious software applications via Bluetooth. This theft of user data via Bluetooth is referred to as a Bluesnarfing attack. Hackers execute Bluesnarfing attacks by scanning for nearby devices with enabled Bluetooth via their smartphone or laptop. Applications used for bluesnarfing can steal data from victim's mobile device in silent and undetectable mode. The worst aspect of bluesnarfing attack is that turning off Bluetooth on the device cannot guarantee security. This is because a mobile device with enabled but hidden Bluetooth can also be discovered and exploited by making a guess of its MAC address through brute force attack [25].

A Bluesnarfing attack causes theft of user data from the device, while a Bluebugging attack leads to the silent broadcast of anonymous and unwanted messages to other Bluetooth-enabled devices without the victim's consent and knowledge. A Bluejacking attack is executed by backdoor bypassing of victim's mobile device access leading to silent compromise of control of their device. A bluejacking attack is capable of creating new entries in the address book, typing and transmitting new text messages and even transferring files via Bluetooth.

12.2.8   Application Platform-Based Threats

Despite thorough scanning, every mobile application submitted even to trusted online download platforms like Apple's iTunes and Android Play Store cannot be guaranteed to be genuine and safe in all terms. Some suspicious applications may lead to unauthorized access to user credentials, siphoning of internet data or even make silent unapproved purchases from the user's account. In the year 2010, a Vietnamese app developer was blacklisted from iTunes store by Apple Inc. The reason for this penalty was that he apparently charged users for books which they never purchased via his app. The developer committed this fraud only to boost his rating in the iTunes store and improve his ratings. To prevent such exploits, the users should try to install and use mobile apps of only trusted vendors and developers [26]. In a case where it is required to install an app from a new developer, a thorough study of app details like developer name, affiliations, user ratings and permissions required by an app, must be done.

A major category of such suspicious apps is free mobile apps available on these platforms. Such suspicious free mobile apps, like games or utility apps, are more likely to exploit device features and compromise user data. They are usually capable of accessing the internet, tracking user location and even accessing sensitive data. For example, 94% of gambling mobile games provided as free apps demand a user's permission to send text messages, use the phone camera and even to make outgoing phone calls [26]. The users must be alert and substantiate the intent of such a free gaming app asking for access to these features.

But parallel to genuine application platforms mentioned above, there are also third-party application stores that provide alternative apps for users. Downloading and installing apps from these unauthorized platforms on a device can be very hazardous for the end user. Such application stores always remain at high risk of being run by cyber criminals by hosting fake copies of legitimate applications altered to execute fraudulent activities.

12.3   Smartphones as a Tool of Crime

The vulnerabilities of mobile computing infrastructures exist in device hardware, application designs, coding standards, wireless connectivity and even in data transfer protocols. Such vulnerabilities always risk the profits of mobile computing at the cost of cybersecurity threats. The increasing attention of cyber criminals on the mobile sector is a matter of serious concern for everyone. High prices, portability and immense computing potential of mobile devices make them a focus of criminal exploits [6]. But above all, the extensive dependence of common folks on their mobile devices for every little thing they require makes these machines a lucrative target for cyber criminals. In this scenario, user data like contacts, emails, bank details, and passwords are at stake.

12.4 Types of Mobile Phone-Related Crimes

Activities associated with criminal usage of mobile phones can be considered as mobile crimes. Such activities make use of one or more potential uses of mobile devices to commit crimes. Here we discuss various types of mobile crimes.

Physical Theft: The ease of carrying mobile devices make them highly susceptible to physical theft. Criminals are able to demand an attractive price for stolen mobile devices on the black market due to their pricey hardware. But for a user, who is a victim of mobile theft or physical loss, the damage extends to the loss of the sensitive and private user information stored on the device [7]. Modern mobile devices are well equipped with character- or sequence-based passwords, biometric access restrictions [19], user data encryption and data erasing mechanisms to minimize the information loss. Also, regular and automatic backup of user data on cloud-based locations can almost neutralize the damage of data loss due to physical theft of a mobile device.

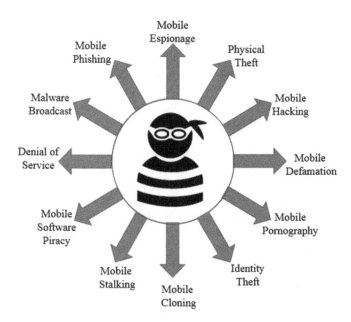

Figure 12.2   Various mobile phone-related crimes.

Mobile Hacking: Any illegitimate intrusion into a computing device and/or network without the consent of its owner can be termed as hacking or,more specifically, cracking. This definition also covers the acts breaching the security of mobile devices, communication systems and/or networks [8]. To implement mobile hacking, intentionally written scripts or malicious applications are utilized by hackers to target mobile devices and systems connected to them.

Mobile Cyber Defamation: Transfer or broadcast of intentionally written derogatory, humiliating and obscene information, offensive to the reputation and/or survival of a person or organization, causing them physical and/or financial loss is referred to as defamation [8]. Use of mobile applications, such as SMS, emails or phone calls, to commit acts of defamation can be classified as mobile defamation.

Mobile Pornography: Pornography is considered a crime in many countries. After the advent of the Internet and computer technology, the spread of pornography has taken a tremendous leap. Use of mobile devices, communication systems, internet and connected mobile-based services for creation and transmission of pornography is covered under mobile pornography [7, 9]. Mobile pornography has kept pace with evolving mobile devices. In India, mobile pornography is a punishable offense under section 67B of the amended Indian Information Technology Act, 2000, with a maximum sentence of 5 years and fine of up to 10 lakhs rupees.

Mobile Identity Theft: User information, such as email conversations, SMS messages, phone contacts, call logs and browsing history are generally stored on mobile devices. In addition, these devices also store and transfer sensitive information like financial details and health records, etc. Therefore, it has become critical to safeguard such information on mobile devices to prevent any unexpected loss.

Every person with a mobile phone has a unique 10-digit number that he willingly shares and exchanges with friends as well as strangers, depending on the required circumstances. People also download and install various mobile apps that require a valid mobile number to continue services [9,10]. They even write and exchange their mobile numbers on public documents like medical prescriptions, official pages and survey forms of grocery stores to claim reward points. With the advent of the internet of things (IoT)-based technologies, now smartphones are being optimized to perform all sorts of remote control functions from controlling the locks and lights in homes to collecting sensor-based data. These data, in turn, are collected and stored in databases, having much more than social security numbers, totally exposed to fraudsters, thieves and scammers which can lead to identity theft via mobile devices.

Mobile Cloning: Transfer of secured device sensitive data from one phone to another phone to make it an exact replica of the original phone is referred to as mobile cloning. After cloning, calls and messages can be exchanged by both phones, while the owner of the original phone is billed for all activities of the cloned phone. In CDMA phones, ESN (electronic serial number) and MIN (mobile identification number) are presented on an EPROM chip. To clone a CDMA phone, the ESN/MIN pair on the EPROM chip must be copied onto an EPROM chip of another CDMA phone. In the case of GSM phones, cloning of an original SIM card to another SIM can complete the task of cloning [8 ,10]. A new generation of devices known as "magic" phones scans their surroundings to copy the identities of nearby phones in use.

Mobile Stalking: Continuous and repeated acts of threatening and harassment targeting a victim's life, public image and property is covered under stalking, Making use of mobile devices like smartphones for following the victim's location without their consent, vandalizing their property, making harassing communications via call or messages, and posting threatening messages or objects is termed mobile stalking. If left unchecked, stalking may lead to serious acts of violence or damage to victims and their belongings.

Denial-of-Service Attack: A DoS attack is another type of cyberattack aimed at flooding the victim's computing resources with fake or bogus input to disrupt normal services. Making use of mobile devices, to flood a victim's email inbox, SMS inbox folder or phone memory, depriving them of normally entitled services, can be classified as a mobile DoS attack.

Mobile Software Piracy: Illegal copying, forging or distribution of genuine and copyright protected mobile software products with an intention to fake or damage the original software is covered under mobile software piracy.

Mobile Malware Dissemination: After the era of desktop and laptop targeted malware applications, new malware threats are constantly evolving along with the improving architectures of mobile devices. Malware, including Trojan, worm, virus, ransomware and spyware, can rigorously damage normal functionalities of mobile devices. Also, malware infected mobile devices also pose a high risk of infecting other connected devices in their networks [3, 28].

Mobile Phishing: To a certain extent, risk of malware propagation can be encountered by using updated anti-virus software products. But another class of social engineering-based attacks that trick the users of mobile devices to fall prey to malicious exploits, is phishing attacks. Phishing attacks can trick a victim mobile user to naively handover their user details, login credentials, financial information, browsing history or download malware on their mobile device [29]. To execute these attacks, a sufficiently harmless and reasonable looking link to a website is sent to the victim's mobile device by the cyber criminals. The link can be embedded into a webpage, a text message or an application-specific message such as WhatsApp, etc. The formal and sophisticated language of the approach of such links generally makes even the experienced user believe the context and click on them. After clicking the link, malicious applications or processes, crafted specifically for target devices, are triggered to execute in the background of the mobile device. After execution, such attacks are capable of stealing sensitive data or even damaging the normal functioning of the device. Phishing attacks via mobile phones can be further elaborated into the following categories [7, 8]:

Vishing: The act of scamming or tricking a mobile user by making use of telephonic conversation to unknowingly surrender his sensitive information to be exploited for identity theft is known as vishing [12]. Generally, in vishing attack, the attacker impersonates a worker or official of a genuine business group and tricks the user by threatening service disruption, official penalty or promising a significant profit.

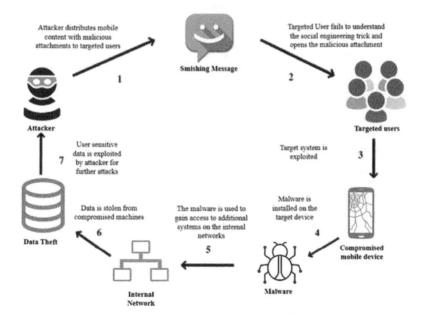

Figure 12.3   The schematic sequence of a SMiShing attack.

The attempt to approach a potential victim when executed via an SMS message instead of a phone call constitutes the next class of mobile phishing attacks called SMiShing. SMiShing attacks prompt the user to unknowingly download and install a malware onto their mobile device by clicking on a deceptive text link. Usually, instead of a clear sender phone number, SMiShing messages are received from a number "3949" like the source. Such messages, instead of a genuine smartphone number, are sent via an email address to hide the identity of the attacker. Often such messages contain a URL or phone number linked to an automated voice response system. These systems ask users about their sensitive user data that requires their immediate attention. Instead of immediate disruption of services, the aim of SMiShing is to track the user or steal sensitive user information by downloading malware [12, 13].

A hybrid format of phishing attacks are lottery scams or advance fee frauds that are delivered by emails or text messages to the target user. The content of such attack messages displays catchy lines like "your credit is waiting," "claim your trip to Australia" or "you have won," and so on. Lottery scam attacks trick the victim into believing that they have won a large sum of money, which will be accessible after handing over their sensitive information or paying a hefty sum of money.

Because the nature of phishing attacks make them difficult to recognize, the best possible strategies to prevent them are to scan the addresses and names of every digital content, read every SMS and email carefully to ensure its origin, check for grammatical errors and totally avoid opening any attachments linked to the message [14].

Mobile Espionage: Espionage refers to silent spying or monitoring of individuals or groups to obtain confidential data without the owner's consent and knowledge. But espionage via mobile devices can be considered as a mobile and more elaborate version of the same. Modern mobile devices are equipped with high computational capacities, huge memory banks, movement tracking GPS, good resolution camera and accessories like the microphone to enhance user experience. With these capabilities, a mobile device becomes an attractive tool for hackers and cyber criminals to execute espionage. Besides these features, the sensitive data shared by users in real time build a sufficient reason for the growing concern of governments and organizations for their data security. The advent of monitoring apps like Mobistealth [11] that exploit aforesaid capacities of a mobile device, raised red flags over the possible exploitation of such features by attackers for cyber espionage. For competitors, unfiltered discussions about strategic plans, innovations, financial information, legal discussions, and more highly desirable business information can be made available through espionage. Espionage is a potential tool for nations for silent monitoring of its citizens' activities and foreign rivals to ensure safety and security. Gathering conversational data, verbal commands and requests and pairing these with location data provide powerful profiling information desired by advertisers. Swept up in this information gathering may be sensitive corporate or client information. For malicious actors like hackers and cyber criminals, motivated by a variety of reasons, including economic, political, social or personal, smartphones serve as a potential attack vector.

12.5   Types of Mobile Fraud

Frauds committed using mobile devices comprise a wide range of cheats and tricks to motivate the potential target to surrender to the malicious intent of the hackers or criminals. Here, the malicious intent may include to influence the victim to purchase substandard, overpriced or non-existent products or services, to make phone calls or send text messages to links of such products, to unknowingly subscribe the expensive subscriptions of these services or in worst case, to surrender their sensitive data, such as financial details, etc., to the criminals. For a user with fair experience of desktop computing and email communication, figuring out a malicious email from its awkward language, misspelt words or poor graphics is not a very tough task. In most cases, the users simply delete such spam emails without even opening them. But the same is not the case with mobile fraud [8, 9]. A reason for this is that because till now, mobile fraud is less widespread as compared to junk email. SMS messages also have much higher delivery and open rates relative to emails. Besides this, a single and comprehensive SMS spam filtering mechanism is far from evolving. In this section, we will discuss various mobile-based frauds.

Missed Call Scams: Generally, every mobile phone user receives missed calls on their device. But in the case of a missed call scam, a missed call may be of a very short duration from an unknown number usually from a foreign location. As the targeted victim is unable to recognize the calling number, they simply call back. This call from victim's device may get redirected to a premium rate service, costing them an unexpected money charge or even more.

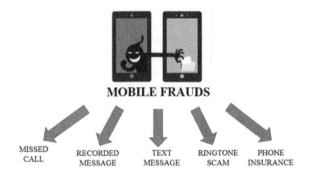

Figure 12.4   Types of mobile frauds.

Recorded Message Scam: In this format of mobile fraud, the user is prompted by a recorded message played on a phone call to call back on another number telling him that he has won a prize, and must call on the next number to claim it. But the next provided number may be the premium rate service number, as discusses in the missed call scam section, resulting in the user incurring a hefty call charge. In addition to this, the above-mentioned prize may also be another fraudulent ringtone or caller tune subscription service, causing further loss to the victim.

Text Message Scams: The user receives an SMS text message from an unknown sender containing a very friendly language, like "Hey, it's Mike. I'm back New Jersey! When can we catch up and hang out?"" Assuming such message to be from the wrong sender, the user naively calls back on the number, just to confirm that it's a wrong number. But in the case of a text message scam, the victim again is charged with a hefty premium rate for the call or a high rate lengthy SMS exchange similar to above formats of mobile fraud.

Ringtone Scams: Ringtone scams prompt the target mobile user with an offer to download or subscribe to a very cheap or even free ringtone. On accepting such offer, the victim user mistakenly subscribes to another costly fraudulent service that keeps on sending more ringtones and continues charging high premium rates for them. A basic difference among such fraudsters and legitimate ringtone selling companies is that, unlike genuine ringtone selling companies, the ringtone scammers keep hiding the true cost of their offers and services.

Phone Insurance Scams: After collecting data from newly registered mobile users from a shop of mobile devices or from a mobile network provider, fraudsters call the target users with offers to sell smartphone insurance for the newly purchased device. On falling victim to such scams, the user ends up with no insurance at all or with a very poor and costly phone insurance policy.

12.6 Case Studies

12.6.1 Mobile Identity Theft

One of the fastest growing types of threats to the security of the common masses is mobile identity theft. A major cause of this is the dominance of mobile devices such as smartphones and tablets in every sphere of modern society [10, 16]. The possible implications of mobile identity theft are discussed in this section.

1. **Gather User Information**: A mobile number is a unique communication entity reserved for an individual user or single group. Due to this uniqueness, many social media platforms, mobile apps and financial applications demand mobile numbers of their users as social identifiers. This fact leads to the possibility of a criminal or hacker to search for a smartphone number in a search engine or a website and collect information about a target user sufficient to exploit it for malicious intent. Such malicious intent may include social engineering scams or even financial damage simply by figuring out the true online identity of the victim. For example, if a user's cell phone number is connected to his Facebook account, someone could use it to try and obtain his name either through the site's general search by using the forgot password feature at login and entering the number instead of a name or email address [15].

2. **Launch SMiShing Attacks and Phone Scams**: If a user's smartphone number gets into the hands of a criminal, they can use it to their advantage and try to scam the user via text messages which may be sufficiently convincing, especially if the scammer has done their homework on the user prior to their attempt.

3. **Take over User's Mobile Account**: People search or reverse-lookup websites allow anyone to find out information about a cell phone number, including the carrier network provider, name and city/state associated with the number. Using information collected about the user, they will impersonate the user either in-person or over the phone to gain access to their mobile account. This enables them to upgrade for new phones for free (which they can sell for a profit), add additional lines or take over their number entirely (known as a SIM swap) [17]. They might also try to open up a mobile account at a different carrier using that information.

4. **Gain Access to Financial Accounts**: Beyond wreaking havoc on a mobile account, access to a mobile phone number enables cyber criminals to exploit the connected accounts by using SMS text message-based two-factor authentication. If the criminals own the control of the phone number linked to these accounts, the text message, email communication or even a phone call sent to verify a victim user's identity will be sent to them instead of the real owner. This could enable them to change the passwords

and get access to victim's accounts, possibly leading to unauthorized charges on credit cards or a siphoning of bank accounts.

5. **Terrorist Uses of Smartphone**: Similar to criminals, terrorists have also worked up elaborate mechanisms to fraudulently acquire random cell phone numbers and devices under unsuspecting victims' names. For extremely low prices, numbers and devices are accessible to terrorists for exploitation in their malicious objectives. Some such issues are presented below.

6. **Burner Phones**: A burner phone is an inexpensive and mostly refurbished mobile phone [18] designed for temporary use, after which it may be discarded. Burner phones are mostly purchased with prepaid minutes and without a contract. Using phones and increasing balances purchased with cash rather than a credit card and having no contract with a service provider clearly imply that no record of the user connected to the phone number can't be traced. If the user suspects that the number has been traced or compromised, they can just dump the phone and purchase a new one, which would have a totally new number. Today, a large civil population uses smartphones, and smartphone numbers are increasingly being used as unique profile identifiers that connect user data across multiple databases. Moreover, phone numbers aren't subject to privacy requirements like credit card details and social security numbers and thus are shared frequently. As a result, mobile number privacy is a growing security issue. An easy method of increasing mobile security is the use of burner phone mobile apps or services rather than using an actual device, which provides a temporary phone number that can be provided instead of the user's actual cell number. One such application is the Burner mobile app [19] service, that has numbers that usually expire after a certain time period. These numbers can be used by paying for them with in-app purchases. If they lapse, they're burned. The premium subscription gives the user a permanent second number. When a user calls via Burner, it actually calls Burner, which in turn replaces a relay call to the number you want to reach. Details of the Paris terror attacks [20] reveal that instead of encryption, consistent use of prepaid burner phones helped the terrorists to remain off the radar of the intelligence services. The three terrorist teams in Paris used only new phones, activated minutes before the attacks and discarded after use. Later, the investigators found a Samsung phone in a dustbin near a theater. The phone had a Belgian SIM card used only since the day before the attack. The phone was used to call just one other unidentified number in Belgium. As police pieced together the movements of the attackers, they found yet more burner phones.

7. **Smartphone Bomb**: Generally, two smartphones are used in the bomb-making process; one to call the other, which then transmits a signal to a circuit board and triggers the explosion [21]. Smartphones are basically small and sophisticated radio devices that translate a radio signal into an equivalent electrical pulse and convert that current into sound. If a smartphone is integrated with a bomb as a triggering device, the electrical impulse generated by the smartphone is adequate to create a detonation charge to trigger the main explosive compound of the bomb. Crafting a mobile phone into a remotely detonable bomb trigger is very easy and cheap due to the availability of online information and spare parts. Exploding such bombs also simply requires dialing the mobile number of the SIM in the phone connected to the detonator. The 28-year-old terrorist, Ahmad Khan Rahami, the suspect in twin bombings at locations in New Jersey and New York, admitted the use of smartphones [22] to detonate his homemade

bombing devices. The Nokia 105 smartphone is a favorite device among ISIS fighters [23]. The cheap, durable and long battery life Nokia 105 phone is the most popular remote bomb-triggering device among ISIS organizations for detonating bombs. ISIS has assembled and deployed improvised explosive devices across the battlefield on a large scale, causing a large number of civilian and military casualties."

12.6.2   Data Theft by Applications

Parallel to malicious mobile applications, in recent times some genuine applications have also been found to be continuously stealing data related to user communications and preferences. Such information is collected from data audio codecs of the call, duration of user calls, timestamps of user activities, frequently accessed contacts and far more. A similar case of data theft by a genuine chat application called "WhatsApp" was brought to light by researchers at the University of New Haven [27, 30].

The information stolen in real time was noted to be transferred to the official servers of WhatsApp[1]. The researchers created some experimental participant users to conduct the experiment and tested the hypothesis of data theft by the app. After that, the users were authenticated by making calls on WhatsApp via a communication channel created by Opus codec at 8 and 16 KHz frequencies. Later, upon analyzing the destination IP addresses and relay servers for the calls, the experiment revealed that the application was stealing sensitive user data like call's audio codec, phone numbers and timestamps of calls. The analysis of message exchange mechanism between the relay servers of the app and an Android version of the app also exposed the collection of data accumulation pattern of WhatsApp via FunXMPP[2] internet protocol. After this experimental case study of WhatsApp, it can be concluded that leakage, theft or silent monitoring of user information is also possible via even the most trusted and safe-looking mobile applications.

12.6.3   SIM Card Fraud

One of the most sophisticated and unusual techniques of mobile fraud that leads the criminals to access victim's financial details is SIM card fraud. A combination of social engineering and exhaustive surveys paves the way for attackers to smoothly conduct this attack.

To start with, loosely handled, stolen or misplaced bank account statements of a potential target provide the access to bank details to attackers. After locating a potential target, the attackers conduct exhaustive social engineering and survey to collect and assemble sufficient personal information about the target from their social media account profiles including the details of their contact number and service provider. This survey enables the attackers to answer basic security questions to be asked by the mobile service provider of the target user.

Now the attackers call the target, convincing them to shut down their phone temporarily, either by repeatedly making blank calls or posing as a call for an upgrade from the mobile service provider. During the period when the phone of the target user is shut down, the attackers call the service provider of the target, pretending to be the target user and claim that their phone is damaged or lost. In such situations, the service provider company asks basic security questions which are successfully answered by the attacker, confirming

[1]https://www.whatsapp.com/
[2]https://github.com/mgp25/Chat-API/wiki/FunXMPP-Protocol

the identity of the target. This leads the service provider to cancel the existing SIM and activating a new SIM possessed by the attacker.

Now, the attacker contacts the bank of the target user with their new SIM card and claims to have forgotten their access password. After asking basic security questions similar to the mobile service provider, the bank also sends a one-time access code or one-time password (OTP) to the phone number of the target user, which is actually received by the attacker.

Now the attacker opens a fake parallel account in the bank of the targeted user in his name and ultimately drains the user's money into this new fake account without the user's consent and knowledge. The worst part of this fraud is that the mobile user victim is totally unaware of this attack until their mobile seizes to operate or they are unable to access financial details of their bank accounts. By then, the attackers drain all the money from the victim's fake account to finalize this attack.

12.7   Preventive Measures and Precautions

12.7.1   Against Physical Loss and Theft of the Mobile Device

Physical loss of device due to theft or misplacement is a severe security threat because in addition to the financial damage of the device's cost, the user also loses total physical control over their data. Concerning human nature and accidental possibilities, such physical losses cannot be guaranteed to stop, but their impacts can be sufficiently reduced if the users adopt the following measures:

1. **Check security features provided by the mobile service provider**: Generally, all mobile service vendors provide sufficiently strict security policies to help the users in protecting their data. Provision of secret security questions and PIN numbers are examples of these securities. Unique password combinations and random security questions, having no connection to the user's social media profile are preferable for best use of these security features. It is also preferable for users to go through the security policy statements of service providers before signing up for any contract with them.

2. **Don't store critical information on the mobile device**: Sensitive information details, such as account passwords, PIN numbers, financial details, etc., are at high risk for loss or theft if stored in texts or emails. Theft or loss of mobile devices must be immediately shared with the service providers to help them remotely deactivate the device as soon as possible. After this, the user must change passwords of all connected online accounts accessible through their stolen device.

3. **Setting up sufficiently strong access passcodes**: In case of theft or loss, a strong passcode safeguards user's data to a satisfactory level. Lack of any passcode or knowledge of this passcode by many people risks the security of the data present on the device to a great extent.

4. **Regular and cloud-based backup**: Mobile users must regularly back up their data stored on their devices on secondary storage devices such as external backup drives or memory cards. To improve the security level and accessibility, same data can also be saved to cloud-based backup services. This will allow the user to remotely access, update and restore their data from any location in case their device is lost, stolen or is even accidentally erased.

5. **Proper erasing of data before switching to a new device**: Before recycling, donating or even reselling the mobile device, erasing the data efficiently from the old device helps to protect its privacy and security. For this purpose, certain devices, as well as software applications, are available that ensure satisfactory deletion of old data.

6. **Installing tracking apps on the device**: Modern mobile devices are equipped with remote tracking, locking and even data wiping features. Multiple unsuccessful login attempts can lead to self-destruction of stored data on the device. Several applications are now also available to provide these features.

12.7.2 Against SMiShing Attacks

As discussed earlier, SMiShing attacks act as bait for mobile users who are potential targets for exploitation by cyber criminals. Generally, SMiShing attempts are social engineering attacks embedded in text or phone call formats to prompt the victim to naively attempt the security violation of their device. But following precautions can save the mobile users from SMiShing attacks to a great extent.

1. **Never click on a suspicious link or number**: On receiving a text message or phone call with a suspicious content or from an unknown source prompting to perform a specific action by clicking on a link or dialing a given number, the user must never perform the suggested action. This inactivity will automatically disarm the thrown bait of the remote fraudster or cyber criminal.

   Even if such a message prompts in a prohibitive way like to stop receiving such messages in the future, click the NO button at the bottom or if you do not wish to receive such messages in the future, simply respond by texting "NO"; the user must avoid performing the suggested negative action, as it might lead to the same consequential exploits mentioned above.

2. **Confirm the validity of the source**: On receiving such doubtful communication, the target user should always try to ensure its originating source or sender. This search for its source can be done on search engines or address directories over the web.

3. **In case of imposters, confirm from the original authorities**: If a doubtful message or call pretending to be from one of the known sources, prompts the user for certain action, it is better to contact the original authority to confirm the message. For example, if a user receives a message from his bank such as "Your policy reward points are about to lapse in 2 days, click on the link to claim your points." Here, instead of clicking on the link, and possibly surrendering their financial information, the user should contact their bank directly to confirm the validity of the message.

4. **Never provide any personal or sensitive information**: The scope of personal or sensitive information ranges from financial details, one time passwords (OTP), user account details to even name and address of the target user. SMiShing links commonly threaten the target mobile users with blocking or disruption of a specific service such as blocking of account or credit card penalties. Surrendering any such information may lead to serious consequences against the security of linked data. Instead, the users must remember that any authorities of any legitimate service will never ask them about their sensitive information. In case of persisting doubt, the users must themselves contact the authorized personnel of the service.

12.7.3   Against App-Based Attacks

1. **Download from trusted application platforms only**: Try to always download a mobile application from trusted mobile app download platforms like "*Google Play Store*"[3] for Android device and "*iTunes*"[4] for Apple devices. Applications loaded on these platforms are thoroughly tested and confirmed for their behavior and security by the authorities to maintain the trust and repute of the hosting companies. Apps downloaded from unknown or untrusted platforms may carry malware or spyware that can risk the security of the user data and device [29].

2. **Exhaustively examine the details of the app before downloading**: Ratings provided by users, history and reviews about the authors and update history of the app must be carefully examined before installation of any app even from the most trusted sources mentioned above. This check can save the user from any unexpected loss or damage due to the app, previously experienced by other users.

3. **Check the app permissions before installation**: The user must cautiously read and then grant permissions to the new app for accessing the device data and services. This scrutiny is extremely important for any app to know its intended future behavior after installation on the device. Any unexpected demand for access permission like access to the camera for a gaming app must be reported accordingly.

4. **Checking phone bill**: In cases of abnormal data exchange, sudden deprecated battery life or heating of the device, do check the bill incurred due to the device. The bill may project unexpected rises due to suspicious calling charges or unexpected text message exchanges.

5. **Install security app**: The users must install a security application that scans the behavior of every app installed on the device. In case of any spyware or malware, the security app will alarm the user of the abnormal behavior of the app.

12.7.4   Against Identity Theft and SIM Card Fraud

To protect cell phone number, there are certainly some actions that the users can take to protect themselves from falling victim to cell phone number identity theft.

1. **Staying vigilant**: The users must get in the habit of checking their bank and phone accounts frequently to make sure there's no suspicious activity. Staying up-to-date with any attacks that have hit companies they shop with will make sure that they aren't among the victims.

2. **Utilizing the safeguards provided by companies**: The email based or one-time password (OTP)-based authentications can certainly be exploited by criminals. But their utter absence can expose the user against higher proximity of attacks.

3. **Creating a PIN number for mobile phone accounts**: Creation of PIN for mobile services is an optional security process provided by the services providers. But a PIN-based access creates an extra layer of security for the user's account by enforcing a 4 or 6 digit access restriction prior to performing any crucial account changes.

---

[3]https://play.google.com/
[4]https://www.apple.com/vn/itunes/

4. **Use of unique and strong security access combinations**: Strong passwords consist of a unique combination of alphabets, special characters and numbers with a sufficient length. Similarly, selection of security questions and their answers must be unrelated to any social media profile of the user.

5. **Do not make personal information public**: Too much exposure of personal information on social media can help criminals to answer security questions to access the details of the target user. If information about common facts like hometown, spouse name, details of family members, own and their birthday, mother's maiden name, the name of the first pet, is available on users' social media profiles, it may risk the security of user data to a great extent. In addition, the users must keep checking their social network privacy settings to ensure that their information isn't easily harvestable.

6. **Use a virtual number for noncritical use**: One of the best ways to limit the amount of personally identifying data tied to a main contact number is to avoid sharing it with anyone except the closest trusted individuals. Use of virtual numbers for non-personal matters can help to sustain privacy in such cases. Virtual numbers can accept text messages and phone calls and can be set to forward to the actual contact number to avoid missing any genuine and important communications.

7. **Establish a PIN or password with the mobile carrier**: All mobile service providers allow their users to set up an additional password or SIM-based PIN code that can be required to make any changes to the mobile account. This safeguard mechanism can critically help in case of SIM card-based fraud. Here, even if the criminal acquires a new SIM with user's number, he won't be able to access it without the SIM-based PIN code.

8. **Report suspicious activity immediately**: If the phone suddenly becomes disconnected and restarting it doesn't make any changes to the signal, or the phone bill has sudden unknown hikes, or the phone is receiving multiple repeated nuisance calls, the user must contact their mobile carrier immediately.

The sooner such abnormalities as observed and acted upon, the lesser is the extent of damage caused. Users must be also on alert for suspicious phone calls or messages pretending to be from their mobile carrier.

12.8   Conclusion

Modern mobile communication technologies have empowered individuals and organizations to utilize them for real-time communication and data transfer to their advantage. This advantage is embedded with risks of cybersecurity of the linked devices and the data they manage. To counter these risks, effective management policies, adequate training and comprehensive knowledge of such exploits and their preventions are crucial for safe and uninterrupted productivity. The quest for the upgrade of security threats and improvement of security mechanisms will go on in parallel with the evolution of the capacities of the mobile devices in order to keep connected mobile users and their resources safe and protected.

References

1. Becher, M., Freiling, F. C., Hoffmann, J., Holz, T., Uellenbeck, S., & Wolf, C. (2011, May). Mobile security catching up? revealing the nuts and bolts of the security of mobile devices. In Security and Privacy (SP), 2011 IEEE Symposium on (pp. 96-111). IEEE.

2. Li, Q., & Clark, G. (2013). Mobile security: a look ahead. IEEE Security & Privacy, 11(1), 78-81.

3. Jain, A. K., & Shanbhag, D. (2012). Addressing security and privacy risks in mobile applications. IT Professional, 14(5), 28-33.

4. La Polla, M., Martinelli, F., & Sgandurra, D. (2013). A survey on security for mobile devices. IEEE communications surveys & tutorials, 15(1), 446-471.

5. Miller, K. W., Voas, J., & Hurlburt, G. F. (2012). BYOD: Security and privacy considerations. It Professional, 14(5), 53-55.

6. Burge, P., Shawe-Taylor, J., Cooke, C., Moreau, Y., Preneel, B., & Stoermann, C. (1997). Fraud detection and management in mobile telecommunications networks.

7. Badhe, A. (2016). Click Fraud Detection In Mobile Ads Served In Programmatic Exchanges. International Journal of Scientific Technology & Research, 5(4), 1.

8. Barson, P., Field, S., Davey, N., McAskie, G., & Frank, R. (1996). The detection of fraud in mobile phone networks. Neural Network World, 6(4), 477-484.

9. Shawe-Taylor, J., Howker, K., & Burge, P. (1999). Detection of fraud in mobile telecommunications. Information Security Technical Report, 4(1), 16-28.

10. Wang, W., Yuan, Y., & Archer, N. (2006). A contextual framework for combating identity theft. IEEE Security & Privacy, 4(2), 30-38.

11. Sivaramarajalu, R. V., Krishna, J. H., & Kumar, R. S. (2012). Security Threats of Smart Phones. International Journal of Data & Network Security, 1(3), 51-53.

12. Candia, J., Gonzlez, M. C., Wang, P., Schoenharl, T., Madey, G., & Barabsi, A. L. (2008). Uncovering individual and collective human dynamics from mobile phone records. Journal of physics A: mathematical and theoretical, 41(22), 224015.

13. Shahriar, H., Klintic, T., & Clincy, V. (2015). Mobile phishing attacks and mitigation techniques. Journal of Information Security, 6(03), 206.

14. Foozy, C. F. M., Ahmad, R., & Abdollah, M. F. (2013). Phishing detection taxonomy for mobile device. International Journal of Computer Science Issues (IJCSI), 10(1), 338-344.

15. Hoofnagle, C. J. (2007). Identity theft: Making the known unknowns known. Harv. JL & Tech., 21, 97.

16. Tachikawa, K. (2003). A perspective on the evolution of mobile communications. IEEE Communications magazine, 41(10), 66-73.

17. Lee, S., & Park, S. (2005, July). Mobile password system for enhancing usability-guaranteed security in mobile phone banking. In International Conference Human Society@ Internet (pp. 66-74). Springer, Berlin, Heidelberg.

18. Liao, K. C., Lee, W. H., Sung, M. H., & Lin, T. C. (2009, August). A one-time password scheme with QR-code based on mobile phone. In INC, IMS and IDC, 2009. NCM'09. Fifth International Joint Conference on (pp. 2069-2071). IEEE.

19. Trewin, S., Swart, C., Koved, L., Martino, J., Singh, K., & Ben-David, S. (2012, December). Biometric authentication on a mobile device: a study of user effort, error and task disruption. In Proceedings of the 28th Annual Computer Security Applications Conference (pp. 159-168). ACM.

20. Chen, C. L., Lee, C. C., & Hsu, C. Y. (2012). Mobile device integration of a fingerprint biometric remote authentication scheme. International Journal of Communication Systems, 25(5), 585-597.

21. Felt, A. P., Finifter, M., Chin, E., Hanna, S., & Wagner, D. (2011, October). A survey of mobile malware in the wild. In Proceedings of the 1st ACM workshop on Security and privacy in smartphones and mobile devices (pp. 3-14). ACM.

22. Chin, E., Felt, A. P., Sekar, V., & Wagner, D. (2012, July). Measuring user confidence in smartphone security and privacy. In Proceedings of the Eighth Symposium on Usable Privacy and Security (p. 1). ACM.

23. Chen, Y., Trappe, W., & Martin, R. P. (2007, June). Detecting and localizing wireless spoofing attacks. In Sensor, Mesh and Ad Hoc Communications and Networks, 2007. SECON'07. 4th Annual IEEE Communications Society Conference on (pp. 193-202). IEEE.

24. Riley, R. D., Ali, N. M., Al-Senaidi, K. S., & Al-Kuwari, A. L. (2010, August). Empowering users against sidejacking attacks. In ACM SIGCOMM Computer Communication Review (Vol. 40, No. 4, pp. 435-436). ACM.

25. Callaghan, M. J., Harkin, J., & McGinnity, T. M. (2006). Case study on the Bluetooth vulnerabilities in mobile devices. IJCSNS International Journal of Computer Science and Network Security, 6(4), 125-129.

26. Lee, G., & Raghu, T. S. (2014). Determinants of mobile apps' success: Evidence from the app store market. Journal of Management Information Systems, 31(2), 133-170.

27. Lim, S. L., & Bentley, P. J. (2013, June). Investigating app store ranking algorithms using a simulation of mobile app ecosystems. In Evolutionary Computation (CEC), 2013 IEEE Congress on (pp. 2672-2679). IEEE.

28. Gutmann, P. (2007). The commercial malware industry. In DEFCON conference.

29. Ramu, S. (2012). Mobile malware evolution, detection and defense. EECE 571B, Term Survey Paper.

30. Karpisek, F., Baggili, I., & Breitinger, F. (2015). WhatsApp network forensics: Decrypting and understanding the WhatsApp call signaling messages. Digital Investigation, 15, 110-118.

31. Barth, A. (2011). Network Working Group J. Hodges Internet-Draft PayPal Intended status: Standards Track C. Jackson Expires: February 6, 2012 Carnegie Mellon University.

CHAPTER 13

CYBERSECURITY: A PRACTICAL STRATEGY AGAINST CYBER THREATS, RISKS WITH REAL WORLD USAGES

Anjana Mishra, Soumitra Ghosh, Brojo Kishore Mishra

[1] Department of Information Technology, C.V. Raman College of Engineering, Bhubaneswar, Odisha, India
Emails: anjanamishra2184@gmail.com, ghosh.soumitra2@gmail.com, brojokishoremishra@gmail.com

Abstract

Cybersecurity consists of all the methods to protect the reliability, veracity, usability, consistency and safety of the data, programs and entire computer networks from illegal access which can be exploited. This chapter mainly discusses the importance and application of cybersecurity in the present era. It defines cyberwar, which refers to knowledge-related conflict at the military level, the ISA which state a number of the key challenges facing the industry, particularly in collecting and distributing information. This chapter also highlights some strategies to maintain the privacy, integrity, confidentiality and availability of cyber information and its real-world impacts like mobile security issues, secure email, online banking, cyber health check, cyber incident response management, cybersecurity risk management, cybersecurity schemes and services.

Keywords: Cybersecurity, threats, risk, cyberwar, ISA, cyberspace, mobile security, cybersecurity healthcare

Dac-Nhuong Le et al. (eds.), Cyber Security in Parallel and Distributed Computing, (207–262)
© 2019 Scrivener Publishing LLC

13.1   Introduction

The attention towards cybersecurity is very important as well as at an all-time high. Numerous countries and enterprises realize that digital dangers stand out as the most genuine monetary security challenge they face and which is quickly increasing step-by-step [1, 2]. They have found that their economic success also depends on cybersecurity. Every day a shadowy group or some unauthorized person creates digital security dangers and these dangers result in more criminal activities, causing loss of private information, certainties, cash and trust. As per Merriam-Webster, digital security is characterized as the arrangement of "measures taken to ensure a PC or PC framework (*as on the web*) against unapproved access or assault." In this manner, obviously every one of the undertakings and organizations must have an inner and outer digital security strategy and plan keeping in mind the end goal to of providing the highest level of protection from digital security dangers which are caused to a great degree by basic circumstances.

Figure 13.1   Issues of cybersecurity [4].

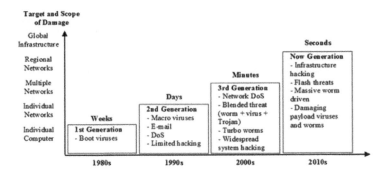

Figure 13.2   Cybersecurity attacks occurring in different years [8].

13.2 Cyberwar

In the year 1993, an article entitled as "Cyberwar is coming!" which anticipated the different difficulties that security experts of western countries would experience throughout the years in a study [12]. Over twenty years earlier, Arquilla and Ronfeldt cautioned that both "Netwar" and "Cyberwar" were coming and may impact the 21st Century security .As purposefully the unified arms movement battling had successfully influenced the security scene of the twentieth. Since that time, the possibility of "Cyberwar" has gotten an unprecedented measure of consideration, while the parallel thought of "Netwar" has blurred away. The Digital opposition affiliations have been vital to challenge Cyberwar and the Netwar [11].

Clearing up the possibility of cyberwar, it coordinating and dealing with, the military exercises as demonstrated by information related benchmarks. By and large described it contain even military culture, on which a foe or adversary depend upon it with a particular ultimate objective to "know" itself: where it is, its personality, what it can do, when it can do, why it is doing combating, which risks to counter first and which to not, et cetera. It infers trying to completely comprehend an adversary while protecting it from knowing much around oneself and using this information against their, with the objective that less proportion of money, effort and business may must be required. This kind of battling may join diverse developments- especially for C3I; for understanding social affair, spread and getting ready; for masterminded correspondences, arranging, and recognizing evidence buddy or-foe (IFF); and for "wise" weapons structures- to give. It may in like manner consolidate electronically blinding, blocking, risky, over-loading, and impeding into an opponent's information and exchanges circuits. Cyberwar isn't only a course of action of measures in light of development. For a military in both intra-and between advantage regions it may demonstrate some specialist remake .The orchestrated structures require some decentralization of bring and control, which is well be restricted that the new development would give more unmistakable central control of military exercises. Various prescriptions of legitimate update recognize decentralization; yet decentralization alone isn't the key issue. The coordinating of decentralization with top sight brings the real increments [11]. Cyberwar may in like manner induce developing new gauges about what sorts of forces are needed, what and how to strike on the adversary's side and where and how to send them. For the course of action of air ship and their upkeep limits the information is necessitated that How and where to position what sorts of PCs and related sensors, databases and frameworks et cetera. It moreover has impacts for the mix of the psychological and political and with the military parts of battling. Cyberwar raise wide issues of military affiliation and course of action, and their methodology, techniques and arms, weapon and rocket diagram. It is considerable in low-and high-constrain wars, in customary and non-conventional condition, and for watched or antagonistic purposes. It moreover addresses an extension of the customary noteworthiness of finding information in war- of having dominating C3I, and of trying to distinguish, read, consider, and swindle the foe before they does in like manner paying little respect to what general strategy is looked for after. In this sense, it infers that information related components are more basic than whenever in ongoing memory in view of new developments. The cyberwar implies an adjustment in war.

Cyberwar is about Association as much as advancement. It deduces new man-machine interfaces that development man's abilities, not an isolating of man and machine. Anyway cyberwar is significantly more than striking an enemy's C3I structures while improving and anchoring one's own. In Clausewitz's sense, it is depicted by the push to change learning into limit. In spite of the way that full arranging and execution requires impelled development, cyberwar isn't penniless after bleeding edge advancement. The continued with change of bleeding edge information and exchanges progressions is fundamental for U.S. military limits anyway cyberwar, does not by any stretch of the imagination require the nearness of bleeding edge advancement whether paid by the Unified States or other. The definitive and mental estimations may be as basic as the specific. Cyberwar may truly be paid with low advancement under a couple of conditions.

13.3   Arms Control in Cyberwar

The U.S. directors have considered the trial of dealing with risks in the computerized zone to that of checking nuclear controlled weapons at the period of the Icy War. China and Joined States and orchestrating what may be the essential advanced arms control agree to blacklist attacks on one another's unstable substructure in peacetime [16]. The U.S Obama organization has conviction that, in such an assention could provoke a more broad "widespread structure" of rules, contracts, and relationship to direct the web. The long-standing U.S. technique are instruments that are Arms control and neutralizing activity which is being vivified and retooled to address current days advanced troubles. In any case, the practicality of these Frosty War approaches, which make principal anyway not tasteful measures, will be fundamentally confined in view of genuine differentiations between the advanced and nuclear spaces. Regardless of this Chinese and Russian can't of recommending digital arms control activities that are genuinely helpful and gainful activities that it would be in the consideration of the United States to help. All nations faces enormous dangers from digital assault, and realized that the arms control methodologies can help it in that, yet they would be delinquent, or surely to propose great ones. In this way, the disparate, contradicting, and conceivably deceptive interests of different nations should made it troublesome for United State starting stand toward such proposals even while they stay open to valuable possibilities. The U.S. overseers have considered the trial of dealing with threats in the computerized zone to that of checking nuclear controlled weapons at the period of the Icy War. China and Joined States and masterminding what may be the essential computerized arms control agree to blacklist strikes on one another's flimsy substructure in peacetime [16]. The U.S Obama organization has sureness that, in such an assention could provoke a more broad "all inclusive structure" of rules, contracts, and relationship to manage the web. The longstanding U.S. methodology are instruments that are Arms control and neutralizing activity which is being enlivened and retooled to address current days advanced challenges. Nevertheless, the practicality of these Frosty War approaches, which make principal anyway not agreeable measures, will be essentially confined in view of genuine complexities between the advanced and nuclear spaces. Notwithstanding this Chinese and Russian can't of recommending digital arms control activities that are sincerely helpful and gainful activities that it would be in the consideration of the United States to help. All nations faces colossal dangers from digital assault, and realized that the arms control methodologies can help it in that, however they would be delinquent, or undoubtedly to propose great ones. In this way, the divergent, contradicting, and conceivably deceptive interests of different nations should made it troublesome for United State beginning stand toward such recommendations even while they stay open to valuable potential outcomes.

13.4 Internet Security Alliance

The cyber security alliance term as the application security forum .It is a swiss activity for developing mindfulness around cybersecurity. It contains the majority of the cybersecurity stuffs from application security, to cryptography, organize security, hazard controlling, enormous information, moral hacking, protection, basic frameworks, digital culpability, dangers insight, personality, disclosing difficulties confronting organizations and experts. The national digital security collusion (NCSA)[1] is just a remarkable relationship among the administration, driving private-division associations, informational affiliations and trade affiliations. ISA is a multi-segment work relationship with alliance from pretty much all of the named basic industry portions, including expansive support from the flying, safeguard managing an account, producing, budgetary administrations ,training, human services, protection, security, innovation and interchanges businesses. ISA accentuations totally on cybersecurity and cybersecurity related issues as is in its activity, which is to make a viable structure of cybersecurity by combining cutting edge innovation with funds and common strategy. ISA is likewise outstanding as it joins the idea direction that may be found in a "think tank," with help one would anticipate from an exchange affiliation, and dynamic security programs.

NCSA Aim is to drive sharpness and reaction to relentless digital security issues. It gives the different assets and instruments to approve, autonomous endeavors, schools, home customers and universities to stay safe on the web. NCSA Objective To interface with more than 50 million home customers, privately owned businesses, school, colleges and enlightening PC customers to engage them to stay safe online through the NCSA website, one of a kind events and phenomenal tasks.

NCSA's Focus: The DHS (*Department of Homeland Security*) national computerized security division authoritatively indicates the NCSA as their principle work is to contacting these three groups of onlookers:

- Home clients

- Small organizations

- Academic foundations

NCSA's principle objective is to engage and support propelled locals to use the Web safely and securely, guarding themselves and the computerized establishment. NCSA, a 501 c(3) set up in 2001, is the eminent open private affiliation, working with the DHS, business building up backings and humanitarian pros to progress computerized security care for home customers, little and medium size associations, school, colleges, or fundamental and discretionary guidance. NCSAM is a multifaceted push to spread security information and messages through conspicuous, regular and online life channels. In advance as found NCSA's persistent work alone reached a probable 29,000,000 people through media and distinctive activities. Finally, it will assess its satisfaction to the degree by which advanced security social benchmarks and best practices have ended up being second nature for all PC customers. NCSA also endeavor to find the new progression framework for the care of advanced security by the help of other standard educating that is generally valuable for subjects, for instance, great abstaining from excessive food intake, and safe driving and exercise, which collect a national appreciation about fitting on the web instruments and lead.

---

[1] https://staysafeonline.org/

13.5   Cybersecurity Information Sharing Act

President Barack Obama denoted a bill on December 18, 2015, which incorporate the cybersecurity data sharing act of 2015 (CISA) into law. It supports open and what's more private part units to share propelled danger data. It stipends Joined States government affiliations and non-government substances to offer data to each remarkable as they study cyberattacks. In this the chief of national knowledge and the organization parts of country security, equity and guard are compulsory to arrange in a managed way and overhaul systems for sharing cybersecurity chance data. The Non-government parts will be required to wipe out individual information, reality and figure before sharing propelled chance pointers, and the department of homeland security (DHS)[2] will be fundamental to facilitate an affirmation investigation of the got data.

As indicated by this law the administration just utilize this mutual data to:

- Discover the motivation behind cybersecurity.

- Distinguish the reason for digital security risk or security helplessness.

- Distinguish digital security dangers which are utilized by a fear based oppressor or outside foe.

- Keep a genuine monetary mischief or gravitating toward risk, containing a psychological militant act or a usage of a weapon of mass damage.

- Alleviate a genuine risk to a minor like sexual maltreatment and blackmails to physical wellbeing.

- Examine, hinder or else make legitimate move and infringement emerging out of a risk or identifying with extortion and data fraud.

The department of homeland security and the department of justice[3] issued course on february 16, 2016, to offer assistance the associations that offer data under CISA with the national government. Around a similar time the additional course moreover issued which give the idea how chosen workplaces would keep the information securely and how they would grant that information to one another, area governments and state, and the private part.

Key Provisions of CISA: On December 2015 rendition law CISA included help inside the two social affairs in Congress and from the Organization, yet was separating by some development associations and private get-togethers .By enabling associations to execute checking and self-guarded instruments on their information structures, the control responded to vulnerabilities that particular such exercises could achieve duty, including under the Electronic Correspondences Protection Act. To ask associations to give information to the organization or diverse social occasions could risk case for harming security and antitrust laws, among others [21].

The going with is a rundown of CISA's key game plans.

- *Secure and Screen Data Frameworks*: An affiliation is affirmed, of law, to "screen" and "work monitored measures" in solitude information structure or, with formed endorsement to another Association system for cybersecurity purposes.

---

[2]https://www.dhs.gov/
[3]https://www.justice.gov/

– *Security from Liability for Monitoring*: In CISA. Area 106(a). Note that there is no nearness of similar commitment security for working watched estimates that go more far off than checking.

▪ ***Get or Offer Digital Risk Markers or Cautious Measures***: For a cybersecurity reason an endeavor is affirmed, to share or get advanced peril pointers and defensive measures "from, the united government, state and close-by governments, and other little associations and private substances". Locale 104(c)(1).

– A "digital risk marker" suggests information that is "required to describe or mastermind" a collection of recorded perils, together with "poisonous examination" and procedures for mishandling a security lack of protection or making a true blue customer unwittingly enable such corruption. Section 102(6) [11].

– A "guarded measure" is portray as something that can be associated with an information structure which perceives, stops, or moderates a known or addressed cybersecurity threat or security shortcoming, anyway measures that disaster area, and banished the outcast data which harmed systems. Section 102(7).

– A "cybersecurity reason" describes as the inspiration driving shielding an information structure or data from a "cybersecurity peril" or "security shortcoming," as shown by the law. Section 102(4) [11].

▪ ***Look over Individual Data previously Sharing***: An affiliation can wanting to share an advanced threat marker must empty, intended to remove or ought to clear any information "not particularly related to a cybersecurity chance" that the association "knows at the period of sharing." Segment 104(d)(2)(A), (B).

▪ ***Insurances for Getting and Offering Data***: In understanding with CISA's necessities i.e., expulsion of individual data should be possible for the assurance.

– *Antitrust Exemption*: With the end goal to anticipate, analyze, or moderate dangers CISA offers that it's definitely not an administration or state antitrust encroachment for associations to share their computerized hazard pointers or watched. Fragment 104(e)(1), (2); Segment 108(e).

– *Non-Waiver of Benefit*: The administration does not swear off advantages and other legitimate confirmations for Offering information to state and adjacent governments or distinctive associations.. Fragment 105(d)(1).

– *Restrictive Data*: The legislature will consider protected estimates markers and computerized chance with it to be the sharing substance's beneficial, money related, and enrolled information when so doled out by that component. Territory 105(d)(2).

– *Exception from Government and State FOIA Laws*: Data shared under CISA is released from admission under the Opportunity of Data Act (5 U.S.C. 552), and moreover under any State or close-by courses of action .Segment 105(d)(3) [21].

– *Information Cannot Be Used to Standardize or Take Administration Arrangements Against Legal Activities*: The Information that common under CISA can't be utilized by any National, State, inborn, or neighborhood government to standardize, including an organization activity, the legitimate exercises of any non-Federal substance or any exercises taken by a non-Federal element ,the data might be utilized, to actualize imaginative cybersecurity controls. Segment 105(d)(5)(D)(i), (ii).

Numerous private and open or others Association should be a bit of cybersecurity program for, sharing cybersecurity information .Despite the way that CISA likely does not on an exceptionally fundamental dimension change the cybersecurity circumstance, yet rather it venture toward sharing the information that to how, why, and for what reason not to share advanced hazard and defensive measure.

13.6   Market for Malware

Malware is a term that interface bug with programming, defiled PC program expected to mischief, hurt or jump in a server, PC or framework without the regard for affirm customers. The quantity of unapproved clients which utilize destructive and taint programming to the PC frameworks is growing [20]. A circuitous methodology have taken by the satiates to battle against the hazard and for farthest point the utilization of malware by putting limitation on the exchange of malware crosswise over limits through fare controls.

The three purpose behind this:

- First, it is difficult to depict great versus awful programming fitting for a fare control.

- Second, trade controls for the most part overlook the unlawful gatherings and unfaithful people.

- Third, send out controls actualized however they represent the danger of hurting self-defensive partnerships and blocking scientists from teaming up and sharing data.

Markets for data on programming vulnerabilities are useful for security. Be that as it may, they can likewise expand moral and good and problems, especially as digital physical dangers,

It very well may be finished by expanding the pace of powerlessness revelation, exposure, fix application and fix improvement, to abbreviate the defenselessness life cycle. The helpfulness of vulnerabilities will end up rarer and in this manner higher in cost with a shorter life cycle.

A solitary working of zero-day endeavor can cost a huge number of dollars. The sum can go increment significantly more if the defenselessness discovered lies in consistently utilized applications like Internet Explorer (IE) and there's no market an incentive for vulnerabilities in only occasionally utilized applications. We can state that the vulnerabilities and endeavors end up known. Presently the Web-related endeavors in applications, for example, programs like Google chrome, Mozilla Firefox progressed toward becoming piece of adventure units, which contains various adventures bundled and packaged together with the goal that when an administrator go to a devilish site will be hit by a few endeavors. At times the cybercriminals can watch the endeavors of legitimate whitehat programmers and other security researchers who post their advancements in online sites. As we realized that the whitehat programmers and analysts or researcher may have great targets, their work might be abused by confirmed association, blackhat programmers or numerous wicked online gatherings to deliver malware. It can likewise be the situation cybercrime association who need to utilize zero-day abuses yet don't have the specialized learning, and after that they enlist different cybercriminals to make bugs in applications.

13.7   Mobile Cybersecurity

At the present time, the habit of utilizing cell phones and their applications have turned out to be rapidly well known in each one of us everyday life. In the past period, versatile cash administrations accessibility, for example, portable installment frameworks and their application markets have expanded fundamentally owing the diverse kinds of applications and availability giving by different cell phones, for example, 3G, 4G, GPRS, and Wi-Fi, and so forth however the quantity of vulnerabilities pointing these administrations and correspondence systems has additionally raised up [13].

Table 13.1   A contrast of the smartphone oses market share over the era of 2011-2017

OS Name \ Factors	Android	Apple iOS	Windows Phone	BlackBerry (RIM)	Symbian and others
Source Code	Open source	Closed source	Closed source	Closed Source	Closed source, previously open source
OS Family	Linux	Unix-Like, Darwin	Windows NT	Unix-Like, QNX	RTOS
Support by	Google	Apple	Microsoft	Blackberry	Discontinued (2012)
Exclusive Company	Unexclusive	Apple	Unexclusive	BlackBerry	Unexclusive
Programming Written in	Java, C, C++, Basic	C, C++	C, C++	C, C++, Qt	C++
Smartphone Market share sold to the end users (%)	74.79 %	16.11 %	3.33 %	3.23 %	4.27 %

In like manner, for pernicious engineers mobile phones have ended up being flawless target devices with significantly extending the proportion of vulnerabilities and strikes and as a result of these causes, portion systems security is a champion among the most key issues in adaptable portion structures. In this investigation, we intend to give a sweeping and sorted out survey of the examination on security answers for PDA devices.

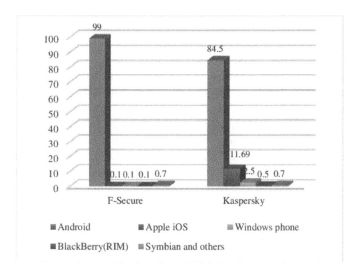

Figure 13.3   Malware attacks on smartphone OSes.

In this part we illuminate the security risks, their answers, and vulnerabilities in the midst of the season of 2011-2017, by giving more complement on programming ambushes which impact the phone applications. It can anchor by using some acknowledgment rules, data aggregations and working systems, especially focusing on open source applications. In this part we give a basic seeing way to deal with customers and furthermore the researchers to assemble their knowledge about the characterization and trustworthiness and security of mobile phones [15].

13.8 Healthcare

The Ex-President of US Obama marked cybersecurity act of 2015 into law which was the primary basic advance toward serving the medicinal services region and furthermore supportive to littler social orders. It sets up standards of the guide similarly as how computerized hazard information should be shared, which HIMSS considers is to a great degree a central steps to hint at enhancement advanced information to the private territory, including social protection affiliations.

The law, most likely comprehended as the cybersecurity data sharing act, contains three essential game plans related to the human administrations part which incorporates the progression of:

- A recommendation inside each division of the branch of wellbeing and human administrations which prescribing the conventional jobs for tending to cyberthreats in the social protection territory.

- A standard course of action of methodology, intentional understanding based guidelines, and best practices to help human administrations relationship against the cyberthreats.

- A HHS industry group to examine, the advanced challenges which are making issues for the restorative administrations section, and furthermore instruct the region that it can pick up from various endeavors.

The fundamental objective is to guarantee that the medicinal services associations ought to get every one of the devices and assets which enhance their cybersecurity on the grounds that cybercriminals have now focuses from banks to human services as the business moved into the best promotion of the rankings. As an overview as indicated by IBM 2016 Cyber Security Intelligence Index[4], it is found that more than 100 million social protection records were in all actuality exchanged off dependent on information gathered between different nations. The health records, quite a bit of which keep on substantial and usable for a considerable length of time, contain profitable information for programmers like portable number, messages addresses, MasterCard data, institutionalized funds numbers, work information and helpful history records can be utilized as a rule of or fraud, theft or trick which can causes an incredible lose to the organization. As precedent it is conceivable to stolen restorative records of another person and sold it to other people who utilized it for their advantages and additionally leaving the whole bill against the principal individual. So, it is, vital for the wellbeing organization to shield themselves from such sort of misrepresentation by utilizing new digital security procedures on the grounds that as long as the information keeps up its esteem, there will be dangers to any organization that holds it.

---

[4]https://www.ibm.com/security

13.9   Human Rights

Having suitable to use the web is coherently evaluated to be a making human right. The global affiliations and national governments have formally begun to know its centrality for the privilege to talk unreservedly, enunciation and information exchange. The ensuing stage is to help confirm cybersecurity to be seen as a human appropriate, also. The United Nations formally had pronounced that the movements of governments cutting off web access as denying their residents' rights to free articulation. Be that as it may, this isn't adequate on the grounds that now a days we have standard web get to which quickly endure from cyber-dangers, assuming our information to be hacked at any minute we are feeling powerless to stop it. An online rights promotion gathering, prominently known as The electronic frontier foundation[5], called all the innovation partnerships to "join with regards to clients," for defending their frameworks against interference by programmers and in addition government examination.

Unhindered internet is the rule that each point on the system can connection to some other point on the system, without segregating based on source, goal or sort of information and this assessment is the principal purpose behind the achievement of the Internet. Unhindered internet give the capacity to Internet to create new methods for human rights, for example, the opportunity of articulation and the privilege to send, get and pass on data and additionally it is essential for insurgency, modularization, competition and for the development of data.

Advantages:

- The incredible telecom organizations can convey the ways however don't have any privilege to coordinate how the general population ought to depend on them.

- Net impartiality secures upheaval, if bigger undertakings like Google and Netflix[6] could pay and get unique treatment like quicker speeds, more transmission capacity, at that point new start-up or the little Organization had extraordinary misfortune.

- If unhindered internet isn't in the situation at that point, the enormous organizations could offer need to TV arranges and back off the signs of others.

- It offers opportunity to each association, from huge undertakings to little new businesses to participate in it.

Disadvantages:

- Nowadays, enormous association like Netflix and YouTube[7] and square the funnels with tremendous measures of information, here changes will put a confinement.

- The different organizations like Google, Facebook gives talk benefits that allow individuals to make free approaches web that portable organizations have consumed billions to manufacture.

[5]https://www.eff.org/
[6]https://www.netflix.com/
[7]https://www.youtube.com/

13.10   Cybersecurity Application in Our Life

Mobiles: Association gave or bring your own device (BYOD), customers with various contraptions and sorts will auto select all of them effectively. Each contraption is painstakingly enrolled and scratched to a customer and can be in a brief moment uncovered lost or stolen. In case uncovered, countermeasures are begun and whenever found, can be viably re-chose for continued with advantage.

Smart Cards: It can provides, authentication, individual recognizable proof, information stockpiling limit, and application preparing inside associations. A solitary contact/contactless keen card can be preset with various keeping money approvals, driver's permit, therapeutic benefit open transport right, club memberships. It can likewise be utilized as an ID, a put away esteem money card, a charge card, and a distribution center of individual data, for example, medicinal history or contacts numbers. On the off chance that it lost or burglary, the card can be effectively supplanted by the security personal identification number (PIN) [14].

Virtual Private Systems (VPN): It gives you on the web privacy and being anonymous by creating a individual network from a open public Internet interconnection. Whilst VPN delivers wonderful network protection, it may just be used from a great appropriately secured computing product. There are several reasons people around the world make use of VPNs: to cover location, gain access to work systems, even to prevent government censorship. A VPN is commonly professional help that keeps the web scouting secure and over general public Wi-Fi hotspots. For example, OpenVPN[8], Juniper[9], Cisco, and so on.

Signing of Documents: It give the e-marks, time-stamps, approved teammates, and encryption/decoding to assertions, reports, bills, approved and financials in record composes like, DOC, XLS, PDF, etc.

Securing Email: Digital Security avoid harming of email content, turn away introduction of email content with encryption, confirm message source, and give adaptable and ensured communication [6].

Strong Authentication: It give the solid Authentication offices by giving the Managing and checking of both gadget and client and personalities, allowing or permitting power over who without a doubt, gets to your information, organizations, data and propelled assets on your web, extranet or intranet assets [14].

Protected Communication: It offers strong connections between SSL (*Secure Sockets Layer*)/TLS (*Transport Layer Security*) servers and SSL/TLS customers for within private frameworks and the financial remittance is less stood out from procuring trader provisioned propelled verifications.

Online Corroboration Facilities: The programmed and solid validation benefit gives the cybersecurity, gives secure association ask for whether the clients signing into a remote application or opening a record on the private gadget or nearby machine. It can process lakhs of solicitations every second.

Code Signing: Digital security giving an innovation known as code marking which ensures that product improvement process is being guaranteed and that the item running on servers, cloud and end customers can't be changed or tainted since it was marked by the validated creator.

---

[8]https://openvpn.net/
[9]https://www.juniper.net/

Time Stamping: It gives the data about who is the maker of online record- who made it, insisted it and the information that when this record was delivered or last refreshed, which are the most required information for the client for their online safety [14].

Single Sign-on: It enables the official customer to get to various applications and servers on the double using master accreditations and furthermore it stop all application logins by someone who gets the opportunity to work region or device which isn't endorsed.

13.11 Conclusion

In this chapter we found that the highest rates of hacking industries now a day is healthcare then the second place for the most attacked industry went to manufacturing, the financial targets fell down from the top to the third place while government and the transportation industry are in the fourth and fifth places, respectively. It is observed in the year 2015 the most of these, approximately 60 percent of cyberattacks were carried out by "insiders", or those who had a right of entry to organization systems and since the beginning of 2016 more than 4,000 ransomware attacks have occurred every day. In the year 2017, 74 percent of organizations feel that they are powerless against insider dangers, with seven percent revealing an extraordinary powerlessness.

As artificial intelligence and machine learning impact more and more industries, it's certain to assume a greater job in cybersecurity [17-19]. The machine learning models foresee and precisely discover the robbery. We ought to be dynamic about ransomware and additionally nimbly overseeing information breaks.

References

1. Kshetri, N. (2010). The global cybercrime industry: economic, institutional and strategic perspectives. Springer Science & Business Media.

2. Dupont A. Time to attack cybercrime with a strong security policy. WWW page, October 2010

3. Powell, A., Stratton, G., & Cameron, R. (2018). Digital criminology: Crime and justice in digital society. Routledge.

4. Thakur, K., Qiu, M., Gai, K., & Ali, M. L. (2015, November). An investigation on cybersecurity threats and security models. In cybersecurity and Cloud Computing (CSCloud), 2015 IEEE 2nd International Conference on (pp. 307-311).

5. Yan, Y., Qian, Y., Sharif, H., & Tipper, D. (2012). A survey on cybersecurity for smart grid communications. IEEE Communications Surveys and tutorials, 14(4), 998-1010.

6. Tonge, A. M., Kasture, S. S., & Chaudhari, S. R. (2013). cybersecurity: challenges for society-literature review. IOSR Journal of Computer Engineering, 2(12), 67-75.

7. Subashini, S., & Kavitha, V. (2011). A survey on security issues in service delivery models of cloud computing. Journal of network and computer applications, 34(1), 1-11.

8. Petric, G., Axinte, S. D., Bacivarov, I. C., Firoiu, M., & Mihai, I. C. (2017, June). Studying cybersecurity threats to web platforms using attack tree diagrams. In Electronics, Computers and Artificial Intelligence (ECAI), 2017 9th International Conference on (pp. 1-6). IEEE.

9. Mauw, S., & Oostdijk, M. (2005, December). Foundations of attack trees. In International Conference on Information Security and Cryptology (pp. 186-198). Springer, Berlin, Heidelberg.

10. The Cisco Secure Services Client: Enabling the Self-Defending Network 2007. [Online] Available: www.cisco.com/c/en/us/products/collateral/wireless/secureservices

11. Karp, B. (2016, March). Federal Guidance on the Cybersecurity Information Sharing Act of 2015. In Harvard Law School Forum on Corporate Governance and Financial Regulation.

12. https://www.rand.org/

13. Ahvanooey, M. T., Li, Q., Rabbani, M., & Rajput, A. R. (2017). A Survey on Smartphones Security: Software Vulnerabilities, Malware, and Attacks. INTERNATIONAL JOURNAL OF ADVANCED COMPUTER SCIENCE AND APPLICATIONS, 8(10), 30-45.

14. http://www.sio2corp.com/cyber-security-applications/

15. https://www.govinfosecurity.com/

16. https://www.wilsoncenter.org/

17. Ristic, I. (2010). ModSecurity Handbook. Feisty Duck.

18. Kordy, B., Kordy, P., Mauw, S., & Schweitzer, P. (2013, August). ADTool: security analysis with attackdefense trees. In International Conference on Quantitative Evaluation of Systems (pp. 173-176). Springer, Berlin, Heidelberg.

19. Dorfman, R. (2004). Extensible Markup Language (XML). The Internet Encyclopedia.

20. Makino, Y., & Klyuev, V. (2015, September). Evaluation of web vulnerability scanners. In Intelligent Data Acquisition and Advanced Computing Systems: Technology and Applications (IDAACS), 2015 IEEE 8th International Conference on (Vol. 1, pp. 399-402). IEEE.

21. Beyer, J. The Cybersecurity Information Sharing Act (CISA). Jackson School of International Studies.

CHAPTER 14

SECURITY IN DISTRIBUTED OPERATING SYSTEM: A COMPREHENSIVE STUDY

Sushree Bibhuprada B. Priyadarshini[1], Amiya Bhusan Bagjadab[2], Brojo Kishore Mishra [3]

[1] Institute of Technical Education and Research, Bhubaneswar, India.

[2] Sambalpur University of Information Technology, Burla, India

[3] C. V. Raman College of Engineering, Bhubaneswar, India

Email: bimalabibhuprada@gmail.com, amiya7bhusan7@gmail.com, brojokishoremishra@gmail.com

Abstract

In recent years, various attacks have increasingly been making their way into the world of information. In this context, security in distributed operating systems is poised to become a crucial element. However, currently entirely new information markets have opened up as playing fields for a number of computer criminals, and therefore it is still the job of the user to protect the data. In the current chapter, we shed light upon security policies, security mechanisms, various categories of attacks such as denial-of-service attacks, Globus security architecture, along with distribution of security mechanisms. Furthermore, we have also investigated the various strategies of attack that occur frequently in any information system under consideration.

Keywords: Access control, cryptography, denial-of-service, distributed operating system, fabrication, threat

Dac-Nhuong Le et al. (eds.), Cyber Security in Parallel and Distributed Computing, (221–262)
© 2019 Scrivener Publishing LLC

14.1 Introduction to Security and Distributed Systems

The phrase "Operating system security" is basically the process of ensuring the integrity, confidentiality as well as availability of the operating systems. Fundamentally, operating system security (*abbreviated as: OS security*) incorporates the measures involved in protecting the OS from various viruses, worms, threats, malware, external hackers, etc. Basically, a distributed operating system is an operating system software for a group of various independent, networked as well as physically distinguished computational nodes. Various jobs are carried out by multiple central processing units (CPUs). Fundamentally, a distributed OS represents an extension of the operating systems employed in networks that assists in higher levels of information interchange and combinations of the machines across the network. The logical organization of distributed systems into various layers is as portrayed in Figure 14.1, where various layers are arranged among one another, including kernel and the hardware.

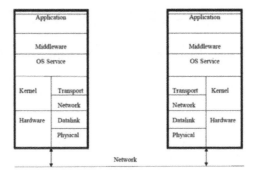

Figure 14.1 Logical organization of distributed systems into various layers.

With the popularity of distributed systems, the demand for security in distributed operating system is growing day by day with the advent of modern technology. However, if the attacker has physical contact with the intended machine, then it becomes hectic to protect the system concerned. Various basic elements of security are as shown in Figure 14.2.

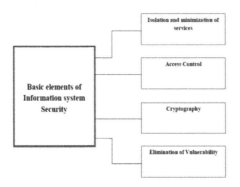

Figure 14.2 Basic elements of information system security.

Cybersecurity involves: isolation and minimization of services, access control, cryptography and elimination of vulnerability. Access control is controlling access to resources present in the system. Cryptography is the process of transforming the plain text into cipher text, in which text before conversion is known as plain text and after conversion is called cipher text [6].

However, preventing external threats are the easiest way for protecting. Normally, most of the attacks prevail owing to social engineering, observation, rummaging in the trash, etc. A distributed system represents a network which comprises of various autonomous computers interconnected through a distribution middleware. In this system, sharing of various resources occur. In other words, a distributed system is that system which is designed to assist in the development of various applications as well as services that can makes use of a physical architecture consisting of multiple, processing elements that are autonomous and which do not share primary memory, which, however, cooperate through transferring asynchronous messages over a communication network of interest. The main motto of using distributed systems is: resource sharing, scalability, extensibility, etc. A schematic of information exchange in distributed systems is as shown in Figure 14.3.

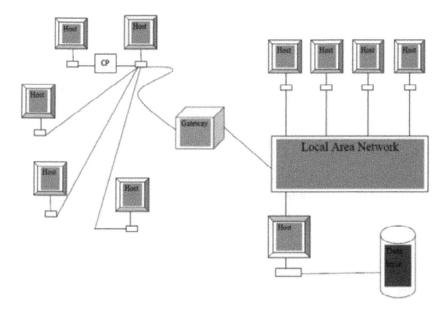

Figure 14.3   Schematic showing the exchange of information in distributed systems.

As shown in the Figure 14.3, all the systems are interconnected through a local area network (LAN). A gateway is present that connects one network to another. In this chapter, we put focus on several mechanisms which are normally integrated into distributed systems for assisting security. Fundamentally, security in distributed systems can be divided into two parts: the first part is concerned with the communication between users or processes, which dwell on distinct machines. The primary technique for making sure such communication is secure is using a secure channel.

In the coming sections, we will discuss message confidentiality, message authentication and message integrity. The second part concentrates on authorization that deals with making sure that a process attains access rights to those resources in a distributed system for which it is assigned to. We will discuss authorization along with access control. Let us first discuss two things which need to be taken into account when considering the security in any distributed system:

- **Security Policy**: This determines what is secure for the system or organization or entity. It basically refers to the constraints on the characteristics of the members and restrictions imposed upon the adversaries by various techniques, viz. locks, keys, walls, doors, etc.

- **Security Mechanism**: A security mechanism is basically designed for preventing or recovering from a security attack. A security service basically uses one or more security mechanisms. Fundamentally, a security service is that which enhances the security of the data processing systems. The following four different types of security threats are commonly present:

    - *Interception*: Refers to the situation where an unauthorized party has access to data or service. Such situation arises when the communication between two parties is overheard by another person.

    - *Interruption*: When something is corrupted or lost, the interruption occurs. Basically, it is a situation in which services or data become unavailable, destroyed, unusable, etc. In denial-of-service attacks, someone maliciously tries to make a service inaccessible to another party.

    - *Modification*: This is concerned with unauthorized change or tampering of data such that it cannot further adhere to its initial specifications; for example, frequently changing the transmitted data.

    - *Fabrication*: Represents the circumstance where additional data or activity gets produced that does not normally exist. For example, an intruder may attempt to append an entry into the password file or the database.

Furthermore, the security mechanisms through which a policy can be enforced are as follows:

- Encryption

- Authentication

- Authorization

- Auditing

Encryption is fundamental to computer security. Encryption transforms data into something an attacker cannot understand. In other words, encryption provides a means to implement data confidentiality. In addition, encryption allows us to check whether data have been modified. Thus, it also provides support for integrity checks. Authentication is used to verify the claimed identity of a user, client, server, host, or other entity. In the case of clients, the basic premise is that before a service starts to perform any work on behalf of a client, it should be known [9].

14.2   Relevant Terminology

The distinct terminology related to DoS [10] security is outlined as follows:

- *Vulnerability*: It indicates a fault in the system that enables an attacking agent to create inappropriate malicious behavior.

- *Threat*: A threat is something aimed at harming the system.

- *Compromise*: It refers to the impact of the vulnerable attack.

- *Exploit*: It means a program exploits the vulnerability/susceptibility of a system.

- *Payload*: This refers to executing the actions pre-planned as the aim of the concerned attack.

- *Root kit*: It refers to a set of programs that that hides the presence of the attacker concerned.

- *Malware*: This is the generic name for programs that are malicious.

    - Virus: It refers to a program that propagates itself by appending its corresponding code to the rest of the programs.
    - Backdoor: It refers to a secret part of the program which enables unauthorized access.
    - Trojan: It indicates a benign program having an undocumented as well as secret impact on others.
    - Logic/time bomb: It refers to a fragment of code that is executed at the time when a particular condition gets satisfied.
    - Worm: It refers to a program that propagates itself actively through the corresponding network under consideration.
    - Bacteria: It refers to the program that can multiply itself for exhausting the system's resources locally.

14.3   Types of External Attacks

The various types of external attacks that can occur are illustrated in Figure 14.4.

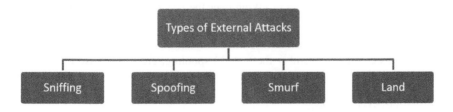

Figure 14.4   Types of external attacks.

- Sniffing attack

    - This attack is also known as a sniffer attack in the context of network security. This attack represents the interception of data by ensnaring the network traffic by employing a sniffer.

    - The term sniffer refers to an application aimed at capturing the network packets.

    - Whenever, the data are transferred across the network, if the packets of the data are not at all encrypted, a sniffer is employed at that time to read the data packets.

    - The attacker can analyze the network and gain information to eventually cause the concerned network to become corrupted.

    - Otherwise, it can read the communications prevailing throughout the network.

- Spoofing

    - Spoofing refers to the process of impersonating the machine that is authorized in the information interchange with the victim.

    - The frequent spoofing example is IP spoofing. Basically, IP spoofing is a technique that is aimed at gaining access to the machines in which an attacker impersonates any other machining by manipulating the IP packets.

    - It involves modifying the packet header with a forged or spoofed IP address, checksum as well as other values.

- Smurfing

    - Smurfing is defined as the process of getting access to a secret account that is different from the main document under consideration such that an user can do anything without being detected by anyone.

    - Smurfing is the phenomenon of impersonating any sort of victim in communication with remaining machines.

- Landing

    - It is defined as the phenomenon of defrauding the victim while in communication with them.

    - Various attacks on machines and processes come under such type of attacks.

- Information Theft

    - This involves the process of taking over the necessary information from various machines.

    - In recent years there has been a huge amount of information concerning thefts, such as credit card number theft, ATM spoofing, electronic cash theft, database theft, etc.

- Denial-of-Service (DoS)

    - A DoS attack refers to a security event which prevails whenever the attacker initiates actions which prevent the legitimate users from getting access to targeted computers under consideration or any other network resources.

- Typically, such attacks flood the servers, systems or networks with the traffic so as to overwhelm the victim resources for the purpose of making it hectic or impossible for the authorized users to access it.

The United States Computer Emergency Readiness Team (US-CERT)[1] affords various guidelines so as to determine when a DoS attack occurs, which are as follows:

- Difficulty in reaching a specific website

- Degradation in the performance of the network

Whenever a suspicion arises regarding a DoS attack, the organizations or enterprises contact their Internet Service Provider (ISP) to check whether it is owing to a DoS attack or due to something else. Afterwards, the ISP assists in mitigating the attack by throttling the malicious traffic by employing the load balancers for reducing the impact of attacks. Similarly, the feasibility of DoS detection can be explored through intrusion prevention systems, intrusion detection systems, etc. Moreover, in distributed operating systems, the network connected devices along with the computer are infected by malware. The various types of DoS attacks are as shown in Figure 14.5.

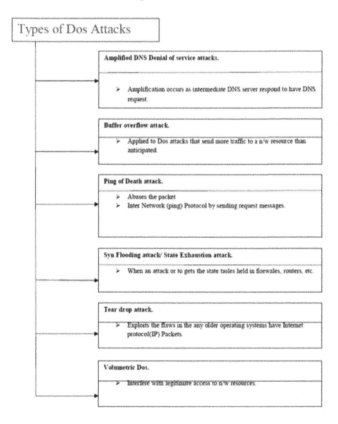

Figure 14.5   Types of DoS attacks.

[1] https://www.us-cert.gov/

14.4   Globus Security Architecture

The idea of security policy and the mode that security mechanisms contribute in distributed systems for enforcement of such types of policies are best established by considering an example. Let us discuss the security policy involved for the Globus wide-area system [3]. Basically, Globus is a system that supports large-scale distributed computations where many hosts, files, and other resources are concurrently employed for carrying out a computation. These environments are also referred to as computational grids. Furthermore, many times resources in these grids are located in distinct domains of administration which may be positioned in several parts of the world.

The security policy for Globus includes the following statements:

- The environment consists of a number of administrative domains.

- Local operations: It represents the operations which are conducted only within a single domain. These are merely subjected to a local domain security policy.

- Global operations: This represents the operations concerning several domains that require the concerned initiator to be known in every domain wherever the operation is being conducted.

- Operations between entities in distinct domains need mutual authentication.

- Local authentication is replaced by Global authentication.

- Controlling access to the resources is mainly merely subjected to local security.

- Users can delegate the right to the processes.

- Credentials can be shared among processes in the same domain.

It is assumed that the environment consists of number of administrative domains, such that every domain possesses its policy for local security. It is further understood that local policies cannot be altered since the domain takes part in Globus. Subsequently, security in Globus prohibits itself from operating, which can hamper several domains relevant to this issue. Furthermore, Globus assumes that operations which are completely local to a domain are subject only to the concerned domain's security policy. The Globus security policy means that various requests for operations can be initiated either locally or globally. The initiator can be a user or process acting on behalf of a user, and must be locally known within each domain.

Once a user or a process acting on behalf of a user gets authenticated, it becomes essential to verify the exact access rights with respect to resources. For example, a user wishing to update a file will first have to be authenticated; afterwards, it can be verified whether or not the concerned user is practically permitted to update the file. The Globus security policy depicts that the access control decisions are framed completely locally within the domain of the location of the accessed resource. Furthermore, Globus focuses on security threats involving multiple domains. Specifically, the security policy demonstrates that the crucial design issues involve the representation of a user in any remote domain, as well as the allocation of resources from a remote domain to a user or his representative. The architecture of the Globus security policy is as shown in the Figure 14.6.

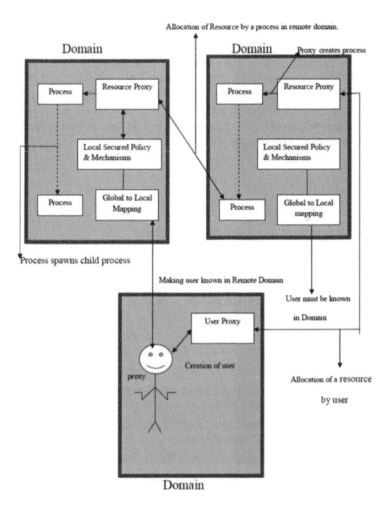

Figure 14.6   Globus security policy architecture.

14.5   Distribution of Security Mechanism

The dependency existing among services concerning trust gives rise to the notion of a Trusted Computing Base (TCB). A TCB represents a set of all security mechanisms in a distributed computer system that are necessary for ensuring a security policy, and which are required to be trusted. The smaller the TCB is, the better it will be. Furthermore, TCB in a distributed system can incorporate the local operating systems at several hosts. A file server in a distributed file system might need to to be believed on the several protection mechanisms afforded by corresponding local operating system. Moreover, middleware-based distributed systems need to trust in the existing local operating systems. If no trust exists, then part of the functionality of the local operating systems has to be incorporated into the distributed system itself.

14.6   Conclusions

This chapter discussed the various types of attacks that frequently prevail in the case of distributed systems by introducing distributed system. Then, we discussed the concept of policy and mechanism concerning distributed systems. Moreover, we detailed the different types of attacks that prevail in distributed systems, including the denial-of-service (DoS) attacks. Thereafter, the concept of Globus security architecture as well as the distribution of security mechanism were briefly discussed.

References

1. http://staff.elka.pw.edu.pl/ akozakie/DOS/lecture_10.pdf

2. Thakur, B. S., & Chaudhary, S. (2013). Content sniffing attack detection in client and server side: A survey. International Journal of Advanced Computer Research, 3(2), 7.

3. Khan, S., Gani, A., Wahab, A. W. A., & Singh, P. K. (2018). Feature selection of denial-of-service attacks using entropy and granular computing. Arabian Journal for Science and Engineering, 43(2), 499-508.

4. Sinha, P. K. (1998). Distributed operating systems: concepts and design. PHI Learning Pvt. Ltd.

5. Stallings, W. (2006). Cryptography and Network Security, 4/E. Pearson Education India.

6. Ogiela, M. R., & Ogiela, L. (2018). Cognitive cryptography techniques for intelligent information management. International Journal of Information Management, 40, 21-27.

7. Firdhous, M. (2012). Implementation of security in distributed systems-a comparative study. arXiv preprint arXiv:1211.2032. https://arxiv.org/ftp/arxiv/papers/1211/1211.2032.pdf

8. https://people.cs.pitt.edu/ mehmud/docs/abliz11-TR-11-178.pdf

9. Tanenbaum, A. S., & Van Steen, M. (2007). Distributed systems: principles and paradigms. Prentice-Hall.

10. Le, D. N., Van, V. N., & Giang, T. T. T. (2016). A New Private Security Policy Approach for DDoS Attack Defense in NGNs. In Information Systems Design and Intelligent Applications (pp. 1-10). Springer, New Delhi.

CHAPTER 15

SECURITY IN HEALTHCARE APPLICATIONS BASED ON FOG AND CLOUD COMPUTING

ROJALINA PRIYADARSHINI[1], MOHIT RANJAN PANDA [2], BROJO KISHORE MISHRA[1]

[1] Department of Computer Science and Information Technology, C. V. Raman College of Engineering, Bhubaneswar, India

[2] Department of Computer Science and Engineering, C. V. Raman College of Engineering, Bhubaneswar, India

Email: brojokishoremishra@gmail.com

Abstract

The last few years have seen remarkable advancements in the e-healthcare system. This is due to the growth of digitization in the healthcare sector, especially the use of wearable devices equipped with sensors, IoT devices and body area network. e-Healthcare is not only limited to storing clinical data. Sophisticated digital applications are able to be designed and developed which cater to an array of varied health-related services. Some examples are telemonitoring of elderly persons, tracking mobility of patients, monitoring sugar levels and blood pressure, and giving early notifications in case of emergencies. This has brought about a revolution in e-healthcare. At the same time, these applications are challenged by different security issues. The security challenges are multi-fold when these solutions are built on a virtual environment like cloud or fog. In this chapter we have tried to accumulate some of the security issues which arise in the healthcare sector. The chapter also discusses existing solutions and emerging threats.

Keywords: e-Healthcare, confidentiality, integrity, availability, threats, vulnerabilities

Dac-Nhuong Le et al. (eds.), Cyber Security in Parallel and Distributed Computing, (231–262)
© 2019 Scrivener Publishing LLC

15.1   Introduction

Recent years have have seen a rise in the use of electronic equipment, such as sensors, for developing digital healthcare solutions. Nowadays, healthcare applications are not limited to digital record keeping of various clinical data generated from patients, doctors, etc. Current healthcare applications focus on telemonitoring patients, tracking their mobility, and giving early notifications to doctors and relatives in case of critical situations. This is possible due to the emergence of Internet of Things (IoT) devices and the use of embedded sensors in a patient's body. The general architecture of the healthcare monitoring system is depicted in Figure 15.1. Reliable communication, handling and mobility, latency control and energy-efficient routing are some of the issues which need to be addressed. Due to the digital transformation, there has been a staggering quantity of unstructured data like video and images generated in the healthcare field. The healthcare field has produced a virtual and connected world of clinical devices which continuously send out unstructured, and potentially unsecured data, which is vulnerable to attack. These data need to be transmitted in a channel, which may not also be secured. But, the physiological data of an individual contain highly personal and sensitive information. So, security is a predominant need of healthcare applications, especially if the solutions use IoT devices equipped with sensors or body area networks.

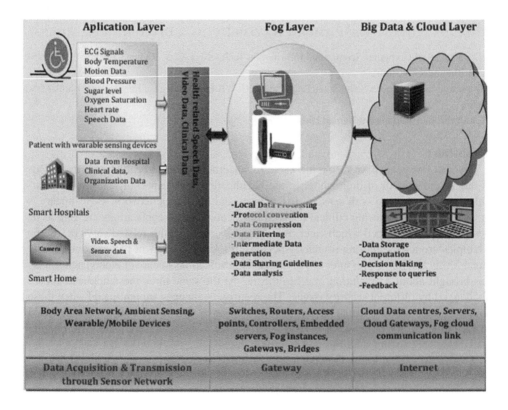

Figure 15.1   General architecture of healthcare monitoring systems.

But, when the healthcare solutions are deployed in cloud and fog environment, the security concerns are doubled due to the following reasons:

- Fog and Cloud are deployed on top of the traditional network computing so they are vulnerable to all kinds of security threats suffered by traditional networks.

- Personal human health-related data are captured from ubiquitous wearable sensors deployed in IoT devices, which are highly scalable and dynamic in nature.

- In most of the cases the communication medium through which the data transmits is wireless and lacks security.

- The captured data from an IP-enabled user device transmitted to the desired site may be routed through an unsecured network infrastructure [46].

15.2 Security Needs of Healthcare Sector

Security and privacy in healthcare solutions is of prime concern, especially when it is deployed in a virtual computing environment. In these cases, authentication and authorization of both users and service providers must be ensured [1]. So, in order to have a secure and foolproof cloud-baed healthcare system, the desirable characteristics must include the following security requirements:

15.2.1 Data Integrity

Data integrity is required to ensure that the patient data transmitted to the service provider is not changed by any means during the transition. In the fog-based healthcare system, most of the communication is wireless. So, there is a risk of integrity loss during transmission. The data integrity can be maintained by adding a cyclic redundancy check (CRC) to the data packets which can detect erroneous packets. Otherwise, message authentication code (MAC) protocols are also used to maintain data integrity [2].

15.2.2 Data Confidentiality

All the relevant health-related sensitive data and personal information are transmitted over a communication network between the user and service provider. To preserve the data in their original form and to prevent them from leakage and middleman attack, the confidentiality of the data is required to be preserved. This could be possible by imposing strong encryption and decryption mechanisms. By the use of encryption and decryption mechanisms, the eavesdropping can be controlled and no middleman can get the access to the data.

15.2.3 Authentication and Authorization

Authentication and authorization are required to validate the identity of the sender and receiver of the health data packets. Any unauthorized access to private medical information can spoil the entire mechanism. Unauthorized access to private data may cause the injection of some invalid spurious data which may damage the system. This can be avoided by using MAC protocols.

15.2.4   Availability

Availability ensures that the health services enabled through the fog-based system are uninterruptedly available to the authorized users as and when required. There may be a chance that the data and service will be unavailable at the time of need due to denial-of-service (DoS) attacks. DoS attacks can consume network bandwidth, kill response time, causes network traffic congestion. Availability can be defined by the policies and principles of a system and resources to be accessible, usable and available when there is a demand by one legitimate users [3, 4] anytime and anywhere in the healthcare system . Ensuring availability prevents service disruptions caused by hardware failures, power failure, maintenance work and system upgradation.

15.2.5   Access Control

This is the capacity to provide controlled access to various resources by authorized users [5]. It involves three different security and privacy requirements: identification, authentication, and authorization. Identification is all about how to identify users. Though it is not a clear goal of security, it can be used to influence the manner in which a user is authenticated. Authentication, in turn, gives a surety that the requested data access is genuine. It also provides a surety that the communication is happening with an authorized party on the other side. Eventually, the authorization process decides which portion of data can be restricted to an outside requester based on some security policy. It is to be noted that an appropriate access control mechanism could ensure patient privacy and also could offer a good balance between availability and confidentiality [6, 7] types of security goals.

15.2.6   Dependability

Dependability guarantees easy recovery and retrieval of medical data at any time, irrespective of the presence of some threats caused by the network dynamic or failure node [8, 9]. Normally, in most medical cases, inability to retrieve accurate data is due to threats caused by the network dynamics, which can threaten the patient's life. Fault tolerance is an essential requisite for dependability.

15.2.7   Flexibility

Flexibility enables an unauthorized participant who is not on the permission list to access specific data in an emergency case to save the patient's life. Inability or prevention the access rules may threaten a patients life [10].

15.3   Solutions to Probable Attacks in e-Healthcare

There are several points in fog environment where patient health-related information containing confidential data can be compromised; for example, by exploiting any system and application vulnerability, unauthorized third-party data access from a data store or during data transmission, malicious insider threat and when the data is shared among some other systems [11]. The data capturing sensors are continuously forwarding data to cloud environment via wired or wireless connection mediums. So, there is a high risk of compromising data privacy, data integrity, and system availability. The reason behind this is that any point, the sensors and capturing devices can be exploited along with the underlying communication network and the data can be forged. The IoT environment usually works in open, unattended and hostile environments. This ease-of-access to data can lead to increase the chances of attacks like DoS, Masquerade, and selective forwarding attacks [12]. In addition, if the fog node manages sensitive data and is lacking in better access control mechanisms, it might suffer from information leakage due to account hijacking, unauthorized access, and other vulnerable points of entry [13]. The attacks in the healthcare system can be broadly categorized into three types, which are depicted in Figure 15.2.

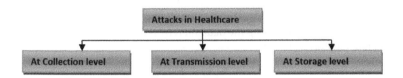

Figure 15.2   Categorization of attacks in healthcare system.

15.3.1 Jamming Attack

In a jamming attack, the antagonist tampers with the content of the original message by transporting radio frequency signals inside the network or by blocking the message and, as a result, it cannot reach the intended receiver. Radio interference attacks are very difficult to be addressed by conventional security methods. An attacker can cause the attack simply by disregarding the medium access protocol and continually sending on a wireless networks. A jamming attack can happen in two ways. Either it could be an external threat model in which jammer is not part of network; or it could be an internal threat model in which jammer belongs to the underlying network. A jamming attack may happen in healthcare applications by interference of the attacker's radio signal with frequencies of the BAN (body area networks) [14].

15.3.2 Data Collision Attack

A data collision attack takes place when two or more nodes attempt to transmit simultaneously. It is a form of jamming attack where an intruder may strategically produce extra collisions by sending repeated messages on the channel [15, 16]. When the frame header is changed due to a collision, the error checking mechanism at the receiving end detects an error and rejects the received data. Thus, a change in the data frame header is a threat to data availability in the BAN [17].

15.3.3 Desynchronization Attack

In this type of attack, the attacker tampers with the message transmitted between sensor nodes by copying it many times by imposing a fake sequence number to one or both endpoints in an active connection; which leads to WBAN (wireless body area networks) overwhelming the network resources and energy, thereby causing the sensor nodes to transfer the message repeatedly [15, 18].

15.3.4 Spoofing Attack

A fog platform where fog devices collaboratively work is more prone to data tampering and spoofing attacks [19]. Stojmenovic *et al.* suggested prevention methods could be built in using a public key infrastructure (PKI), Diffie-Hellman key exchange, intrusion detection techniques and monitoring for modified input values. In a health fog platform both security, performance and latency are the important factors to be considered, and mechanisms like encryption methodologies, known as fully homomorphic [20] and somewhat homomorphic [21] can be used to preserve data security during data transmission. These methods constituted by a hybrid of symmetric and public-key encryption algorithms, as well as other variants of attribute-based encryption. The homomorphic encryption schemes allow doing normal operations without decrypting the data, thereby reducing the key distribution which helps to maintain data privacy.

The algorithm for homomorphic encryption is given below:

Algorithm Homomerphic encryption

Input: Encrypted data from individual fog nodes.
Output: Secured private data at receiver end
BEGIN
     Step 1. Let PT_1 and PT_2 be encrypted data collected from sensor and fog nodes from edge devices.
     Step 2. Apply either additive or multiplicative homomerphic (EH) on PT_1 and PT_2 given by equation 15.1 and 15.2 respectively.

$$EH(PT_1)\Theta EH(PT_2) = EH(PT_1 + PT_2) \qquad (15.1)$$

$$EH(PT_1)\Theta EH(PT_2) = EH(PT_1 \times PT_2) \qquad (15.2)$$

Where, Θ is a mathematical operator.
     Step 3. Receive data at in a double encrypted mode.
END

Processing should be done on the data in fog node without decrypting the original message, thus preserving data confidentiality.

15.3.5 Man-in-the-Middle Attack

In fog computing, there is high chance of going through man-in-the-middle (MITM) attack [22]. During this attack, fog devices serving as gateways might be compromised or substituted by forged ones [23]. Traditionally these attacks can be prevented by using encryption and decryption algorithm methods [22]. But it is difficult to protect communication between fog node and IoT devices using the encryption method. Encryption and decryption methods devour a considerable amount of time and battery on a mobile device. It is often a risk factor against the QoS (quality of service) requirement of the healthcare monitoring system in fog environment.

Kulkarni *et al.* [24] suggested a method to handle an MITM attack. On the extracted data, they insert Gaussian noise in some part of data to reduce the chance of eavesdropping. They split the data into blocks and shuffled their order. Koo and Hur [25] have proposed a data deduplication scheme based on a proper key management principle. This scheme is suitable for the deduplication of encrypted data in fog storage by efficient ownership management schemes. They employed the idea of updating the user-level public keys and ciphertext saved in the central cloud server without using the private keys of users, thereby reducing computation and communication overheads. So this can be a feasible choice for healthcare applications.

Figure 15.3 depicts a situation where an eavesdropper is capturing a communication between the sender and receiver, e.g., from a phone to personal computer; wireless local area network; time division synchronous code division multiple access; wideband code division multiple access; code division multiple access.

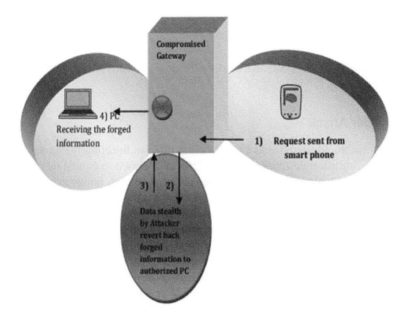

Figure 15.3   Schematic diagram of a captured communication by an eavesdropper in fog environment.

15.3.6 Denial-of-Service (DoS) Attack

A fog platform is highly vulnerable and more prone to DoS attack [26]. The FC (fog computing) platform runs in a distributed environment, where the data centers work in a cooperative way. So it is very difficult to identify the roots of the attack. To protect against DoS attack, network monitoring is often done. Intrusion detection systems (IDS) are used to guard network behavior and to monitor access control policies [27].

DoS attacks on a Fog platform, either from end-users or external systems, can prevent legitimate service use as the network becomes saturated. In addition, all communication is wireless and hence susceptible to impersonation, message replay, and message distortion issues. Protection from these attacks is significant as human life is involved. The most common way of eliminating such issues is by implementing strong authentication, encrypted communication, key management service, perform regular auditing, and implement private network and secure routing [41]. Figure 15.4 presents a snapshot of a DoS attack.

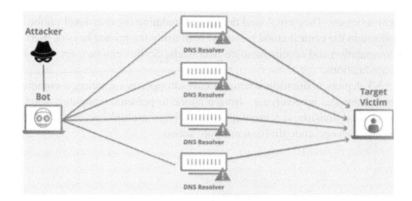

Figure 15.4   Schematic diagram of a distributed denial of service attack.

15.3.7   Insider Attack

In a fog platform the insider attacks may be caused due to injecting malicious code into the stored data. Intrusion detection systems (IDS) can be used to handle these problems, but they face more challenges in fog environment because high power consumption and intensive computing are not feasible in fog environment. Lee *et al.* [27] introduced a hybrid intrusion detection system which uses a signature-based engine. Here, anomaly detection happens at cloud end whereas a signature of identified anomaly is produced and saved in local fog server. Dsouza *et al.* [28] proposed a policy-driven security management framework which employs an attribute-based authentication scheme, in which all users and associated devices are substantiated on the basis of a set of attributes which are the representative attributes. They have employed eXtensible Access Control Markup Language (XACML) to specify operational security, and network policy monitoring in the framework. These security policies are structurally modular in design where each security policy module could be plugged and played in real-time upon particular applications and devices so well-suited for fog platform. Shi and colleagues [29] suggested a cloudlet mesh architecture based on a collaboration of the cloudlet members inspecting and detecting malware, malicious attacks, and other threats. This type of collaborative intrusion-detection technique is well-suited for fog environment, and could be used among fog nodes to observe IoT environmental components.

15.3.8   Masquerade Attack

A masquerade attack happens when a malicious fog node pretends to be a legitimate one to exchange and collect the data generated by other IoT devices for any ill intention. These types of nodes are said to be rogue nodes [30]. Ma *et al.* [32] introduced a hybrid framework [31] that can sense the rogue access points in WiFi-based access networks. Their proposal was meant to provide protection to the networks from rogue access points, and also in situations where the attacker uses customized equipment. A rogue fog node is vulnerable to data integrity and possesses the ability to interpret user data or provide unadulterated data to neighboring nodes. These issues are difficult to handle in IoT and fog environment due to the complexity in trust management in various schemes. A schematic diagram of a masquerade attack is depicted in Figure 15.5.

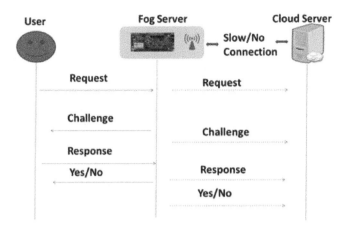

Figure 15.5   Masquerade attack.

The authentication and authorization between the user and fog server fails when there is a fragile or broken connection between the fog server and cloud server. The mechanisms to deploy authentication and authorizations schemes are deployed in the cloud server. This may lead to a masquerade attack.

15.3.9   Attacks on Virtual Machine and Hypervisor

The healthcare-related services provided by fog and cloud are deployed in a virtual environment. If the virtual machine is compromised, it can communicate with the rest of the virtual machines belonging to the same physical host. If the hypervisor is compromised, it can give access to the host operating system and the hardware [32, 33]. There is no significant research concerning this in the literature, especially in cloud computing. Wu *et al.* [34] proposed an access control model to prevent virtual machine escape attack in cloud environment. Their model is based on the Bell-LaPadula model [35]. Yet this is not tested in fog environment. Harnik *et al.* pointed out some potential side channels that can be found in a traditional client-side duplication [36], in spite of using secure encryption methods. They suggested client-side and server-side deduplications based on a random threshold. But the feasibility of using this in a FC platform is yet to be tested. So a proper lightweight network monitoring system is required to avoid these attacks in a hostile environment like fog [37].

From the above discussion the noticeable key points which can be drawn regarding security requirement in healthcare security protocols can be summarized as follows:

(i) Fog/Cloud nodes have limited resources in terms of processing power and computational resources. So, security solutions should not be computationally intensive.

(ii) Healthcare-based solutions work with IoT device, sensors etc. These usually have low battery life. The solutions should be energy efficient and light weight.

Table 15.1 summarizes potential security attacks and some existing solutions in fog computing environment which can also be considered as threats in fog-based healthcare solutions.

Table 15.1   Security attacks and their existing solutions.

Possible Attacks	Security Threats	Existing Solutions
Man-in-middle-attack	Data confidentiality, Data privacy	Encryption and Decryption algorithm, splitting data to data blocks
DoS Attack	Data availability	Network Fire walls, Network monitoring system, IDS
Insider Attack	Data integrity, Data privacy, Data Confidentiality	Network access control protocols, IDS
Masquerade Attack	Authentication, Authorization, Data integrity	Network access control protocols
Attacks on virtual machine and hypervisor	Data availability, Data privacy	Network access control protocols
Spoofing Attack	Data integrity	Public Key based algorithms, Diffie-Hellman key exchange algorithms, IDS

15.4   Emerging Threats in Cloud- and Fog-Based Healthcare System

This section discusses some of the emerging threats which are found in the healthcare system, which are discussed below.

15.4.1   Software Supply Chain Attacks

A supply chain attack mainly targets the supplier of an organization. Here, the targets of the attackers are the business associates and partners, especially in relation to healthcare providers. A attacker always tries to find a backdoor entry, which is through the people who are connected with an organization or those who provide its software. These entryways are built on the supply chains. Recently, in January 2018, Hancock Health was hit by SamSam ransomeware, where the hackers were able to penetrate the hospital's data center through a backdoor entry with the help of a hardware vendor of the backup system [38].

15.4.2   Ransomware Attacks

Ransomware was a main concern in 2017 throughout the entire public and private sectors. Some examples of high-profile and high-impact attacks are WannaCry and Petya/NotPetya. But when the attack victim is the healthcare system, the reaction is different from other sectors. For example, when Hancock Health was attacked by SamSam ransomeware, it fixed the ransom at $55,000 approx. The ransom amounts in the healthcare sector are much higher than in other sectors [39].

15.4.3   Crypto-Mining and Crypto-Jacking Malware

This malware is basically used by hackers to try to overwhelm the organizations computing resources to process and verify the truncations made on bitcoins or any other cryptocurrency. e-Healthcare systems require more availability [40].

15.5 Conclusion

Many security lapses are still present in e-healthcare solutions based on cloud. There are certain points which should be taken into consideration when looking at the security requirements in cloud. The ubiquitous devices used in wearables rely on battery for power, so any security solution used should not consume large amounts of energy. The computational intensive algorithms cannot be used in these scenarios, because they may increase the communication latency and delay. With the growth of sophisticated adversaries, some emerging threats are affecting the healthcare system which need to be addressed. Standardized protocols and business policies need to be developed for seamless use of e-healthcare services.

References

1. Garcia Lopez, P., Montresor, A., Epema, D., Datta, A., Higashino, T., Iamnitchi, A., ... & Riviere, E. (2015). Edge-centric computing: Vision and challenges. ACM SIGCOMM Computer Communication Review, 45(5), 37-42.

2. Moosavi, S. R., Gia, T. N., Rahmani, A. M., Nigussie, E., Virtanen, S., Isoaho, J., & Tenhunen, H. (2015). SEA: a secure and efficient authentication and authorization architecture for IoT-based healthcare using smart gateways. Procedia Computer Science, 52, 452-459.

3. Kraemer, F. A., Braten, A. E., Tamkittikhun, N., & Palma, D. (2017). Fog computing in healthcareA review and discussion. IEEE Access, 5, 9206-9222.

4. Lye, J., Kaylor, R., Lindsay, J., & Everhart, D. (2004). U.S. Patent Application No. 10/305,263.

5. Oussous, A., Benjelloun, F. Z., Lahcen, A. A., & Belfkih, S. (2017). Big Data technologies: A survey. Journal of King Saud University-Computer and Information Sciences. DOI: 10.1016/j.jksuci.2017.06.001.

6. Dastjerdi, A. V., & Buyya, R. (2016). Fog computing: Helping the Internet of Things realize its potential. Computer, 49(8), 112-116.

7. Sun, J., et al., Security and Privacy for Mobile Healthcare (m-Health) Systems. 2011, Amsterdam, The Netherlands: Elsevier.

8. Fatema, N. and R. Brad, Security Requirements, Counterattacks and Projects in Healthcare Applications Using WSNs-A Review. arXiv preprint arXiv:1406.1795, 2014.

9. Wang, J., et al., A Research on Security and Privacy Issues for Patient Related Data in Medical Organization System. International Journal of Security and Its Applications, 2013. 7(4): p. 287-298

10. Darwish, A. and Hassanien, A.E., 2011. Wearable and implantable wireless sensor network solutions for healthcare monitoring. Sensors, 11(6), pp.5561-5595.

11. M. Li, S. Yu, K. Ren, W. Lou, Securing personal health records in cloud computing: Patient-centric and ne-grained data access control in multi-owner settings., in: SecureComm, Vol. 10, Springer, 2010, pp. 89106.

12. K. Ren, W. Lou, Y. Zhang, Leds: Providing location-aware end-to-end data security in wireless sensor networks, IEEE Transactions on Mobile Computing 7 (5) (2008) 585598.

13. K. Lee, D. Kim, D. Ha, U. Rajput, H. Oh, On security and privacy issues of fog computing supported internet of things environment, in: Network of the Future (NOF), 2015 6th International Conference on the, IEEE, 2015, pp. 13.

14. Altamimi, Ahmad Mousa. "Security and Privacy Issues In eHealthcare Systems: Towards Trusted Services."

15. Saleem, S., S. Ullah, and K.S. Kwak, A study of IEEE 802.15. 4 security framework for wireless body area networks. Sensors, 2011. 11(2): p. 1383-1395.

16. CHELLI, K. Security Issues in Wireless Sensor Networks: Attacks and Countermeasures. in Proceedings of the World Congress on Engineering. 2015. R. Roman, J. Zhou, J. Lopez, On the features and challenges of security and privacy in distributed internet of things, Computer Networks 57 (10) (2013) 22662279

17. Habib, K., A. Torjusen, and W. Leister. Security analysis of a patient monitoring system for the Internet of Things in eHealth. in Proceedings of the International Conference on eHealth, Telemedicine, and Social Medicine (eTELEMED'15). 2015

18. Kumar, P. and H.-J. Lee, Security issues in healthcare applications using wireless medical sensor networks: A survey. Sensors, 2011. 12(1): p. 5591.

19. I. Stojmenovic, S. Wen, X. Huang, H. Luan, An overview of fog computing and its security issues, Concurrency and Computation: Practice and Experience 28 (10) (2016) 29913005.

20. C. Gentry, et al., Fully homomorphic encryption using ideal lattices., in: STOC, Vol. 9, 2009, pp. 169178. [65] J. W. Bos, W. Castryck, I. Iliashenko, F. Vercauteren, Privacy-friendly forecasting for the smart grid using homomorphic encryption and the group method of data handling, in: International Conference on Cryptology in Africa, Springer, 2017, pp. 184201.

21. J. W. Bos, W. Castryck, I. Iliashenko, F. Vercauteren, Privacy-friendly forecasting for the smart grid using homomorphic encryption and the group method of data handling, in: International Conference on Cryptology in Africa, Springer, 2017, pp. 184201.

22. E. Petac, A.-O. Petac, et al., About security solutions in fog computing, Ovidius University Annals, Economic Sciences Series 16 (1) (2016) 380385.

23. I. Stojmenovic, S. Wen, X. Huang, H. Luan, An overview of fog computing and its security issues, Concurrency and Computation: Practice and Experience 28 (10) (2016) 29913005.

24. S. Kulkarni, S. Saha, R. Hockenbury, Preserving privacy in sensor-fog networks, in: Internet Technology and Secured Transactions (ICITST), 2014 9th International Conference for, IEEE, 2014, pp. 9699.

25. D. Koo, J. Hur, Privacy-preserving deduplication of encrypted data with dynamic ownership management in fog computing, Future Generation Computer Systems 78 (2018) 739752.

26. S. J. Stolfo, M. B. Salem, A. D. Keromytis, Fog computing: Mitigating insider data theft attacks in the cloud, in: Security and Privacy Workshops (SPW), 2012 IEEE Symposium on, IEEE, 2012, pp. 125128.

27. K. Lee, D. Kim, D. Ha, U. Rajput, H. Oh, On security and privacy issues of fog computing supported internet of things environment, in: Network of the Future (NOF), 2015 6th International Conference on the, IEEE, 2015, pp. 13.

28. C. Dsouza, G.-J. Ahn, M. Taguinod, Policy-driven security management for fog computing: Preliminary framework and a case study, in: Information Reuse and Integration (IRI), 2014 IEEE 15th International Conference on, IEEE, 2014, pp. 1623.

29. Y. Shi, S. Abhilash, K. Hwang, Cloudlet mesh for securing mobile clouds from intrusions and network attacks, in: Mobile Cloud Computing, Services, and Engineering (MobileCloud), 2015 3rd IEEE International Conference on, IEEE, 2015, pp. 109118.

30. Chen, N. and Jiang, R., 2014. Security analysis and improvement of user authentication framework for cloud computing. Journal of Networks, 9(1), p.198.

31. S. Yi, C. Li, Q. Li, A survey of fog computing: concepts, applications and issues, in: Proceedings of the 2015 Workshop on Mobile Big Data, ACM, 2015, pp. 3742.

32. L. Ma, A. Y. Teymorian, X. Cheng, A hybrid rogue access point protection framework for commodity wi- networks, in: INFOCOM 2008. The 27th Conference on Computer Communications. IEEE, IEEE, 2008, pp. 12201228.

33. D. Hyde, A survey on the security of virtual machines, Www1. cse. wustl. edu/ jain/cse57109/ftp/vmsec/index. html.

34. J. Wu, Z. Lei, S. Chen, W. Shen, An access control model for preventing virtual machine escape attack, Future Internet 9 (2) (2017) 20.

35. S. R. Moosavi, T. N. Gia, E. Nigussie, A. M. Rahmani, S. Virtanen, H. Tenhunen, J. Isoaho, End-toend security scheme for mobility enabled healthcare internet of things, Future Generation Computer Systems 64 (2016) 108124.

36. D. Harnik, B. Pinkas, A. Shulman-Peleg, Side channels in cloud services: Deduplication in cloud storage, IEEE Security Privacy 8 (6) (2010) 4047. doi:10.1109/MSP.2010.187.

37. I. Stojmenovic, S. Wen, The fog computing paradigm: Scenarios and security issues, in: Computer Science and Information Systems (FedCSIS), 2014 Federated Conference on, IEEE, 2014, pp. 18.

38. https://csrc.nist.gov/CSRC/media/Projects/Supply-Chain-Risk-Management/documents/ssca/2017-winter/NCSC_Placemat.pdf , accesses on 20-8-2018

39. Mohurle, S., & Patil, M. (2017). A brief study of wannacry threat: Ransomware attack 2017. International Journal of Advanced Research in Computer Science, 8(5).

40. Tahir, R., Huzaifa, M., Das, A., Ahmad, M., Gunter, C., Zaffar, F., ... & Borisov, N. (2017, September). Mining on someone elses dime: Mitigating covert mining operations in clouds and enterprises. In International Symposium on Research in Attacks, Intrusions, and Defenses (pp. 287-310). Springer, Cham.

41. Khan, S., Parkinson, S., & Qin, Y. (2017). Fog computing security: a review of current applications and security solutions. Journal of Cloud Computing, 6(1), 19.

CHAPTER 16

MAPPING OF E-WALLETS WITH FEATURES

ALISHA SIKRI[1], SURJEET DALAL[1], N.P SINGH[2], DAC-NHUONG LE[3]

[1] Department of Computer Science & Engineering, SRM University, Sonepat, Haryana, India
[2] MDI, Gurugram
[3] Haiphong University, Haiphong, Vietnam
 Email: profsurjeetdalal@gmail.com, Nhuongld@dhhp.edu.vn

Abstract

This chapter includes various types of models operating in the e-commerce/e-business domains in India. In addition, the chapter also presents the mapping of e-wallets and its features. It is observed that the features such as digital only, text based etc are common to all types of wallets and the features like one touch, CoF etc are specific to open wallets only. This chapter tries to give a brief insight of the various technological, operational, legal and also security features available in different types of e-Wallets. It can also be concluded from the paper that all the three wallets have the same security features which includes: Anti-fraud, 3D SET or SSL, P2P, data encryption and one-time password (OTP).

Keywords: e-Commerce, e-Wallets, OTP, security

Dac-Nhuong Le et al. (eds.), Cyber Security in Parallel and Distributed Computing, (245–262)
© 2019 Scrivener Publishing LLC

16.1 Introduction

16.1.1 e-Wallet

E-wallet can be defined as a type of electronic card which can be used for transactions made online through a computer or a Smartphone. It can also be said that its utility is same as that of a credit or debit card. An E-wallet must be linked with the individual's bank account for the purpose of making payments [59].

The mobile wallet, which can also be called as m-Wallet, digital wallet, or e-Wallet, defines a mobile technology which can be used similarly to a real wallet. The Mobile Wallet also provides a very convenient solution for any business which is looking forward to allow its customers to purchase their products online with greater ease, therefore driving sales [60].

A mobile wallet is a technique to carry your credit card or debit card information in a digital form on our mobile device. Instead of using our physical plastic card to make the required purchases, we can also pay with our Smartphone's, tablets, or smart watch. Heres an overview of the various benefits of the mobile wallets and also how mobile wallet services generally work [61].

A mobile wallet is a replica of a type of physical wallet. Customers can add credit and debit cards, as well as prepaid cards, gift cards and rewards cards. Mobile wallet's also allow users to store and carry an endless amount of cards in their phone. This use case not only replaces the physical plastic of cards, but allows those cards to be enhanced by value added services [62].

As reported in the literature CY 2016 (Annual) Edition the year growth of e-wallets from the Year 2013 to 2015 is 332% i.e. from $0.2 Billion to $2.6 Billion and the growth from the year 2015 to 2016 is 123% i.e. $2.6 Billion to $5.8 Billion. The e-wallet is one of the most popular instrument in India having approximately $9 Billion mobile wallet transactions in April, 2017 versus 1 billion 2 years ago6 .Morgan Stanley estimates that Indias addressable digital consumer payment market to be worth $350-400 billion in 2017 which is however lower than a year ago [6].

Out of the many technological advancement or innovations e-wallets based SSL (*Secure Socket Layer*) and SET (*Secure Electronic Transaction*) for security of Online Systems [5]. The various other technologies include NFC (*Near Field Communication*), Bluetooth, QR Codes, Mobile Web payments, Bluetooth and even Biometrics [7], anti-fraud and data-encryption (*B2B Directory*) [8], Server-side digital Wallets also know was thin wallets [5]. These are one of the legal instruments used for making electronic payment possible in India. (*Ref. Govt Notification*).

Keeping in view the many features of e-wallets and its market share, the ease of use of the various e-wallets can be identified. The presented paper is an attempt to map e-wallets with its features NFC, One Touch, QR Code, and Digital Touch which are the technological features. The various operational features include requirement on KYC, the various entities required to operate etc. Security features for the e-wallets can be data encryption, SET (*Secure Electronic Transaction*) and anti-fraud. Various legal features are PPI License requirement [30], etc.

E-wallet can be defined as a type of electronic card which can be used for transactions which are made online through a computer or may be with a smartphone. Its utility is quite similar as that of a credit or debit card. An E-wallet needs to be linked with the individual's bank account to make payments [1].

16.1.2   Objectives

1. To study the market share of different PPI's (*Prepaid Payment Instruments*).

2. Identification of major features of PPI e-wallets.

3. To map these major features with the existing popular PPI's.

Types of PPI's: PPIs are known as the payment instruments that facilitate the purchase of goods and services, including the financial services, remittance facilities etc. against the value stored on such instruments [20]. According to the norms of the Reserve Bank of India (RBI) the e-wallets are classified as follows [2-4, 18, 20]:

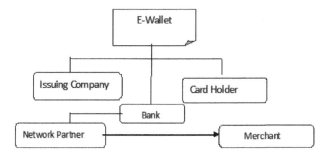

Figure 16.1   Ecosystem for setting up of an Open, closed and semi-closed e-wallet respectively [2]

Table 16.1   Examples of types of e-wallets.

Types of E-wallets	Example	Date and Year of introduction	Type of promoter	Source
Open Wallet	i) M-Pesa by Vodafone, ii) Pockets by ICICI Bank iii) PayPal iv) Amazon Pay	i) Nov 7, 2014 ii) Sep 24,2013 iii) Dec 1, 1998 iv) Oct 8,2013	i) ii) Bank iii) PayPal Pte. Ltd iv)E-Commerce Company (Amazon)	i) ii)ICICI Bank iii) PYMNTS (2015), Paypal iv) Amazon
Closed Wallet	i)Flipkart e-wallet ii)Chase Pay iii)Walmart Pay iv)Google Wallet	i) ii) October 26, 2015 iii)First Half of 2016 iv)May 26,2011	i) Online- retailer ii) Banking business iii) Store (Walmart Stores Inc) iv) Technology (Google Inc)	i) ii) Morgan iii)Ramakrishnan et al. iv)Google Wallet Story
Semi-Closed Wallet	i)Paytm (Pay Through Mobile) ii) Mobikwik iii) Oxigen-Wallet iv) PayU v) Freecharge	i) 2010 ii) 2009 iii) 2004 iv)2002 v)	i) Privately Owned ii) iii) Oxigen Services Pvt.Ltd iv) Private (Nasper's Group (South Africa)) v)Bank(Axis)	i) Paytm Story ii) Agarwal (2013) iii) Oxigen iv) Dalal(2016) v) Variyar (2017)

1. *Open Wallet*: It is the one type of wallet which allows user to buy goods and services, withdraw cash at ATMs or banks, and also to transfer funds. These services can only be jointly launched with a bank. Additionally, it allows its various users to send money to any mobile number bank account. Only banks are allowed to issue these instruments [4].

2. *Closed Wallet*: This type of mobile wallet is quite popular with the e-commerce companies. Here, a certain amount of money is locked with the merchant in case of a cancellation or return of the order or gift cards .Example: Flipkart e-wallet[1].

3. *Semi-Closed Wallet*: In this type of wallets, we can do shopping and transfer virtual fund to any other user in the same wallet network. These types of wallets are very popular in India. It has a drawback that it does not allow to permit cash Withdrawal or redemption, but allows users to buy goods and services at the listed merchants. Example: Paytm[2], Mobikwik[3].

Unique features:

1. One Touch Feature: One Touch is an feature that allows you to complete purchases faster while still helping to keep your full financial information secure. We can easily de-activate One Touch by turning it off within your account [12].

2. NFC (*Near Field Communication*)[4]: NFC is one of the latest technologies which are used for short range wireless communication. NFC also provides safe communication technique between electronic gadgets [10]. The three modes of communication of NFC as defined by the NFC forum are Read/Write mode, Tag emulation mode and peer-to-peer mode [11].

3. CoF (*Cloud based Card-on File*): Cloud-based digital wallets, as the name suggests, carry out transaction processing and store user account information on web based servers. PayPal, Google, MasterCard and Visa all support cloud-based implementations [7].

4. *Optical/QR Code*: QR code stands for quick response code, which is a type of trademark for the type of matrix barcode. QR code is said to be a two dimensional i.e. matrix type symbol with a cell architecture arranged in a square [63].

5. *POS (Point-on Scale)*: In order to ensure wider acceptance and also to reach merchants, NFC POS payments are required to accept payments without tap card [24].

6. *FIPB Approval*: The FIPB (*Foreign Investment Promotion Board*) is a well known designated institution which considers the FDI proposals that further require a government approval. Further, it also sanctions composite approvals which involve foreign investment/foreign technology [65].

7. *Under NBFC's Act*: Under the NBFC's act the various Licensed or the Scheduled Banks and also the registered Non-Banking Financial Companies (NBFCs) are permitted to issue PPI's obtaining approval/authorization from the Reserve Bank of India [64].

8. *KYC requirement*: According to the norms of RBI, the requirement of full KYC for PPI's is a step taken towards interoperability [13]. Those wallets which do not comply with the KYC norms shall not be allowed to load money into their respective wallet

---

[1] https://www.flipkart.com/
[2] https://paytm.com
[3] https://www.mobikwik.com/
[4] http://nearfieldcommunication.org/

accounts or to carry out remittance-based transactions and also will not be allowed to transfer the cash in the wallet account to their bank accounts [14].

9. *IMPS (Immediate Payment Service)*: IMPS is a system that links mobile numbers to bank accounts. IMPS helps customers with debit cards or net banking accounts to transact on e-wallets using their mobile phones [40].

10. *Anti-Fraud*: Fraud, anyhow remains a sensitive issue across every sector of business, whether it may be public or private businesses. It is a critical issue to rather prevent fraud than to nurse the effects of fraud [66].

11. *3D-SET (Secure Electronic Transaction)*: SET is a system which ensures the security of the financial transactions on the Internet. With SET, a user is given an electronic wallet (digital certificate) and a transaction is conducted and verified using a combination of digital certificates and digital signatures among the purchaser, a merchant, and the purchaser's bank in a way that ensures privacy and confidentiality [15].

12. Data Encryption: Encryption is defined as the procedure of encoding the information so that the information cannot be read by normal means. Encryption will also change the data on the information that will be hard to read and also time-consuming if the encryption result data decoded without using any special rules or codes [16].

Actors in Electronic Cash Payment Systems [77]:

Table 16.2   Electronic cash payment systems.

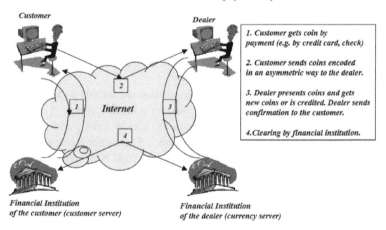

1. *Customers*: Customers are the ones who use the digital cash payment systems to carry out purchases.

2. *Dealers*: Dealers are the ones who bear the costs of payment transactions.

3. *Providers for digital payment systems*: Providers are a type of intermediaries between the dealers and the financial institutions. They provide services as well as training.

4. *Development vendors for digital payment systems*: Financial institutions: Banking systems or organizations that use electronic payment systems.

5. *Trust Centers*: Trust centers are the ones which control digital signature keys, and also helps to secure the customer's confidence in certain payment systems. They are responsible for the integrity of transmitted data and authenticity of contractors.

The chapter is divided into various sections. The first section consists of the Introduction part; Section 2 includes the review of literature part. Section 3 consists of the description about the market share of e-wallets, such as the various technical features of the e-wallets, the various economic features, the operational features of various e-wallets, and the various security features. Section 4 defines the research methodology part and a research model. The result of the analysis is contained in Section 5. Finally, section 6 consists of conclusion and recommendations.

16.2 Review of Literature

The literature of the review was done in order to study the usefulness of the various e-wallets. Rawat *et al.* [2] reported that the growth of the m-wallet's segment can be considered to be in conjunction of rising in the smartphone usage and internet penetration in the nation. The authors also stated that demonetisation in India has also proved to be a lucrative opportunity for m-wallet players in India. It led to the flooding of the m-wallet companies' will millions of transactions and double the number of users. The paper also tries to explain the categories of in which the m-wallets are divided and also explains the various operational features available in these e-wallets. The various operational features mentioned in this paper are entities which are allowed to operate like banks, NBFCs (*Non Banking Financial Companies*), and various other entities, KYC requirement weather it is required or not etc. It also shared the amount which can be stored in the PPI by the card holder like for example INR 10,000 can be stored in the closed wallets and an amount of 10,000 can be stored, in Semi-closed PPI without KYC while an amount of 50,000 can be stored in the same with KYC.

Pandy *et al.* [22] wrote a definition of mobile wallets and for this paper the mobile wallet can be defined as "a digital container accessed by a mobile device (*i.e., Smartphone*) that stores wallet applications, payment credentials, loyalty cards, and coupons, and is used to make proximity and remote mobile payments". The author wrote about the various technological features available in e-wallets and these include NFC (*Near Field Communication*), cloud based card-on file (CoF) and merchant or financial institution (FI) QR code closed wallets. The FRBB wallet team field-tested all the wallet models. They also tested the NFC Pay wallets with the device-specific mobile operating systems like the Apple iOS and Android KitKat (*4.4 or higher*). The various cloud-based mobile wallets, such as PayPal, master pass, pay with Amazon, visa checkout, chase pay, and walmart pay, are also device-agnostic, although some only function in the remote payments environment (*Amazon*[5]) or the POS environment (*Walmart Pay*[6]). They also discussed the various security controls for the mobile wallets which secures the mobile wallet payment method. These are payment tokenization, one-time password (OTP) protection etc.

Agarwal [33] summarizes the law governing the mobile wallets in India, market scenario and other aspects leading to the popularity of the m-Wallet industry. The principal law governing payment systems in India is The payment and settlements act, 2007 (*the*

---

[5]www.amazon.com
[6]https://www.walmart.com/

Act) read along with payment and settlement systems regulations, 2008 and amended up to 2011 and board for regulation and supervision of payment and settlement systems (BPSS) Regulations, 2008, the payment and settlement systems (*Amendment*) act, 2015- No. 18 of 2015. The definition of PPIs as per Para 2.3 of the afore-mentioned policy is "Pre-paid payment instruments are the payment instruments that facilitates the purchase of goods and services, which includes the funds transfer, against the value stored on such instruments". In this chapter it is concluded that the semi-closed wallets are the most commonly used payment methods which are grabbing the attention of the customers. The chapter mentions the various legal acts which are needed in the PPI's and these are FEMA (*Foreign Exchange Management Act*) to issue foreign exchange pre-paid payment instruments. NBFC's (*Non Banking Financial Companies Act*) is also one of the acts required for payment Instruments. Closed and semi-closed wallets have this act while the open wallet does not have this act. It can be concluded in this paper that the core reason of growing digital industry is the unavailability of bank accounts to a substantial population of the economy. Therein, the m-Wallet industry plays a major role in facilitating that part of population to transact day to day transactions.

Kanimozhi et al. [58] wrote on the security aspects of mobile based e-wallets. The paper tries to answer for certain queries related to the operational procedure of e-wallet, kinds of e-wallet and also the security issues related to the mobile e-wallets. The author elaborates the security issues of closed e-wallets and according to the author the security protection for e-wallets is given in two ways in which one is the SET, i.e. secure electronic transaction, it ensures the security of confidential transmissions and digitized financial transmissions and the other is SSL i.e. Secure socket layer which provides an authentication of the buyer and the merchant. It also ensures the security which identifies purchaser and also checks the customer using digital signature, passwords etc. The paper also mentions the OTP feature available in Paytm which is an acronym for "Pay through Mobile" in which an OTP is generated which is to be entered in case the money is being transferred from bank to the wallet. It also concluded that RBI has reported that there are about 20 million active users of e-wallets post demonetizations.

Bezhovski [57] analysed the various systems of electronic payment, the future of the mobile payment as electronic payment system and also the security issues related to them. The paper examined the various factors affecting the adoption of the mobile payment method by the consumers. The various online payment systems are electronic payment cards, e-wallets, mobile payments, electronic-cash etc. According to the study it is clear that the mobile payment has various features like the NFC, sound waves, QR codes and cloud-based solutions etc. which make them more secure and also it is the most convenient payment solutions to the customers in the coming future. It is also clear that the Electronic payment systems have to follow an efficient security protocol in order to ensure high level security for online transactions and for this we have protocols named SSL and SET.

16.3 Market Share of e-Wallet

Mobile wallet transaction is one the fastest growing paperless modes of payment or banking, and it is expected that the majority of transactions will go paperless in the next 10 years [2]. The e-wallet transactions have flown from Rs. 10 billion of transactions in year 2012-2013 to more than 480 billion of transactions in the year 2015-20164. It is also anticipated that the market value of m-wallet transactions in India will grow at a CAGR of 211% during the period FY 2016 to FY 2022, and reach INR 275 Trillion [2]. The various e-wallet companies are benefited with millions of transactions and also with double the number of users. The average wallet-spending for retail was about INR 500-700 prior to the demonetization move; drastically increasing to INR 2,000-10,000 post this event18. The RBI November 2017 Bulletin disclosed that as of September 2017, PPI volumes stood at 240.29 million (as opposed to 97.07 million in September 2016), and PPI values stood at INR 109.77 billion (as opposed to INR 56.28 billion in September 2016) [19].

16.3.1 Technical Features

This section presents technical features of e-wallets used in e-commerce domain in India. These features include NFC (Near field Communication) [28], CoF (Cloud-based Card-on file) [29], QR Code [21, 22], and Point-on Scale [27], Digital Only [21], Text-based [21].

These are compiled in the following Table 16.2.

Table 16.3   Technological features of e-wallets in India.

Types of e-wallets	Technological Features						
	One-Touch or Tap & Pay	NFC (Near field Communication)	CoF (Cloud-based Card-on file)	Optical/ QR Code	POS (Point-on Scale)	Digital Only	Text Based
Open Wallet	YES (Paypal)	NO [22]	YES [7, 22]	NO [21]	YES	YES [21]	YES [21]
Closed Wallet	NO [28]	NO [22, 25]	YES [29]	YES [22]	YES [22]		
Semi-Closed Wallet	YES [21, 23]	YES [24]		YES [26]	YES [24]	YES [21]	

16.3.2 Legal Features

This section presents Legal features of e-wallets used in e-commerce domain in India. These features include PPI License requirement [30], FIPB Approval (Foreign Investment Promotion Board) [31], RBI Approvals [32] and the wallets under NBFCs (Non-Banking Financial Companies) [33] Act.

These are compiled in the following Table 16.3:

Table 16.4   Legal features of e-wallets in India.

Types of E-wallets	Legal Features			
	PPI License Requirement	FIPB Approval (Foreign Investment Promotion Board)	RBI Approvals	Under NBFC's (Non-Banking Financial Companies) Act
Open Wallet	YES [30]	YES [35]	YES [36]	NO [34]
Closed Wallet	NO [30]		NO [32]	YES [33]
Semi-Closed Wallet	YES [30]	YES [31]	YES [37]	YES [33]

16.3.3   Operational Features

This section presents operational features of e-wallets used in e-commerce domain in India. These features include KYC requirement, Entities allowed to operate [2], PIN code for purchase [38], IMPS (*Immediate Payment Service*) [40] and Redemption or Cash Withdrawal [39]. These are compiled in the following Table 16.4:

Table 16.5   Operational features of e-wallets in India.

Types of e-wallets	Operational Features						
	KYC Requirement	PIN Code for Purchase	Entities Allowed to operate			IMPS (ImmediatePayment Service)	Redemption or Cash Withdrawal
			Banks	NBFCs	Other Entities		
Open Wallet	YES [2]	YES [38]	YES [2]	NO [2]	NO [2]	YES [41]	YES [39]
Closed Wallet	NO [2]	YES [44]	YES [2]	YES [2]	YES [2]	YES [42]	NO [39]
Semi-Closed Wallet	NOT Mandatory [2]	YES [43]	YES [2]	YES [2]	YES [2]	YES [40]	NO [39]

16.3.4   Security Features

This section presents security features of e-wallets used in e-commerce domain in India. These features include anti-fraud [45], data encryption [22], 3D SET (*Secure Electronic Transaction*) [5], P2P communication [47] and one-time password [46]. These are compiled in the following Table 16.5:

Table 16.6   Security features of e-wallets in India.

Types of e-wallets	Security Features				
	Anti-fraud	3D SET(Secure Electronic Transactions) or SSL(Secure Socket Layer	Data Encryption	P2P	One Time Password(OTP)
Open Wallet	YES [48]	YES [41]	YES [22]	YES [47]	YES [56]
Closed Wallet	YES [55]	YES [53]	YES [50]	YES [49]	YES [56]
Semi-Closed Wallet	YES [45]	YES [52]	YES [54]	YES [47]	YES [46]

16.4   Research Methodology

Based on PPI Literature and RBI Guidelines category of wallets are identified as i) Open e-wallets ii) Closed E-wallets iii) Semi- closed E-wallets. The major features of the e-wallets are: i) Technical Features ii) Operational Features iii) Legal Features iv) Security Features. Further, each category of feature is expanded to elaborate the availability of different features in various e-wallets.

Table 16.7 Mapping framework of e-wallet features.

Types of e-Wallets	Features
Open Wallet	**Technical Features:** • **One Touch or Tap Pay** (PayPal) • **CoF (Cloud Based Card-on File)** (Pandy et.al, Ovum(2017)) • **POS(Point-on Scale)** (Editorial Staff) • **Digital only** (Peterson et al.(2016)) • **Text Based** (Peterson et al.(2016)) **Operational Features:** • **KYC Requirement** (Rawat et al. (2016)) • **PIN Code for Purchase** (Olsen et al.(2012)) • **Entities Allowed to operate (Banks)** (Rawat et al. (2016)) • **IMPS** (Business Line(2014)) • **Redemption or Cash Withdrawal** (Jamwal(2017)) **Legal Features:** • **PPI License Requirement**(Siddarth(2017)) • **FIPB Approval(Foreign Investment Promotion Board)** (PTI(2013)) • **RBI Approvals** (Chengappa(2017)) **Security Features:** • **Anti-fraud**(PayPal) • **3D SET or SSL** (Nitrosell(2009)) • **Data Encryption** (Pandy et al. (2017)) • **P2P** (Bemoneyaware(2017)) • **One Time Password** (Woodford(2017))
Closed Wallet	**Technical Features:** • **CoF(Cloud Based Card-on File)** (Pandy et.al. (2016)) • **Optical/ QR Code** (Pandey et. al(2017)) • **POS (Point-on Scale)** (Pandey et. al(2017)) **Operational Features:** • **PIN Code for Purchase** (Jolly(2016)) • **Entities Allowed to operate (Banks, NBFC's, Other Entities)** (Rawat et al. (2016)) • **IMPS** (Team Flipkart(2017)) **Legal Features:** • **Under NBFC's (Non- Banking Financial Companies) Act** (Agarwal(2017)) **Security Features:** • **Anti-fraud**(Rampton(2016)) • **3D SET or SSL** (Chase Payment)) • **Data Encryption** (Akin (2017)) • **P2P** (Ryan(2014)) • **One Time Password** (Woodford(2017))
Semi-Closed Wallet	**Technical Features:** • **One Touch or Tap Pay** (Peterson et al. (2016), Paytm Blog(2017)), • **NFC (Near Field Communication)** (ANI(2018)) • **Optical/ QR Code** (PTI(2017)) • **Point-on Scale** (ANI(2018)) • **Digital Only**(Peterson et al.(2016)) **Operational Features:** • **PIN Code for Purchase** (Singh(2017)) • **Entities Allowed to operate (Banks, NBFC's, Other Entities)** (Rawat et al. (2016)) • **IMPS** (Chamikutty(2013)) **Legal Features:** • **PPI License Requirement**(Siddarth(2017)) • **FIPB Approval(Foreign Investment Promotion Board)** (Dutta(2012) • **RBI Approvals** (Tiwari(2017)) • **Under NBFC's (Non- Banking Financial Companies) Act** (Agarwal(2017)) **Security Features:** • **Anti-fraud**(Aulakh(2016)) • **3D SET or SSL** (Pathak(2016)) • **Data Encryption** (Pandy et al. (2017)) • **P2P** (Bemoneyaware(2017)) • **One Time Password** (Kamnath et al.(2017))

Data Collection: To fulfill the first objective which is to know about the market share of different e-wallets proper data is collected and also the effect of demonetization is also depicted on the usage of e-wallets by showing the increase in the market share of e-wallets which is amenable for rational analysis. The major features of e-wallets are given in the table in the form of mapping framework. Data for mapping is collected from various news articles like the Business Line, Economic Times and also from ASSOCHAM, articles by Mahindra Comviva etc. The data is also which was not available online or in research articles is collected from the official website of various e-wallet companies like PayPal, Paytm, CHASE Payment, HERO Pay etc. The data is collected and subjected to trend and content analysis. For the purpose of content analysis, the dictionary in the feature of e-wallet is examined.

16.5   Result Analysis

The result of the above done analysis is combined in the form of the given diagram.

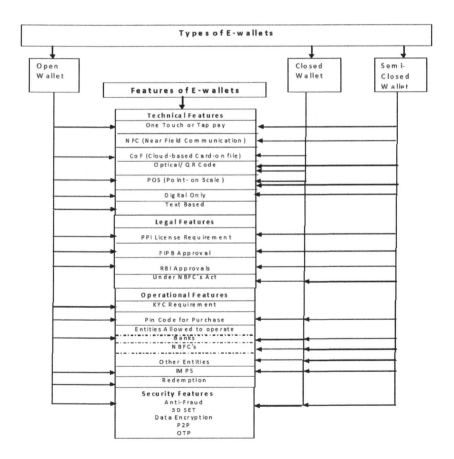

Figure 16.2   Research Model for the mapping of features of E-wallets with the types of e-wallets

16.6 Conclusions and future work

It can be concluded that the upcoming future of the digital payments is very bright. India is also experiencing a remarkable growth in the digital payment mode. In 2015-2016, a total of Rs. 4018 billion transacted through mobile banking as compared to Rs. 60 billion in 2012-2013. The percentage of the digital payments through other modes is also increasing in a significant speed [17]. It can also be concluded that India is all set to evolve as the world's fastest growing economy in the coming years, leaving behind China. Semi-closed wallets have immense potential to add value to the overall GDP striving to make the country a cashless economy.

References

1. The Economic Times. (2018), E-Wallet Definitions available at https://economictimes.indiatimes.com/definition/e-wallets.(Accessed on 7 June 2018)

2. Rawat D. S. and Maheshwari S. (2016). M-Wallet Scenario Post De- monetization ASSOCHAM, INDIA. Retrieved on May 27, 2018 from http://www.assocham.org/upload/docs/M-Wallet_Report_press.pdf.

3. Manikandan, S., & Jayakodi, J. M. (2017). An empirical study on consumer adoption of mobile wallet with special reference to Chennai city. International Journal of Research-Granthalaya, 5(5), 107-115.

4. Nair, A., Dahiya, M., & Gupta, N. (2016). Educating Consumers about Digital Wallets.

5. Upadhayaya, A. (2012). Electronic Commerce and E-wallet. International Journal of Recent Research and Review.

6. Abbas .M. (2017), Indias mobile wallet transactions up at $9 billion in 2017: Mor- gan Stanley, June 16, available at https://telecom.economictimes.indiatimes.com/news/indias- mobile-wallet-transactions-up-at-9-billion-in-2017-morgan-stanley/59174647(accessed on 10 June 2018)

7. Ovum. (2012). Digital Wallet Dynamics: Opportunities Challenges and Rec- ommendations, Mahindra Comviva. Retrieved on June 2, 2018 from chrome- extension://ngpampappnmepgilojfohadhhmbhlaek/captured.html?back=1.

8. Jeannette (2017). PayPal Review, December 29, available at https://reviews.financesonline.com/p/paypal/ (accessed on 11 May 2018).

9. CY 2016 (Annual). (2016). Mobile Wallets Market in India. Retrieved on May 13, 2018 from redseer.com/wp-content/.../02/7.-Analyst-Report-Mobile-Wallets_CY16-Review.pdf.

10. Rahul, A., Gokul Krishnan, G., Unni Krishnan, H., & Rao, S. (2015). Near Field Communica- tion (NFC) Technology: A Survey. International Journal on Cybernetics & Informatics (IJCI), 4(2), 133-144.

11. Al-Ofeishat, H. A., & Al Rababah, M. A. (2012). Near field communication (NFC). Interna- tional Journal of Computer Science and Network Security (IJCSNS), 12(2), 93.

12. PayPal, One Touch available at https://www.paypal.com/us/webapps/mpp/one-touch- checkout/faq (accessed on 25 May 2018)

13. Prasad. N. (2018), KYC compliance needed only for reloading e-wallets, February 27 available at http://www.thehindu.com/business/Economy/kyc-compliance-needed-only-for-reloading-e- wallets/article22859593.ece (accessed on 20 June 2018)

14. Pani.P. (2018). KYC norms for e-wallets made mandatory from March 1, February 26, available at https://www.thehindubusinessline.com/economy/kyc-norms-for-e-wallets-made-made-mandatory-from-march-1/article22859974.ece (accessed on 10 May 2018)

15. Rouse   .M,   Secure   Electronic   Transaction,   available   at https://searchfinancialsecurity.techtarget.com/definition/Secure-Electronic-Transaction (accessed on 11 May, 2018).

16. Husni, E. (2017). Dynamic Rule Encryption for Mobile Payment. Security and Communication Networks, 2017.

17. Pandey .P. (2017), Digital Payments in India 2016-2017: Definition, Types, comparison and Apps, January 2, available at https://upipayments.co.in/digital-payment/ (accessed on 11 May 2018).

18. Danish. (2018), What is a Semi-Closed Wallets?, February, available at https://enterslice.com/learning/semi-closed-wallets/ (Accessed on 15 May 2018).

19. Kamath. A, Maheshwari.K, Reddy.J and Kalra.K. (2017), India: Revamped Prepaid Payment Instrument Law Focuses on KYC, Interoperability, Consumer Protection and Data Security, December 11, available at http://www.mondaq.com/india/x/654638/Financial+Services/Revamped+   Prepaid+Payment+Instrument+Law+Focuses+On+KYC+Interoperability+Consumer+Protection +And+Data+Security (Accessed on 11 May 2018).

20. Dave. N. (2017), All Prepaid Payment Instrument Issuers, System Providers, System Participants and all prospective Prepaid Payment Instrument Issuers, March 20, available at https://rbi.org.in/scripts/BS_ViewMasDirections.aspx?id=11142 (accessed on 24 May 2018).

21. Peterson.T and Wezel.R. (2016), The Evolution of Digital and Mobile Wallets, Whitepaper, Mahindra Comviva. Retrieved on May 15, 2018 from http://www.paymentscardsandmobile.com/wp-content/uploads/2016/10/The-Evolution-of-Digital-and-Mobile-Wallets.pdf.

22. Pandy. S and Crowe.M. (2017), Choosing a Mobile Wallet: The Consumer Perspective, March 7. Retrieved on May 15, 2018 from chrome extension://ngpampappnmepgilojfohadhhmbhlaek/captured.html?back=1.

23. Paytm Blog. (2017), 8 Things you didnt know you could do on Paytm, March 20, available at https://blog.paytm.com/10-things-you-didnt-know-you-could-do-on-paytm-62a1b200faa6. (Accessed on 25 May 2018).

24. ANI. (2018), Paytm Tap Card Launched, Allows Offline Payments in Less Than a Second, April 28, available at https://gadgets.ndtv.com/apps/news/paytm-tap-card-launch-how-to-use-nfc-pos-terminal-1844179. (Accessed on 30 May 2018).

25. Boden.R. (2016), Mahindra Comviva wins GTB innovation award, June 7, available at https://www.nfcworld.com/2016/06/07/345356/mahindra-comviva-wins-gtb-innovation-award/ (accessed on 25 May 2018).

26. PTI. (2017), Paytm QR to help shopkeepers get payments directly to bank a/c, December 18, available at https://economictimes.indiatimes.com/small-biz/startups/newsbuzz/paytm-qr-to-help-shopkeepers-get-payments-directly-to-bank-a/c/articleshow/62122872.cms (accessed on 15 May 2018).

27. Editorial Staff. (2017), PayPal Here- POS Systems Review, December 18, available at https://www.business.com/reviews/paypal-here-pos-systems/ (Accessed on 30 May 2018).

28. Perez.S. (2015), The Problem with Chase Pay, The Banks Forthcoming Apple Pay Competitor, October 10, available at https://techcrunch.com/2015/10/27/the-problem-with-chase-pay-the-banks-forthcoming-apple-pay-competitor/ (Accessed on 4 June 2018).

29. Pandy. S and Crowe.M. (2016), Getting Ahead of the Curve: Assessing Card-Not-Present Fraud in the Mobile Payments Environment, November 10. Retrieved on June 30, 2018

from https://www.frbatlanta.org/-/media/documents/rprf/rprf_pubs/2016/11-getting-ahead-of-the-curve-assessing-card-not-present-fraud-2016-11-18.pdf.

30. Siddarth. (2017), Teaming up to serve our customers better, May 30, available at https://www.fonepaisa.com/blog/go-cashless-and-cardless/the-different-types-of-wallets (Accessed on 30 May 2018).

31. Dutta.S. (2012), Oxigen Gets FIPB Approval for FDI Investment, February 14, available at https://www.medianama.com/2012/02/223-oxigen-gets-fipb-approval-for-fdi-investment/ (accessed on 31 May 2018).

32. Sethi.L. (2017), E-Wallet License Approval from RBI, February 15, available at https://www.gstonlinefiling.com/e-wallet-license-approval-rbi/ (accessed on 29 May 2018).

33. Agarwal. S. (2017), Mobile Wallets- Technology Re-defined, March. Retrieved on May 29, 2018 from http://vinodkothari.com/wp-content/uploads/2017/03/Mobile-_Wallets_Technology_Re-defined.pdf.

34. Jose. T. (2016), What are Prepaid Payment Instruments (PPIs)?, December 1, available at https://www.indianeconomy.net/splclassroom/what-are-prepaid-payment-instruments-ppis/ (accessed on 2 June 2018).

35. PTI. (2013), Vodafone seeks FIPB approval for 100% stake in India unit, October 29. Available at https://www.business-standard.com/article/current-affairs/vodafone-seeks-fipb-approval-for-100-stake-in-india-unit-113102901049_1.html (accessed on 4 June 2018).

36. Chengappa. S. (2017), Amazon gets RBI approval for e-wallet, April 12, available at https://www.thehindubusinessline.com/info-tech/amazon-receives-rbi-approval-for-ewallet/article9634488.ece (accessed on 4 June 2018).

37. Tiwari. S. (2017), Paytm Gets RBI's Approval to Become A Payment Bank, You Can Now Deposit Your Money Here, January 4, available at https://www.indiatimes.com/news/india/paytm-gets-rbi-s-approval-to-become-a-payment-bank-you-can-now-deposit-your-money-here-268756.html (accessed on 4 June 2018).

38. Olsen. M, Hedman. J and Vatrapu. R. (2016)., Designing Digital Payment Artifacts, January 5. Retrieved on May 29, 2018 from http://openarchive.cbs.dk/ bitstream/handle/10398/8502/Olsen_Hedman_Vatrapu.pdf?sequence=1.

39. Jamwal.M. (2017), 10 Digital Wallets in India, December 21, available at http://www.iamwire.com/2017/12/mobile-wallets-best-10-digital-wallets-in-india/170127 (accessed on 29 May 2018).

40. Chamikutty. P. (2013), Paytm implements IMPS mode of payment, a method that allows online recharge through SMS, June 26 available at https://yourstory.com/2013/06/paytm-become-the-first-online-portal-to-implement-imps-mode-of-payment-a-method-that-allows-online-recharge-through-sms/ (accessed on 4 June 2018).

41. Business Line. (2014), M-Pesa starts inter-bank money transfer service, March 22, available at https://www.thehindubusinessline.com/economy/m-pesa-starts-inter-bank-money-transfer-service/article20739747.ece1 (accessed on 5 June 2018).

42. Team Flipkart. (2017), 7 THINGS YOU MUST KNOW ABOUT THE PHONEPE APP FROM FLIPKART, January 2, available at https://stories.flipkart.com/phonepe-app-flipkart/ (accessed on 5 June 2018).

43. Singh.N. (2016), Prepaid Cards by Oxigen Wallet- Features and Advantages, March 25, available at https://www.techmesto.com/oxigen-wallet-prepaid-cards-info/ (accessed on 5 June 2018).

44. Jolly. J. (2016), How to pay for everything with your Smartphone, July 24, available on https://www.usatoday.com/story/tech/columnist/2016/07/24/how-pay-everything-your-smartphone/87434966/ (accessed on 5 June 2018).

45. Aulakh. G. (2016), How wallet companies like Paytm, MobiKwik, Oxigen Wallet are trying to prevent fraudulent mobile transactions, January 16, available at https://economictimes.indiatimes.com/small-biz/startups/how-wallet-companies-like-paytm-mobikwik-oxigen-wallet-are-trying-to-prevent-fraudulent-mobile-transactions/articleshow/50598068.cms (accessed on 20 May 2018).

46. Kamath. A, Maheshwari. K, Reddy. J and Kalra. K. (2017). India: Revamped Prepaid Payment Instrument Law Focuses on KYC, Interoperability, Consumer Protection and Data Security, December 11, available at http://www.mondaq.com/india/x/654638/Financial+Services/Revamped+Prepaid+Payment+Instrument+Law+Focuses+On+KYC+Interoperability+Consumer+ Protection+And+Data+Security (accessed on 30 May 2018).

47. Bemoneyaware (2017). Go Cashless: Digital Wallets, NEFT, IMPS, UPI, Debit Cards, Credit Cards, March 15, available at https://www.bemoneyaware.com/blog/cashless-digital-wallets-neft-imps-upi-debit-cards/ (accessed on 5 June 2018).

48. Paypal, Safer from threats, available at https://www.paypal.com/in/webapps/mpp/paypal-safety-and-security (accessed on 6 June 2018).

49. Ryan. P. (2014), Walmart Enters P2P Space, April 21, available at https://bankinnovation.net/2014/04/walmart-enters-p2p-space/ security (accessed on 6 June 2018).

50. Akin. J. (2017), Payment Security Evolves with Advances in Encryption, April 21. Available at https://www.experian.com/blogs/ask-experian/payment-security-evolves-with-advances-in-encryption/ (accessed on 6 June 2018).

51. Nitrosell. (2009), Feature Spotlight: PayPal Website Payments Pro with 3D Secure, December 11, available at https://www.nitrosell.com/blog/feature-spotlight-paypal-website-payments-pro-with-3d-secure-509.html (accessed on 7 June 2018).

52. Pathak. P. (2016), Is Paytm Safe? The app answers safety questions with a blog post, December 28, available at https://www.indiatoday.in/technology/news/story/is-paytm-safe-the-app-answers-safety-questions-with-a-blog-post-359903-2016-12-28 (accessed on 7 June 2018).

53. Chase Payment, CHASE PAYMENTECH EUROPE 3-DSECURE (3-DS) MPI, Retrieved on June 7, 2018 from https://mage2.pro/uploads/default/original/2X/f/f1171caec005135894253f6ca1bf b7f0b95126d6.pdf.

54. Sharma.R. (2016), What Is Paytm, and How to Use Paytm Wallet?, November 14, available at https://gadgets.ndtv.com/apps/features/what-is-paytm-and-how-to-use-paytm-wallet-1625271 (accessed on 7 June 2018).

55. Rampton. J. (2016), Your Security Concerns about Using Mobile Payment Are Valid, October 4, available at https://www.entrepreneur.com/article/282722 (accessed on 10 June 2018).

56. Woodford. C. (2017), Two-factor authentication, October 15, available at https://www.explainthatstuff.com/how-security-tokens-work.html (accessed on 11 June 2018).

57. Bezhovski. Z. (2016). The Future of the Mobile Payment as Electronic Payment System, available at http://eprints.ugd.edu.mk/15691/1/The%20Future%20of%20the%20Mobile%20Payment%20as%20Electronic%20Payment%20System.pdf (accessed on May 16, 2018).

58. Kanimozhi. G and Kamatchi. K.S. (2017). Security aspects of Mobile Based e-wallets, June, available at www.ijritcc.org/download/browse/...5_Issues/.../1499068565_03-07-2017.pdf (accessed on May 16, 2018).

59. The Economic Times (2018).E-Wallet Definitions, available at https://economictimes.indiatimes.com/definition/e-wallets.

60. Kony(2018). Mobile Wallets, available at https://www.kony.com/resources/glossary/mobile-wallet (accessed on May 16, 2018).

61. Fargo,W. (2017). The Benefits of your Credit or Debit Card. The Convenience of your mobile, available at https://www.wellsfargo.com/mobile-payments/mobile-wallet-basics/.

62. HERO PAY (2015). Mobile Wallet, available at https://www.heropay.com/glossary/mobile-wallet/.

63. Pandya, K. H., & Galiyawala, H. J. (2014). A Survey on QR Codes: in context of Research and Application. International Journal of Emerging Technology and Advanced Engineering, 4(3), 258-262.

64. RBI. (2017). Master Directions on Issuance and Operation of Prepaid Payment Instruments in India, March 20, available at https://www.rbi.org.in/Scripts/bs_viewcontent.aspx?Id=3325 (accessed on June 20, 2018).

65. Jose. T. (2016). What is FIPB (Foreign Investment Promotion Board)? What is its role in FDI approval?, August 17, available at https://www.indianeconomy.net/splclassroom/what-is-fipb-foreign-investment-promotion-board-what-is-its-role-in-fdi-approval/ (accessed on July 30,2018).

66. Rorwana. A, Tengeh. R and Musikavanhu. T. (2015). A FRAUD PRE-VENTION POLICY: ITS RELEVANCE AND IMPLICATION AT A UNIVERSITY OF TECHNOLOGY IN SOUTH AFRICA, available at https://www.researchgate.net/profile/Robertson_Tengeh/publication/286879136/inline/jsViewer/566ecde908ae62b05f0b62cf?inViewer=1&pdfJsDownload=1&origin= publication_detail &previewAsPdf=false (accessed on July 31, 2018).

67. ICICI Bank. ICICI Bank launches Pockets by ICICI Bank, available at https://www.icicibank.com/aboutus/article.page?identifier=news-icici-bank-launches-pockets-by-icici-bank-20131712171049400 (accessed on August 1, 2018).

68. PYMNTS. (2015). Throwback Thursday: PayPal's Biggest Days in History, July 2, available at https://www.pymnts.com/in-depth/2015/throwback-thursday-paypals-biggest-days-in-history/ (accessed on August 1, 2018).

69. Amazon. Amazon Launches Login and Pay with Amazon for a Seamless Buying Experience, available at http://phx.corporate-ir.net/phoenix.zhtml?c=176060&p=irol-newsArticle&ID=1862641 (accessed on August 2, 2018).

70. Paytm Story. Available at https://successstory.com/companies/paytm (accessed on August 3, 2018).

71. Agarwal. M. (2013). Mobikwik becomes India's first Mobile Consumer Wallet, September 28, available at http://www.iamwire.com/2013/09/mobikwik-indias-mobile-consumer-wallet/20344 (accessed on August 4, 2018).

72. Mugdha Variyar. (2018). Demonetization impact? E-payments make up 60% of Amazon Indias business. Retrieved on January 19, 2018 from https://economictimes.indiatimes.com/small-biz/startups/newsbuzz/demonetisation-impact-e-payments-make-up-60-of-amazon-indias-business/articleshow/62563623.cms (accessed on August 5,2018).

73. Oxigen. Available at http://www.myoxigen.com/about-us/our-history.php (accessed on August 6, 2018).

74. Dalal. M. (2016). PayU to launch new businesses in bid to become payments hub, December 12, available at https://www.livemint.com/Companies/7JsiourmFrNANYwZqFzqTP/PayU-to-launch-new-businesses-in-bid-to-become-payments-hub.html (accessed on August 5, 2018).

75. Google Wallet Story. Google Wallet Success Story, available at https://successstory.com/products/google-wallet (accessed on August 9, 2018).

76. Morgan. J.P. Chase Announces CHASE PAY, available at https://investor.shareholder.com/jpmorganchase/releasedetail.cfm?releaseid=938397 (accessed on August 5, 2018).

77. Wright, G. and Gupta.A. (2016). Payment Systems in India and Current Status: A Perspective, available on http://blog.microsave.net/payment-systems-in-india-and-current-status-a-perspective/ (accessed in March 2018)

Printed and bound by CPI Group (UK) Ltd, Croydon, CR0 4YY

27/10/2024

14580478-0002